IMAGES
of America

HONOKAA TOWN

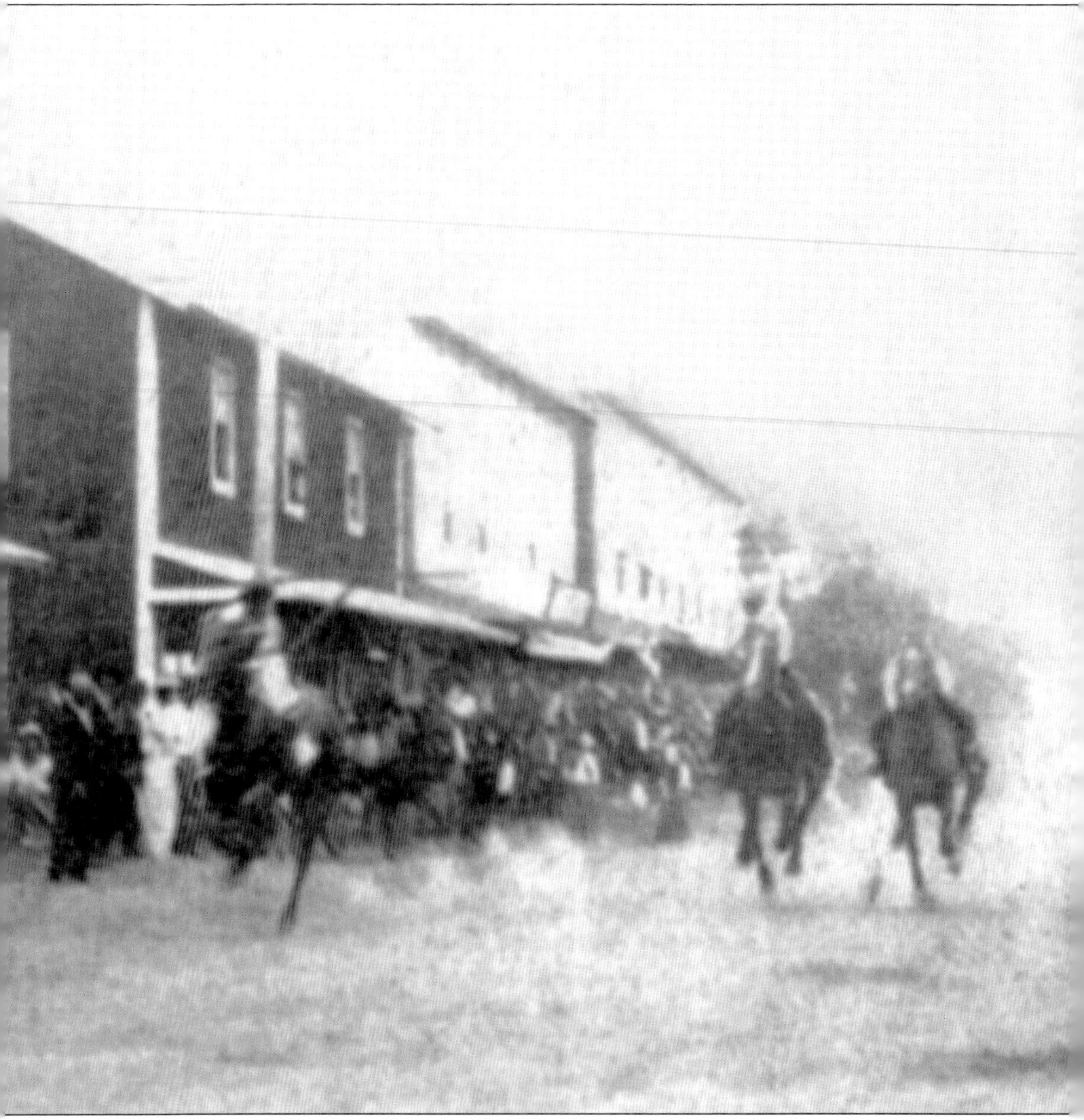

Lots of Horse-Racing Dust. Weekend horse racing on Mamane Street was always a crowd pleaser. Lots of dust kicked up, but spectators enjoyed the excitement. In this undated photograph, the Jesus, Souza, and Rice Buildings are visible in the background. Horse racing and rodeoing still go on today in Honokaa. (*Hawaii Tribune-Herald*, North Hawaii Educational and Resource Center Heritage Center.)

On the Cover: The Original Ujiki Shoten on Mamane Street, c. 1925. The banner reads "Japanese and Western Goods." The Ujiki family lived behind the store in a three-bedroom cottage. Both buildings were erected around 1915. From left to right are Masao (son, 13 years old), Masajiro (father, 49 years old), Miseo (daughter, 15 years old), Takeshi (son, 8 years old), and Momoyo (mother, 46 years old). Note the Honokaa Soda Works boxes on the left. (Ujiki Family Collection.)

IMAGES
of America

Honokaa Town

Laura Ruby and Ross W. Stephenson

ARCADIA
PUBLISHING

ISBN 978-1-4671-3335-7

Published by Arcadia Publishing
Charleston, South Carolina

Printed in the United States of America

Library of Congress Control Number: 2015941673

For all general information, please contact Arcadia Publishing:
Telephone 843-853-2070
Fax 843-853-0044
E-mail sales@arcadiapublishing.com
For customer service and orders:
Toll-Free 1-888-313-2665

Visit us on the Internet at www.arcadiapublishing.com

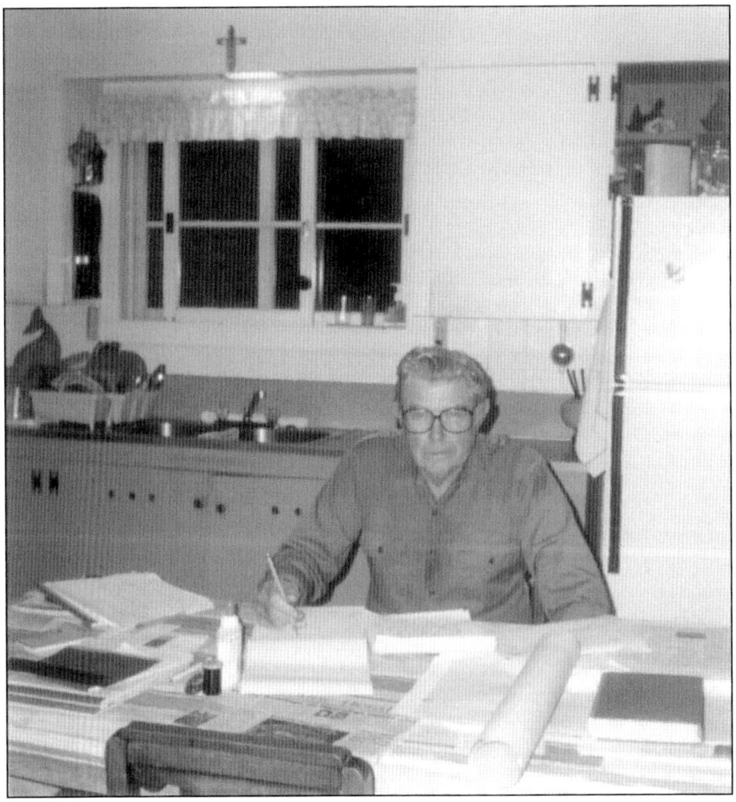

Dr. P. Quentin Tomich, 1920–2014. "Community Matters" was Quentin Tomich's mantra, which he both lived and espoused. Quentin's life certainly personifies the positive spirit of the community and the importance of remembering who we are. Thank you Quentin. This book is dedicated to you. (Peter Tomich.)

Contents

Acknowledgments

Mahalo nui loa to the following: Dr. Edmund Akioka, Charles Anderson, Monica Bacon, Dr. Billy Bergin, Florence Botelho, Helen Botelho, George Bowers, Angela Brandt, Brian Breakstone, DeSoto Brown, Ed Castillo, Sheila Chambers, William Chambers, Stuart Ching, Suisin Coloma, Joe Costa, Julie Costa, Romel De La Cruz, Claudette DeMello, Gerald DeMello, Barbara Dunn, Milo Ferreira, Barbara Franklin, Harue Furumoto, George Garcia, Elizabeth Glenn, Linda Gonsalves, Marlene Hapai, Joan Harper, Les Harunaga, Ken Hasegawa, Tatsumi Hayashi, Dr. Don Hibbard, Jennifer Higa, Larry Ignacio, Alan Ikeuchi, Daisy Ikeuchi, Hideo Imoto, Kerri Inglis, Patsy Iwasaki, Brenda Johnson, Betty Jose, Cynthia Juan, Jan Kamiya, Marilyn Watanabe Kamiya, Roland Kaneshiro, Rona Kaneshiro, Alton Kanioka, Yolanda Martin Keehne, Phaethon Keeney, Dr. Tawn Keeney, Annalise Kehler, Marcia Kemble, Mayor Billy Kenoi, Rev. Olivia Latu, Annelle Lee, Gay Mathews, Mikoko Hasegawa Matsuo, Kathernie Mendes, Dr. Lorraine Minatoishi, Roy Miyasaki, Dana Morifuji, Naomi Morita, Rep. Mark Nakashima, Dr. Momi Naughton, Michael Olival, Kathleen Painton, Council Member Val Poindexter, Martha Reber, Tia Reber, Randy Rickard, Ryon Rickard, Berni Ruis, Wally Sakamoto, Rick Sakata, Franco Salmoiraghi, Neil Sananikone, Patty Sananikone, Renee Watanabe Scudder, Rae Shiraki, Jack Smith, Stanley Solamillo, John Roy Souza, Carol Stephenson, Paul Takamatsu, Earl Tanaka, Susan Ikeuchi Tanoue, Ronald Thiel, Wendy Tolleson, P. Quentin Tomich, Peter Tomich, Sue Kuwaye Toyama, Gerald Ujiki, Jory Watland, Cary Yamada, Maria Yano, and George Zweibel.

Archives and collections (and some photographers) that contributed images include:

Bishop Museum (BM)
Episcopal Church in Hawai'i Archives (EC)
Fathers of the Sacred Hearts, Hawaii Province Archives (CA)
Hawai'i State Archives (HSA)
Hawai'i State Library (HSL)
Hawai'i State Historic Preservation Division (SHPD)
Hawai'i State Survey Office (HSSO)
Hawai'i Tribune-Herald (HTH)
Hawaiian Historical Society (HHS)
Honokaa High School yearbook (HHSY)
Honokaa People's Theatre (HPT)
Honolulu Star-Advertiser
ILWU Local 142 Archives
Japanese Cultural Center of Hawaii (JCCH)
Lyman Museum (LM)
North Hawai'i Education and Research Center (NHERC)
Laura Ruby (LR)
Carol Stephenson (CCS)
Ross W. Stephenson (RWS)
University of Hawai'i Center for Oral History
University of Hawai'i Libraries (UHHL)
University of Hawai'i Libraries, Hawaiian Collection
University of Hawai'i Libraries, Map Collection
Waimea Gazette website (WG)

A full index can be found at www.historichonokaaproject.com.

Numbers in brackets after courtesy lines refer to locations on the map on pages 126–127.

INTRODUCTION

Honokaa Town is located on the Hamakua Coast of the Island of Hawaii in a *moku* (district) of the same name. Honokaa fronts two sides of an old government route to Waipio Valley known as Mamane Street. The town developed linearly along the arterial route since it was first settled as a stage stop in the 19th century, and its limits gradually extended across the *ahupuaa* (land divisions) of Koloaha, Kulihai, Lauka, Nienie, Papuaa, Namoku, Haina, Papaanui, Paalaea, and Kalua (page 10). Honokaa takes its name from the sound of the sea nearby, which translated from the Hawaiian means "rolling [as stones] bay."

Traditionally, in Native Hawaiian culture, the highly organized and productive *loi* (taro terraces) of Waipio Valley supported the largest population concentration in the Hamakua District. Wetland *kalo* (taro) production also was developed "up top" Hilo side of Waipio, between Kukuihaele and Honokaa, through terracing and irrigation from Waikoekoe Stream.

The introduction of non-indigenous plants and animals, disease, technology, Western law, and capitalism greatly changed the appearance and lifestyles of the Hamakua District after outside contact. First ranching on the *mauka* (toward the mountain) slopes, then sugar plantations, coffee, homesteading, and macadamia nut production tied Hawaii to the world economy. Sugar, fostered by a generation of entrepreneurs, evolved into a corporate model, as capital, labor, and technology requirements overwhelmed the resources of individuals.

Sometime between 1881 and 1904, new government roads were developed mauka of the main coastal Hilo-Waipio Government Road, cutting travel time and effort on the route between Hilo and Waimea. It seems logical that a road be developed that ran nearly *makai* (seaward) from the new Hilo-Waimea cutoff to the important points of the mill at Haina and the Honokaa Landing. The route chosen followed much of the boundary between G.M. Coffin's Royal Patent Grant 1155 and George Hardy's Grant 1073 down to the main Government Coast Road and then makai between Keaweopala and Kapokukohana's Grant 1774 and William H. Rickard's Grant 3156. A similar Hilo route, which ran from near the Rickard family homestead on the Government Road to Rickard property mauka, also connected to the new Hilo-Waimea thoroughfare. These two intersections were important, because Hilo-Waimea and Hilo-Kukuihaele traffic met between them, which helped focus commercial development along this section of the main coastal Government Road (Mamane Street).

Government services became concentrated near the Mamane-Pakalana intersection, while religious organizations favored the Mamane-Lehua area. In between grew a multitude of "mom-and-pop" stores. These small independent firms developed as the norm in rural areas throughout the Hawaiian Islands outside the plantation hegemony. Contrary to popular myth, the entrepreneurs who founded these companies often came to Hawaii with mercantile experience gained in the old country or had acquired such skills working in stores run by the plantations themselves. Establishment of a business by an entrepreneur required capital, often acquired through years of saving while working for others and/or through resources such as the Japanese *tanomoshi* (pooling of money between friends for those who needed it most). The entrepreneurs initially catered to their own ethnic group, but they had a major incentive to increase their sales by learning other languages and customs in order to cater to the widest range of potential customers.

The development of commercial buildings on Mamane Street was heavily influenced by the plantations themselves. The Hawaii Sugar Planters' Association (HSPA) developed designs popularly known as plantation architecture, featuring single-wall construction, standardized components such as double-hung windows, and *totan* (corrugated iron) roofs. These structures were erected by succeeding waves of Native Hawaiians, mainland Americans, Chinese, Portuguese, Japanese, and others. Buildings were not known by addresses but by family ownership (for example, the Andrade Building). The contractors were usually Japanese.

The most common type of business is the mom-and-pop general store. The entrepreneur founders usually called upon their family members to contribute to the business. Children, as soon as they were able, were expected to perform increasingly complex tasks. (Having attended the local public schools, where instruction was in English and play yard activities occurred in the local pidgin, children were expected to cater to customers from other ethnic groups.) Particular functions, such as accounting, stocking, paying bills, and so forth would be assigned to individual family members based upon ability and knowledge. These establishments would on average be approximately 1,000 square feet in size and occupy a plantation-style single-wall commercial building. Commercial activities would occur on the first floor, and family living quarters were either above or behind the store. Products included a cross-section of plantation worker needs, including such items as handmade raincoats, cloth, and sewing supplies, hats, tools, car parts, non-refrigerated foods such as rice and bread, children's candy, dolls, and cultural icons for ethnic holidays. If the proprietors could afford refrigeration, then meats, milk, and soda would be included. Specialty items in some shops could include liquor in a separate enclosed area. The proprietors differentiated their shops from similar establishments through specialization, personal relationships with customers, and service. It was not uncommon to have a member of the proprietor's family fill a customer's order in the shop, drive to the customer's home, place perishables in the refrigerator (if there was one) and nonperishable items on the kitchen table. This occurred under an honor system, wherein the customer was expected to visit the store monthly to settle up accounts. This honor system is still practiced in Honokaa.

Honokaa offered attractions unavailable elsewhere on the coast because, as the second-largest town on the island, Honokaa had the population base to support such activity. Merchants, for example, sold real estate or specialized in hardware. Services included several movie theaters, soda fountains, pool halls, automobile sales, banking and investments, pharmacies, hotel rooms, commercial laundries, and even matchmaking for families seeking suitable spouses for their children. A court, fire station, and rat vector control lab were operated by the government. Five religious organizations conducted services.

Today, original territorial-era plantation-style buildings still line Mamane Street, and the social interactions of that period that contributed so much to Hawaii's self-identity remain also. It is no wonder that many long-term residents of the state continue to go back to places such as Honokaa to reclaim their roots.

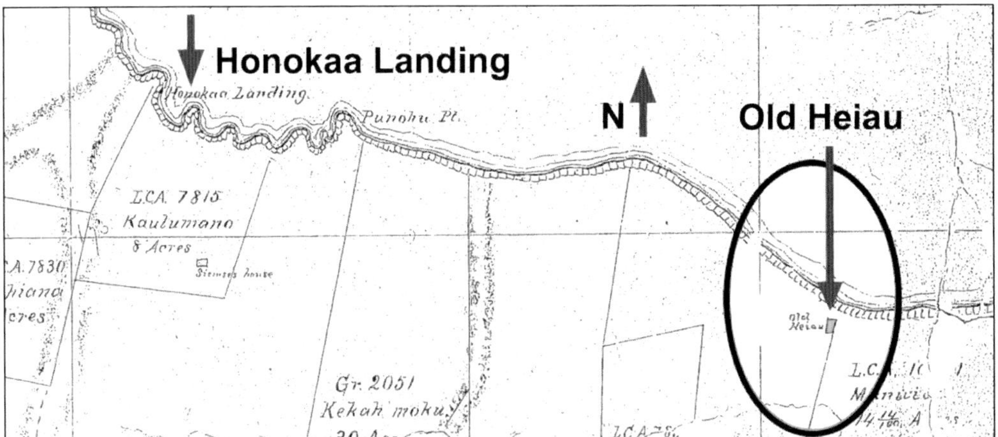

FEW NATIVE HAWAIIAN STRUCTURES. This 1879 map detail locates the old *heiau* (temple) in Haina ahupuaa, at the edge of the *pali* (cliff). John Stokes in *Heiau of the Island of Hawaii* (1906–1907) records Ka Loa heiau in Ahualoa ahupuaa about 400 to 500 feet from the pali and a quarter mile west of the Honokaa Landing. Quentin Tomich in *Perspectives on Hamakua History* (2008) documents the still-extant *ahu* (rock) enclosures on a *puu* (hill) at Haukoi ahupuaa (Waipio side of Honokaa) featuring walls and platforms. (See Δ, page 10.) Intensive sugarcane production destroyed most traces of Native Hawaiian culture along the Hamakua Coast. (HSSO.)

One

On the Way to Honokaa

The topography of Hamakua, with its deep valleys separating plateaus along the coast, has always made overland transportation difficult. The Native Hawaiians first created a system of trails for movement by foot across the many narrow ahupuaa. The introduction of Western wagons led to the development of a Government Road along the Hamakua Coast. This wagon road was constructed well above the rough seashore, along flatter ground, in order to facilitate construction. The high cost of transportation forced the plantation management to innovate. They first employed gravity to move cane—either by floating it downhill in flumes or bundling cane and attaching it to devices similar to modern overhead zip lines (page 14). Riders had to be careful when crossing these gravity cane-haul lines to prevent being knocked off their horses.

The development of roads by 1903 led to regular stage routes (page 11). Land-based transportation, however, advanced with development of the Hilo Railway/Hawaii Consolidated Railway (page 18), which stretched from Puna to Paauilo by 1913. The Hamakua section required high trestles and long tunnels but offered spectacular views of both natural and manmade scenery. Such views fostered a new tourist industry, whose patrons anxiously began their journey by crossing the Wailuku River Bridge. Regular passengers and freight from Hamakua Coast sugar plantations reached Hilo by rail on a scheduled basis for over 30 years.

While the railroad did not reach mauka ranch and homestead developments, an increasing number of secondary roads did. Paauilo, as the actual rail terminus (the line never did reach Honokaa, its designated objective), thrived during the rail era. Unfortunately, destruction of rail bridges by the tsunami of April Fool's Day 1946 and the decision by plantation managements to switch cane hauling to trucks (instead of rebuilding the railroad) spelled doom for railroad-related communities along the coast. After World War II, this situation worsened as a series of federally funded highways bypassed established communities. Consolidation of plantations, relocation of camps, and the end of sugar production in 1994 have exacerbated the abandonment of older settlements and isolated numerous cultural treasures within Hamakua.

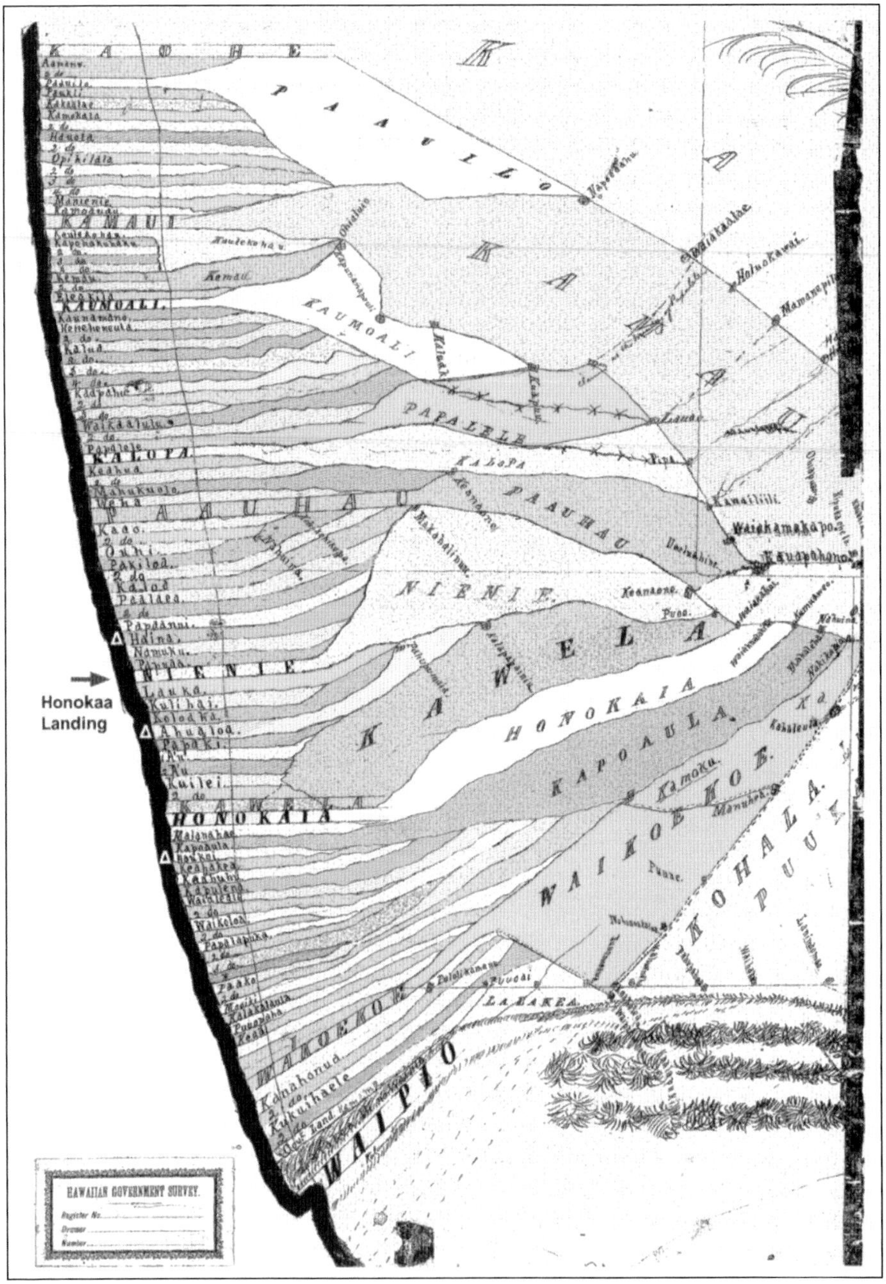

MAP OF AHUPUAA WITHIN HAMAKUA DISTRICT. Located on the windward side of the Big Island, perpendicular to the prevailing winds and geologically too young to develop a fringing reef, the Hamakua District features numerous deep valleys and high sea cliffs. The Native Hawaiian tradition of dividing areas to ensure a mixture of resources for inhabitants (from the sea, lowlands, and highlands), combined with this topography, resulted in numerous small land divisions, or ahupuaa. The ahupuaa in the general Honokaa area going from Hilo to Waipio are Paauhau, Kaao 1, Kaao 2, Kaloa, Paalaea 1, Paalaea 2, Papaanui, Haina, Namuka, Nienie, Lauka, Kulihai, Koloalia, Ahualoa, Papaki, A'u 1, A'u 2 , Kuilei 1, Kuilei 2, Kawela, and Honokaia. Note the Δ symbols, which represent stone structure locations. (HSSO.)

HARVESTING CANE BY HAND, THE OLD-FASHIONED WAY. Early immigrant plantation laborers faced difficult work conditions. These included 10 hour work days, heat, sunburn, frequent contact with skin irritants in the sugar cane, and heavy physical labor. Cutting cane required use of sharp cane knives. Workers were also exposed to smoke inhalation when cane was burned to remove trash in the fields, pesticides used to control pests, and herbicides to control weeds. Pay was meager and many workers and their families found it necessary to buy necessities on credit from the company stores to make ends meet, often forcing them into debt. For these reasons, most plantation laborers did not renew their contracts. (Christensen Collection, NHERC.)

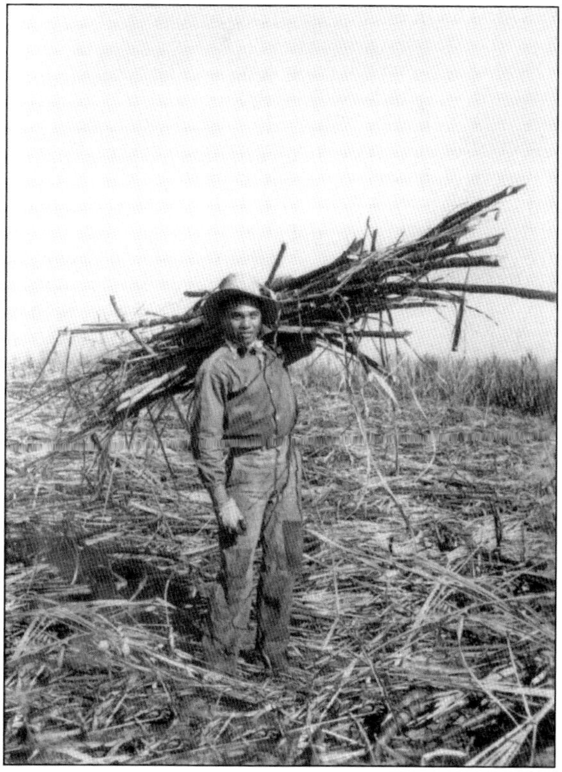

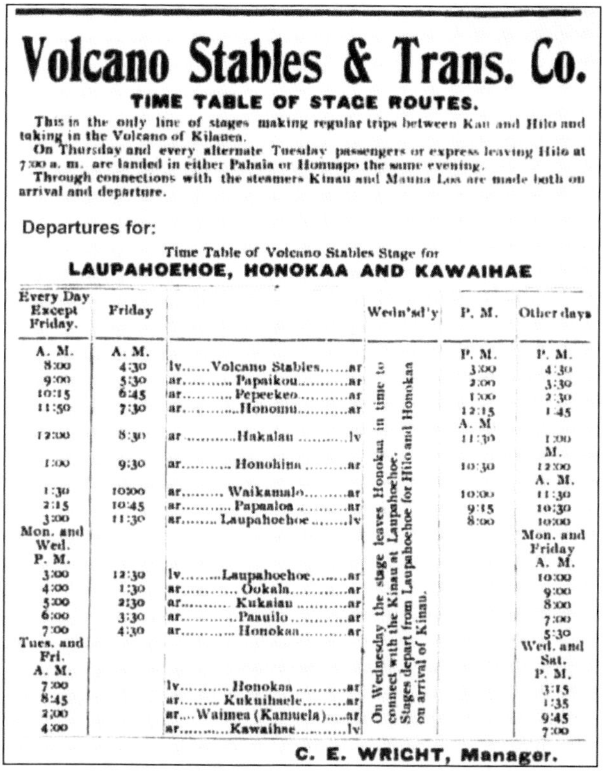

Volcano Stables & Trans. Co.

TIME TABLE OF STAGE ROUTES.

This is the only line of stages making regular trips between Kau and Hilo and taking in the Volcano of Kilauea.

On Thursday and every alternate Tuesday passengers or express leaving Hilo at 7:00 a. m. are landed in either Pahala or Honuapo the same evening.

Through connections with the steamers Kinau and Mauna Loa are made both on arrival and departure.

Departures for:

Time Table of Volcano Stables Stage for

LAUPAHOEHOE, HONOKAA AND KAWAIHAE

Every Day Except Friday.	Friday		Wedn'sd'y	P. M.	Other days
A. M.	A. M.			P. M.	P. M.
8:00	4:30	lv......Volcano Stables......ar	On Wednesday the stage leaves Honokaa in time to connect with the Kinau at Laupahoehoe. Stages depart from Laupahoehoe for Hilo and Honokaa on arrival of Kinau.	3:00	4:30
9:00	5:30	ar.......... Papaikou..........ar		2:00	3:30
10:15	6:45	ar.......... Pepeekeo..........ar		1:00	2:30
11:50	7:30	ar..........Honomu..........ar		12:15	1:45
				A. M	
12:00	8:30	ar ....Hakalau lv		11:30	1:00
					M.
1:00	9:30	ar.......... Honohina ....ar		10:30	12:00
					A. M.
1:30	10:00	ar......... Waikamalo.........ar		10:00	11:30
2:15	10:45	ar.......... Papaaloa ....ar		9:15	10:30
3:00	11:30	ar........ Laupahoehoe lv		8:00	10:00
Mon. and Wed. P. M.					Mon. and Friday A. M.
3:00	12:30	lv.........Laupahoehoe.........ar			10:00
4:00	1:30	ar........... Ookala...........ar			9:00
5:00	2:30	ar.......... Kukaiau ....ar			8:00
6:00	3:30	ar..........Paauilo ....ar			7:00
7:00	4:30	ar.......... Honokaa..........ar			5:30
Tues. and Fri. A. M.					Wed. and Sat. P. M.
7:00		lv.......... Honokaa ....ar			3:15
8:45		ar........ Kukuihaele.........ar			1:35
2:00		ar.... Waimea (Kamuela).....ar			9:45
4:00		ar..........Kawaihae..........lv			7:00

C. E. WRIGHT, Manager.

19TH CENTURY TRANSPORTATION. Early 19th century missionaries such as the Rev. Lorenzo Lyons wrote home about the necessity of using trails overland because Western-style roads did not exist within Waimea, Kohala, and Hamakua. By 1903, road systems had improved somewhat, but regular scheduled transportation still required a combination of travel on the inter-island steamers *Kinau* or *Mauna Loa* to Laupahoehoe and then overland stagecoach service into Honokaa itself. This was in itself considered a great improvement, as transportation to and from Hilo had improved from "days" to "all day." (HTH.)

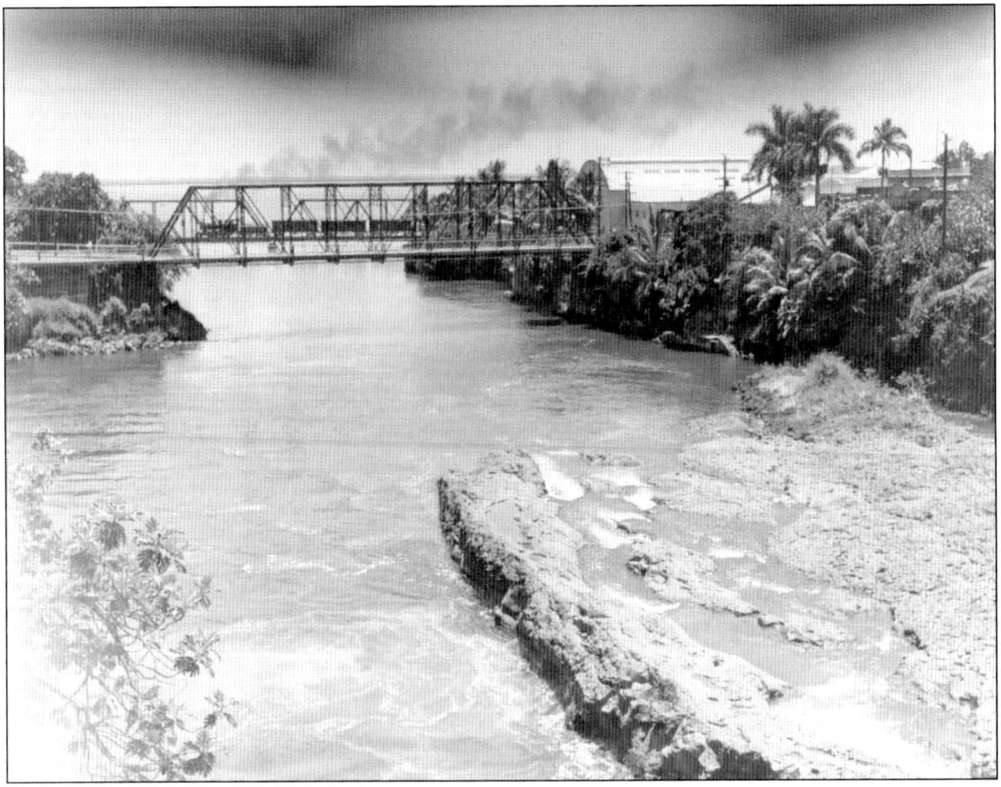

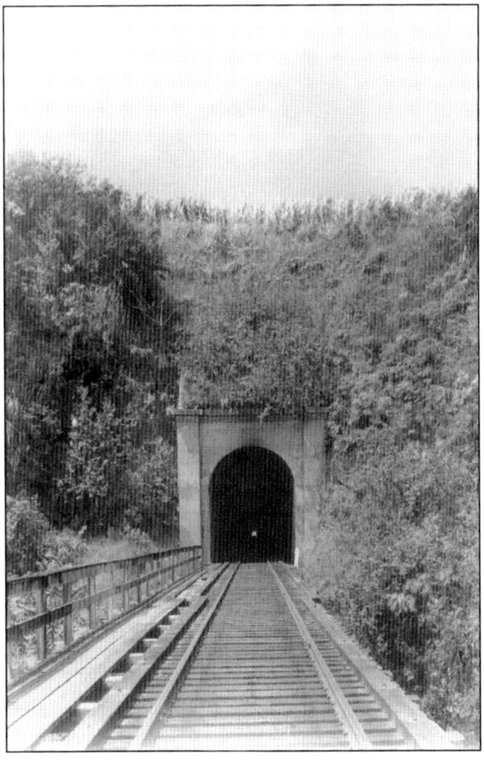

Wailuku River Bridge, Gateway to Hamakua from Hilo. The second-longest river in Hawaii, the Wailuku River's name means "River of Destruction." The often-turbulent estuary has claimed many lives. Entrepreneur Benjamin Franklin Dillingham, who had constructed the Oahu Railway to great success, established his Hilo Railway terminal on vacant land along the Hilo waterfront near Waianuenue Street. The bridge pictured, now the site of a highway bridge, took the shortest, if most precarious, route. (HSA.)

Light at the End of the Tunnel. Maulua Gulch Bridge and Tunnel is pictured here in 1912. The tunnel extends over 2,700 feet into the Hilo side of the gulch and opened onto the bridge at a height of 144 feet. The Hilo Railway (later Hawaii Consolidated Railway) was truly an engineering marvel, crossing 211 streams. However, it cost $6 million to construct between 1908 and 1913, bankrupting its backers and forcing a reorganization under Theo. H. Davies, Ltd., in 1916. (BM.)

Massive Investment in Sugar. Sugar is a very thirsty crop, requiring development of extensive water diversion and distribution systems through Hamakua's difficult terrain. Plantation managers were willing to invest to increase yields. This photograph shows a flume constructed over a deep gulch. To give an idea of scale, a single ditch worker can be seen walking atop the flume at right center. (Davey Photography Company, HHS.)

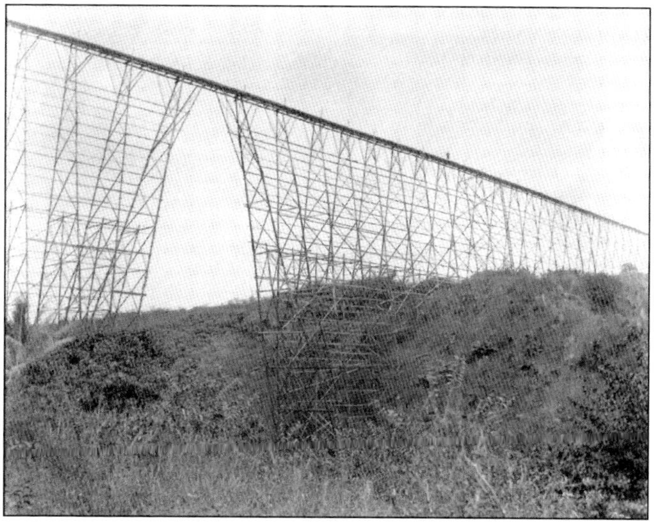

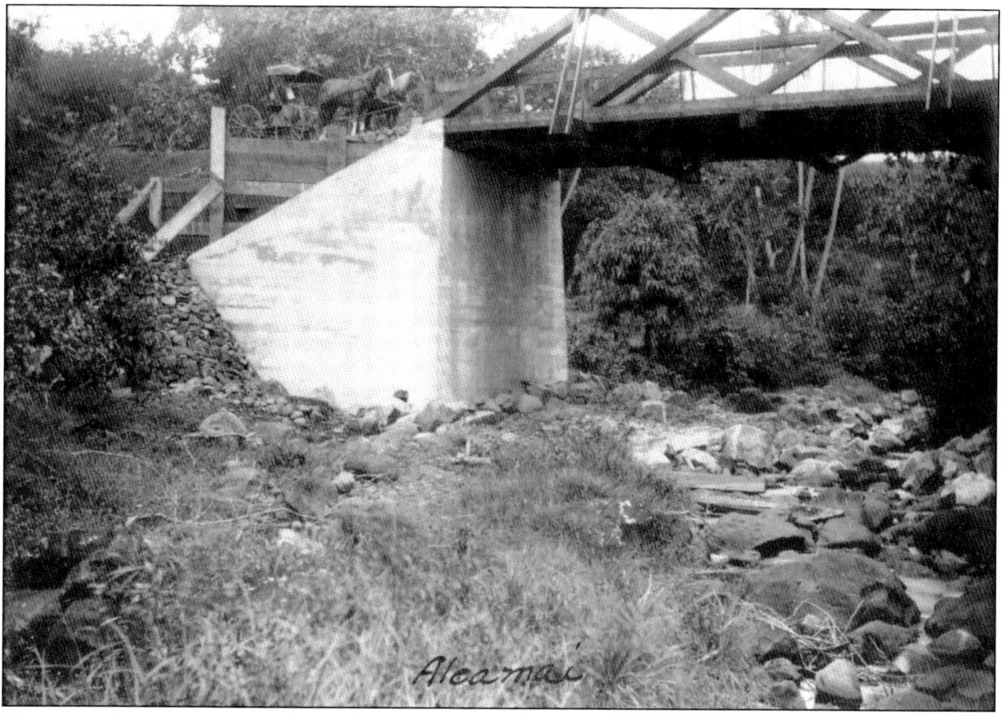

Highway Improvements. Initially, everyone walked everywhere. This photograph, from the territorial government in 1904–1905, celebrates an increasing standard of living (note the horse and buggy at upper left) and the ability to construct permanent bridges across the Hamakua landscape. This elaborate bridge over Aleamai Stream has both a concrete abutment and a wooden Warren truss—just in time for the introduction of automobiles. (HSA.)

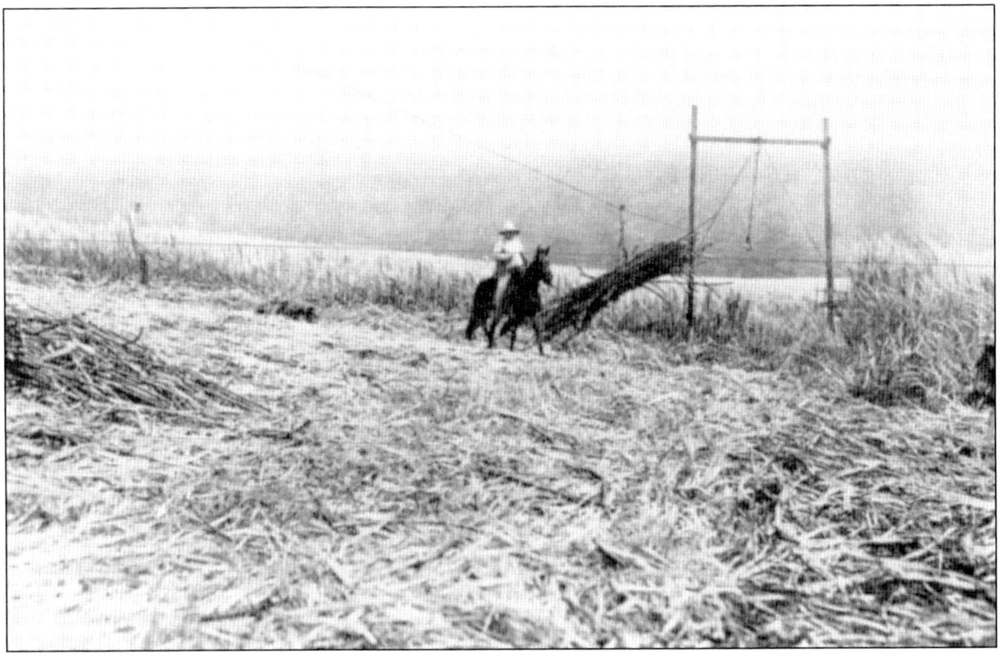

Gravity Method of Cane Transportation. *The Hawaiian Sugar Planters' Association Committee on Labor Saving Devices for Year 1932* noted that one of the earliest methods of transporting sugar cane from mauka fields was through the use of overhead lines using gravity. This involved collecting the cane, placing it in a wagon, carrying it to the line, loading it, monitoring its descent, and unloading it back into a wagon for transport to the mill. (NHERC.)

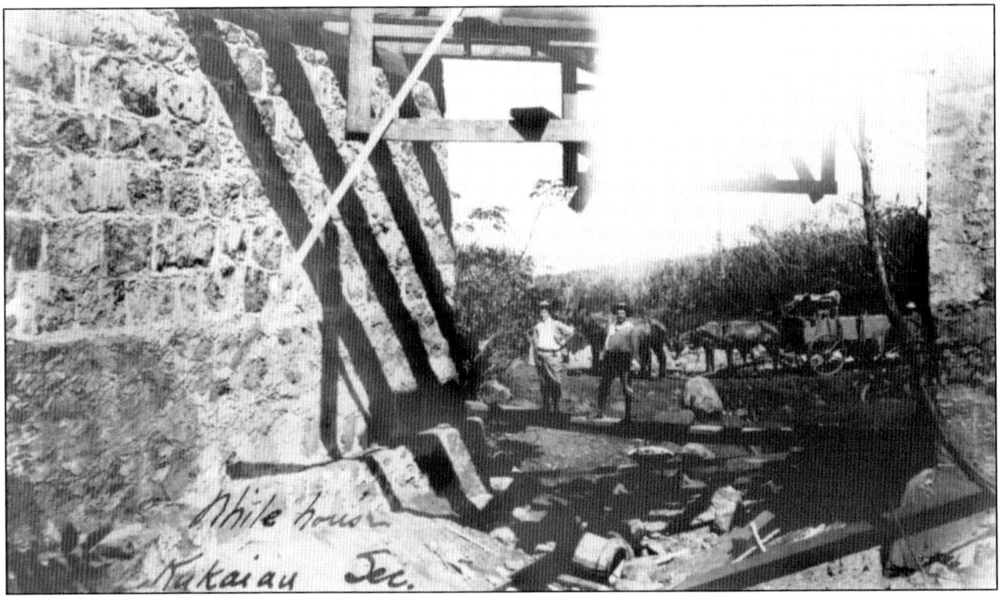

Bridge Building at Kukaiau. When the first roads were constructed, mules carried supplies because the animals were sure-footed and could endure long treks with heavy loads. Retaining walls, such as this one erected to support a bridge, were constructed of rock gathered on site. The rock was hand-chiseled to fit together tightly, much like Native Hawaiian dry stack walls, but minimizing the need for transporting concrete. (HSA.)

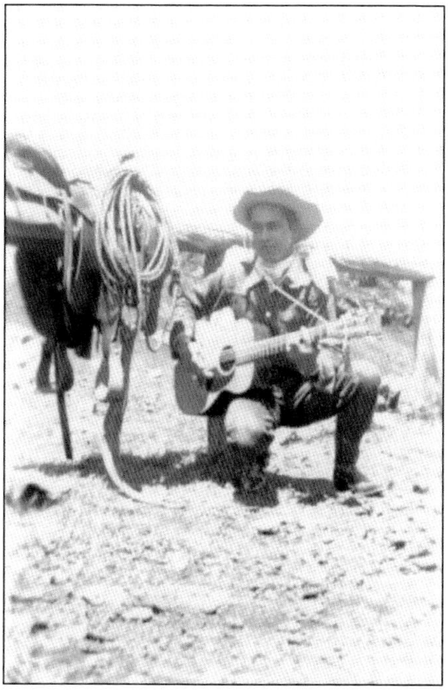
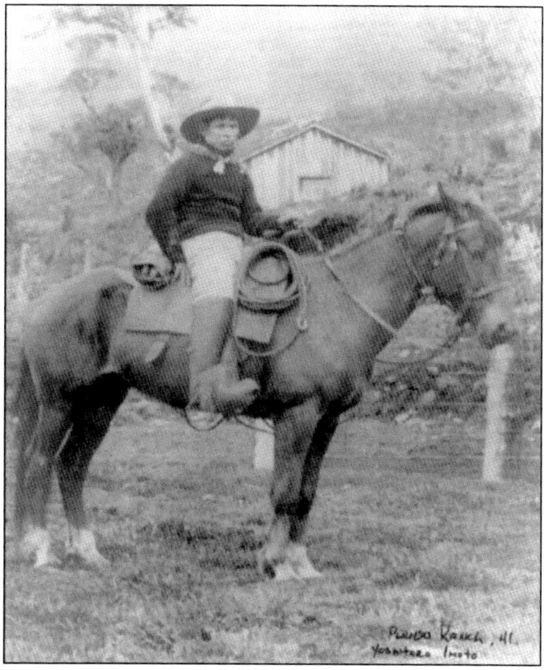

Two Paniolo—George Kealoha and Yoshitaro Imoto. The Kukaiau Ranch was founded around 1887 by Charles Notley on lands above the sugar belt. The ranch was soon sold to John M. Horner of Kukaiau Plantation, whose son Robert Horner acted as manager until 1912. The ranch has included over 5,000 cattle, nearly 300 horses, and 100 mules, employing 18 men on a regular basis and additional *paniolo* (cowboys) for special work. About 700 cattle were driven annually to the Kukaiau rail station for shipment to Hilo and Honolulu. George Kealoha is pictured at left and Yoshitaro Imoto is at right. (Corrine Kealoha Collection and Imoto Family Collection.)

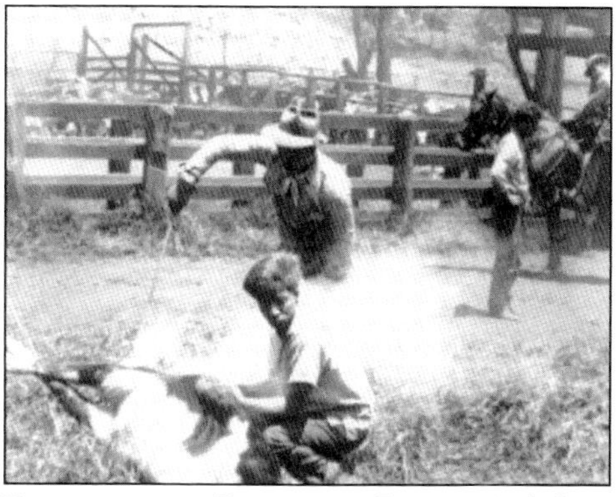
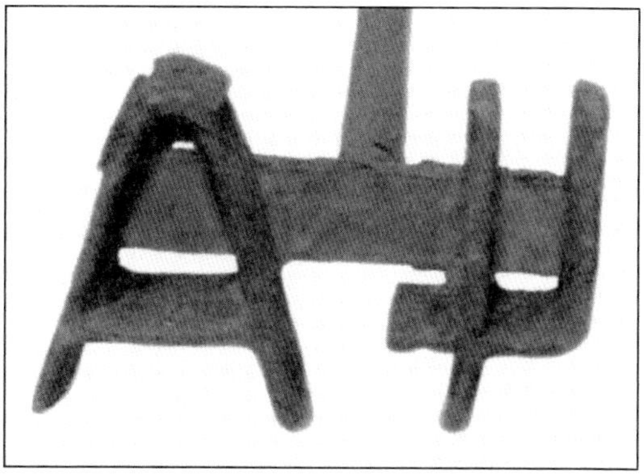

Branding the Pipi in the Pa-eke. At left, George Kealoha holds down a *pipi* (calf) for branding. An example of a local brand, that of the Antone Luce Ferreira family of neighboring Kalopa Homesteads, was personalized to read "4A," signifying the number of his children. (Left, Miranda Family Collection; right, DeMello Family Collection.)

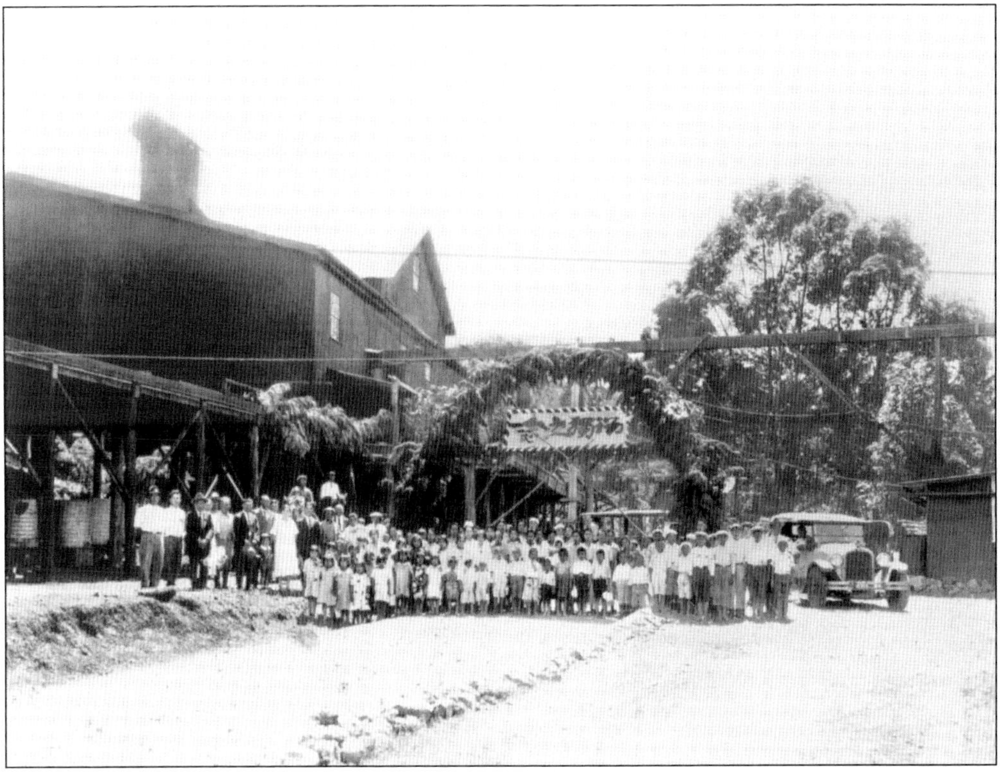

LOUISSON BROTHERS COFFEE MILL. Paauilo Mauka had several coffee mills; the largest was the Louisson Brothers' Mill, shown here around 1925. The conveyor belt that connected the processing and drying operations above the road and the operations below is visible. Many area residents were small-time coffee growers, picking their own beans and then husking, drying, and bagging them before sending them to the mill. (Kimura Collection, courtesy of Jim Reddekopp and Peter Tomich.)

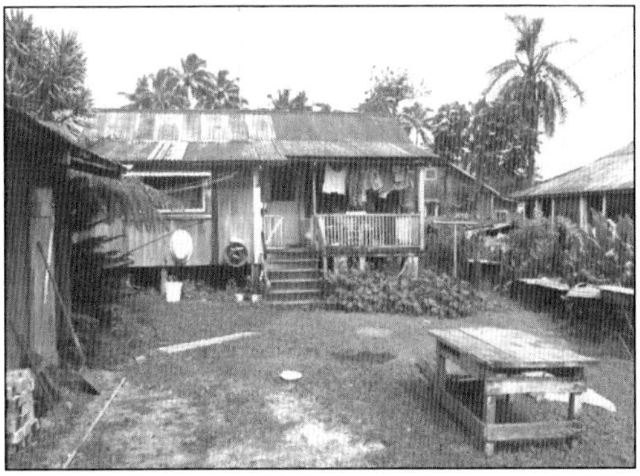

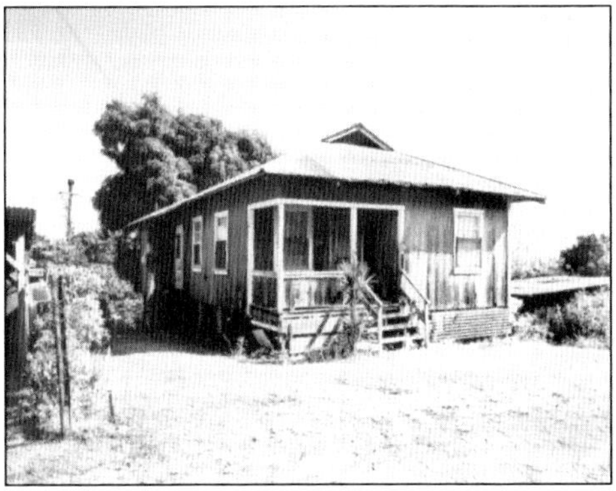

HAMAKUA CAMP HOUSES. Improvements in housing are evident compared to the hovels that workers were relegated to at the end of the 19th century. Increasingly, structures featured platforms supported by post and piers, open *lanais* (verandas), vertical wood single-wall construction, and double-pitched corrugated-iron roofs. Such architectural elements were reflected even in ranch outposts. At left is a Paauhau house for a skilled worker; at right is a Kukaiau house that has undergone many changes. (SHPD.)

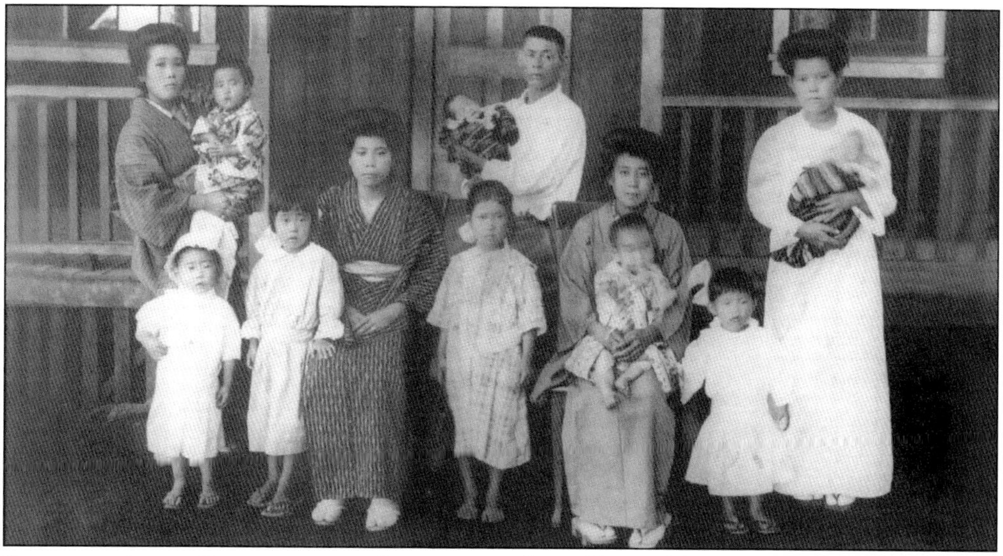

YOSHITARO IMOTO FAMILY AT THEIR PLANTATION CAMP HOUSE, MARCH 1920. From left to right are (first row) Manabu Umoto (nephew), Natsuko (daughter), Osue Matsumoto (sister), Toshiko (daughter), Tsuchiyo Umoto (sister) with baby Yachiko, and Stella Ishii (niece); (second row) Tsuyo with baby Fusako (daughter), Yoshitaro Imoto with baby Yukiko (daughter), and Tsurue Ishii (sister) with baby Yukio (nephew). Tsuyo moved from Puu OO Ranch to Paauilo Plantation to work and send the children to school. Yoshitaro journeyed from his paniolo job to be with his family each weekend. The Imoto family lived in half a plantation house, with three rooms for the entire family—the children slept on the floor in the living room or kitchen. (Imoto Family Collection.)

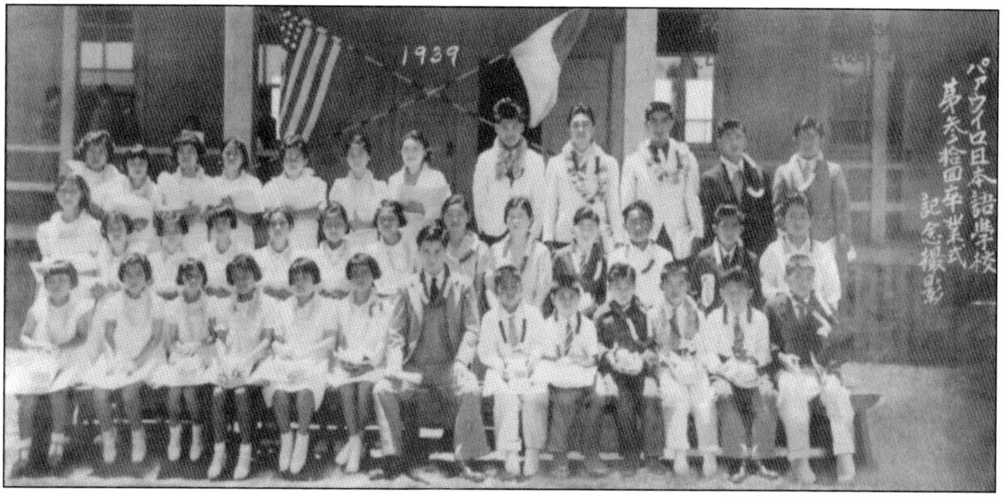

Language Schools Win In Washington

LAW ENACTED HERE DECLARED VOID BY U.S.SUPREME COURT

PAAUILO JAPANESE LANGUAGE SCHOOL, 1939. In the early 1920s, Japanese-language schools were viewed by the territorial government as impeding its Americanization campaigns for immigrants. The territory passed laws to curtail the schools; the schools sued, and the Supreme Court, in Farrington v. Tokushige (February 21, 1927), overturned the legislation. Honokaa had three Japanese-language schools on different sites over time. (Top, Imoto Family Collection; bottom, HTH.)

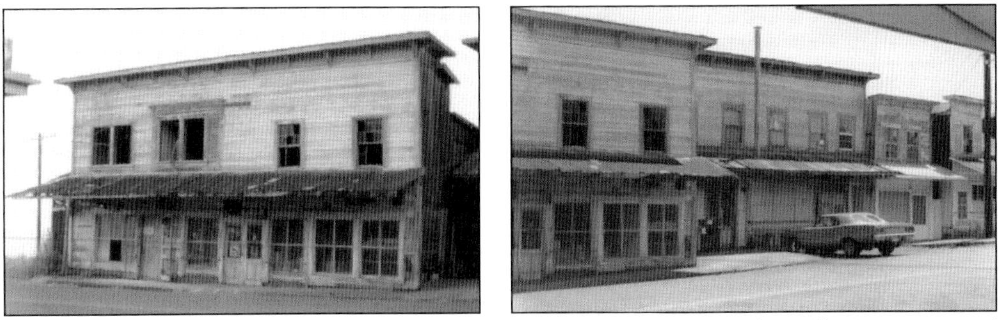

PAAUILO. Paauilo boomed after 1913, when the railway reached Paauilo Mill. A commercial district of small shopkeepers sprouted a mile above and Honokaa-side of the railhead. This was land not owned by the plantation, and so was outside of plantation control and thus allowed small merchants to compete with the Hamakua Sugar Company plantation store. Many single-wall, two-story buildings, similar to those in Honokaa, were built, with businesses on the ground floor and living quarters on the second. Dick's Bar, a jeweler, Takamune Barber Shop, Bataan Store, Miyasaki Store, Nakahara Store, a hotel, Higashi Gift Shop, Arakawa Store, and the Hamakua Theatre were located here. (Miyasaki Family Collection).

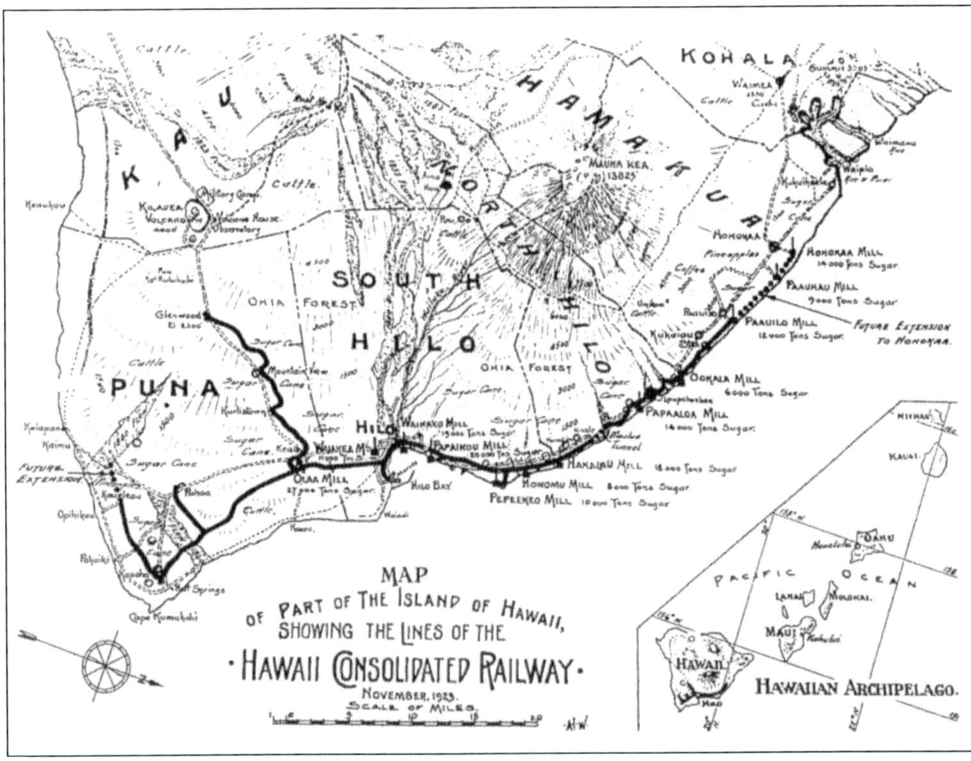

HAWAII CONSOLIDATED RAILWAY MAP, 1923. In 1899, Oahu Railroad pioneer Benjamin F. Dillingham and supporters were granted a charter for the Hilo Railroad. The first line, to Olaa, was completed the next year, and lines eventually went to Glenwood, Pahoa, and Kamaili (Puna). As part of an agreement to gain government assistance in Hilo Harbor improvements, Dillingham agreed to a branch into Hamakua, to extend into Honokaa. (HHS.)

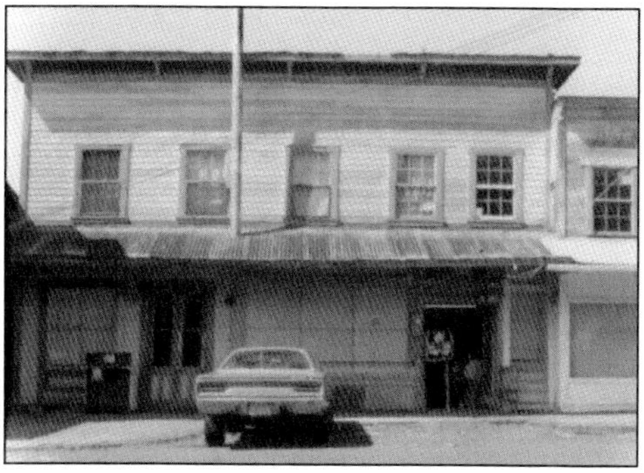

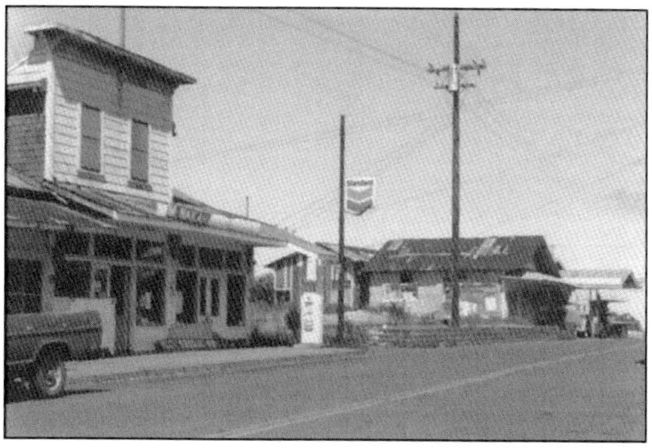

Decline of a Town: Paauilo, 1975. The Paauilo commercial area lost its customer base in the mid-20th century because plantations mechanized, shrinking the number of plantation jobs in Hamakua; plantation consolidations closed the Paauilo Mill; plantation owners decided not to rebuild the Hawaii Consolidated Railway after the 1946 tsunami, and a new highway constructed by the government makai of the original road bypassed the area. Business dropped off, stores closed, and the buildings became unkempt. All buildings (except the gas station) pictured here no longer exist. (Miyasaki Family Collection.)

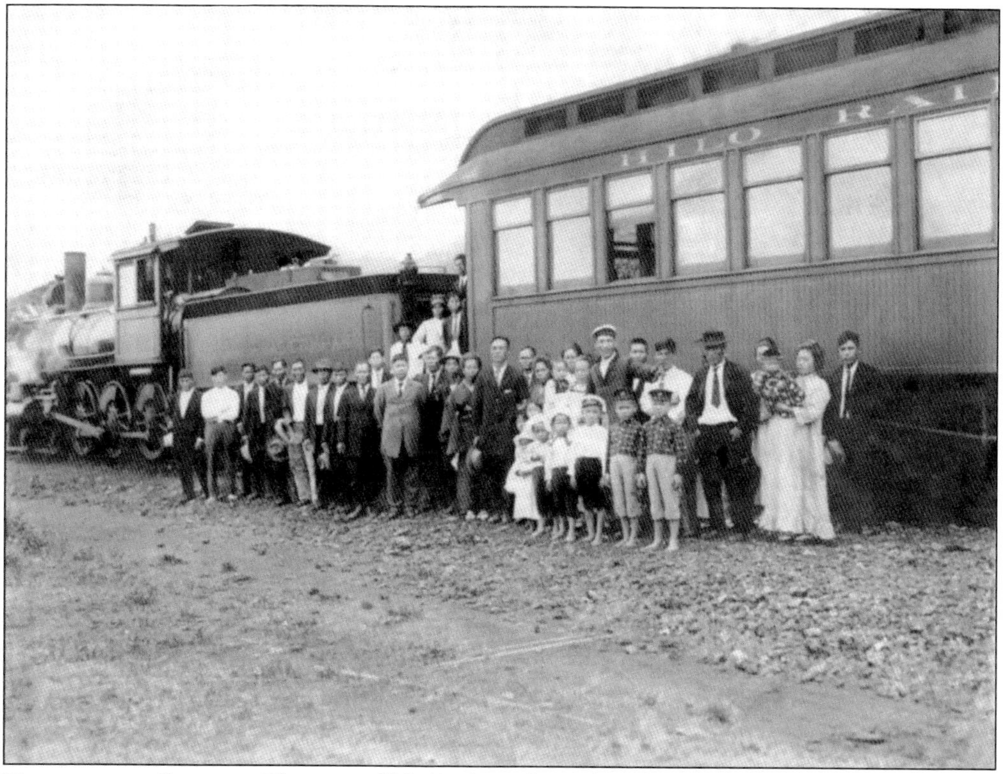

Down to the Station. The name Hilo Railway dates this photograph between approximately 1913, when rail reached Paauilo, and 1915, when bankruptcy led to a name change to Hawaii Consolidated Railway. These people are in their best clothes. The children's bare feet illustrate the hardscrabble life of recent immigrants. The children's military headdresses are reminiscent of the then-recent Japanese naval victory over Russia at Tsushima in 1905, a source of great pride to the Japanese community. (Miyasaki Family Collection.)

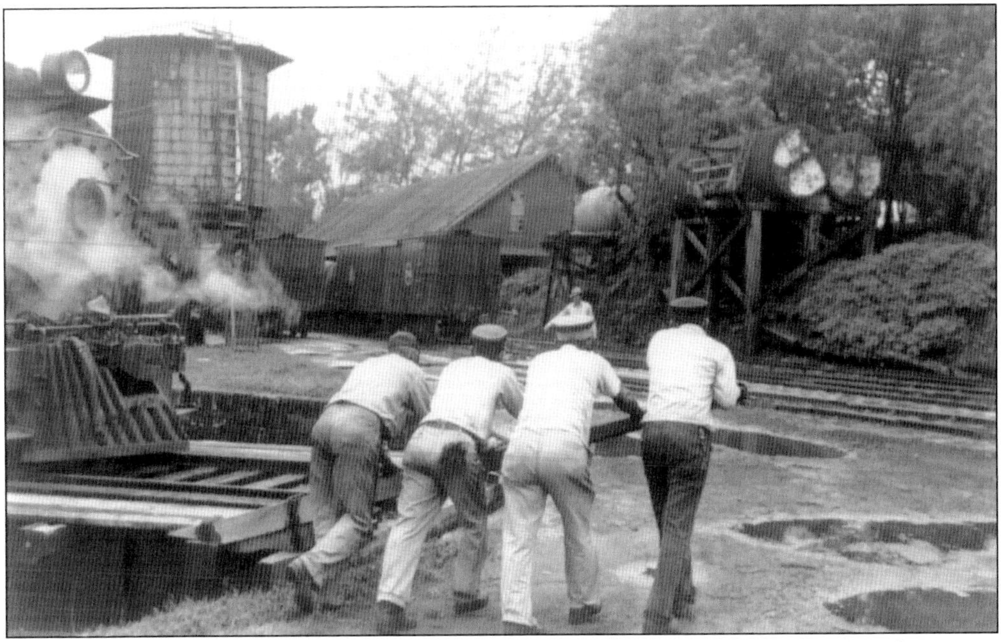

END OF THE LINE. Honokaa was the planned terminus of the Hilo Railway. Plans for a major station and roundtable makai of the Botelho Building in Honokaa were scrapped after the Hilo Railway filed for bankruptcy. Instead, a roundtable was constructed at the last of the track laid near the Paauilo Mill. In this photograph, four men manually turn a steam engine around for the return trip to Hilo. (BM.)

HILO RAILROAD COMPANY

TIME TABLE

Effective Sept. 15, 1913

HAKALAU-PAAUILO DIVISION

Outward

LEAVE HILO for Hakalau and Way Stations: Daily: 7:25 a. m., 11:30 a. m. and 4:30 p. m.

LEAVE HILO for Paauilo and Way Stations: Daily: 9:15 a. m. and 3:15 p. m.

LEAVE HILO for Laupahoehoe and Way Stations: Daily: Saturday Only: 10:30 p. m.

Inward

LEAVE HAKALAU for Hilo and Way Stations: Daily: 9:15 a. m., 12:30 p. m. and 5:30 p. m.

LEAVE PAAUILO for Hilo and Way Stations: Daily: 6:15 a. m. and 12:15 p. m.

LEAVE LAUPAHOEHOE for Hilo and Way Stations: Saturday Only: 12:19 p. m.

RAILROAD TIMETABLE, 1913. The trip back to Hilo was just under two hours, a significant improvement over earlier travel times by either land or sea, much safer, and also much more comfortable. The spectacular views of valleys, mills, fields, flumes, and the coast led to the development of a tourist business. A 1916 German-made film of the trip is available today for viewing at the Laupahoehoe Train Museum. (HTH.)

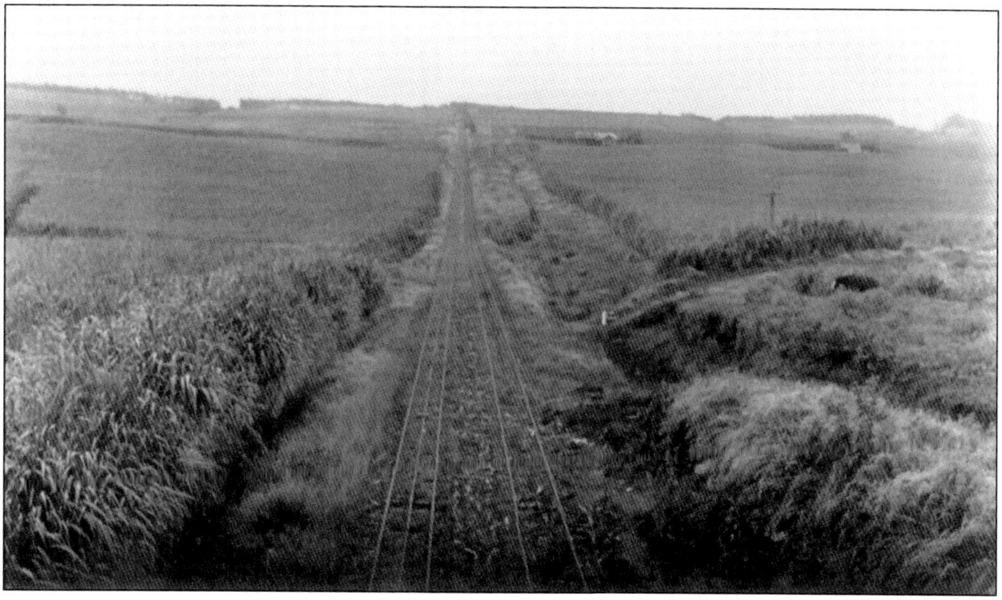

Gravity Crossing at Paauhau. As land travel across Hamakua became more common in the late 19th century, road users had to be aware of the dangers imposed by the passage of fast moving makai-bound cane bundles overhead or on rails at surface level. Material could simply fall on travelers, but more likely, people, horses, and wagons could be struck. The answer was, much like with modern highways, grade separation. Today, maps still show a "Gravity Road" makai of Kalopa State Park that crosses Mamalahoa Highway. However, the mauka-makai rails are long gone. (HSA.)

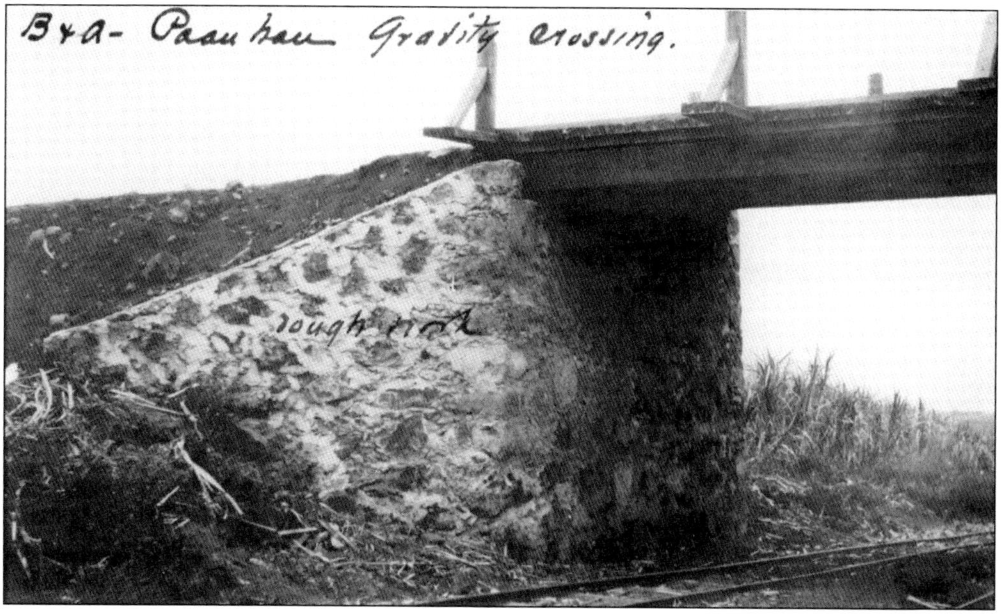

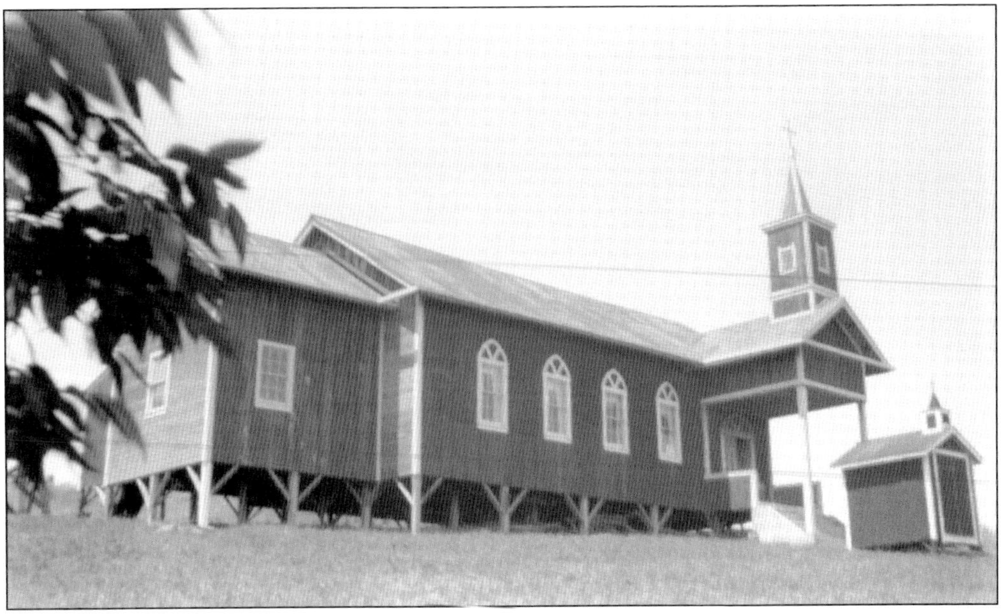

Our Lady of the Mount, Kalopa. There have been two Catholic churches and cemeteries constructed in Kalopa. The first was makai of the original belt road and the second above the present Mamalahoa Highway in Kalopa Homesteads. These photographs are of the second church exterior and interior. Note the plantation-influenced architecture and materials. Today, only the cemeteries remain. (CA).

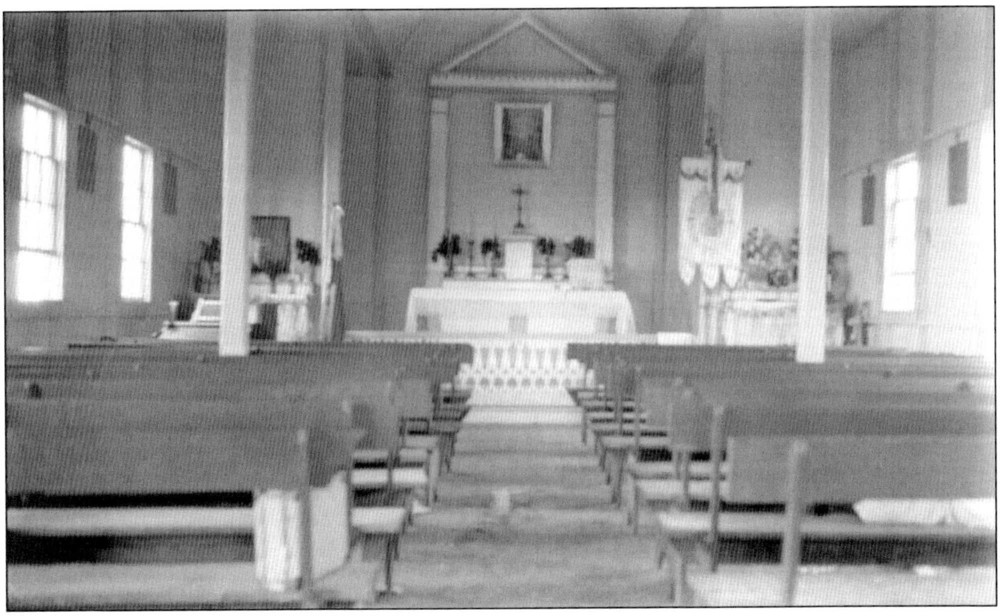

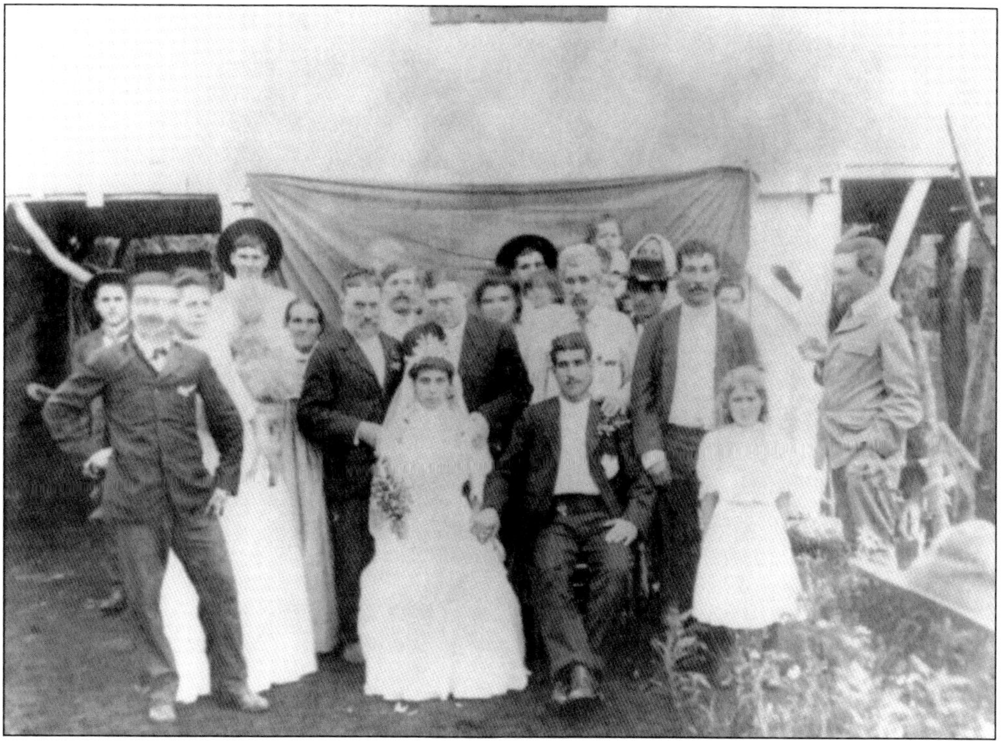

Marriage Ceremony. The families of Virginia Gouvea and Antone Luce Ferreira were joined in the Catholic church that stood in lower Kalopa in 1910. Virginia's parents, Emelia and Bento Gouvea, stand to the left; Antone's father, Lucio, has his hand on Antone's shoulder on the right. Both Virginia and Antone spent their lives in Hamakua; they now rest together in Kalopa Catholic Cemetery. (DeMello Family Collection.)

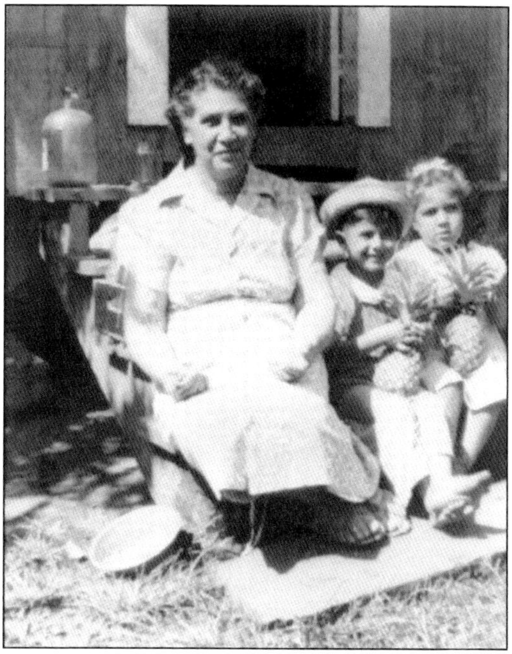

Savoring Homestead Pineapple. Families with small landholdings undertook much more diversified agricultural pursuits than did the plantations. Foremost, of course, were items for their own consumption. These included figs, oranges, avocados, papaya, sweet potato, corn, pumpkins, Portuguese parsley, sweet guava, *wiwi* (strawberry guava), Portuguese cabbage, *pipinola* (chayote), chickens, turkeys, and goats. Products grown for income included coffee, macadamia nuts, pineapple, and grapes. Here, Virginia Ferreira sits on the steps next to her grandson Gerald DeMello and niece Jeannie Freitas with pineapples grown on the extended family's Kalopa property. (DeMello Family Collection.)

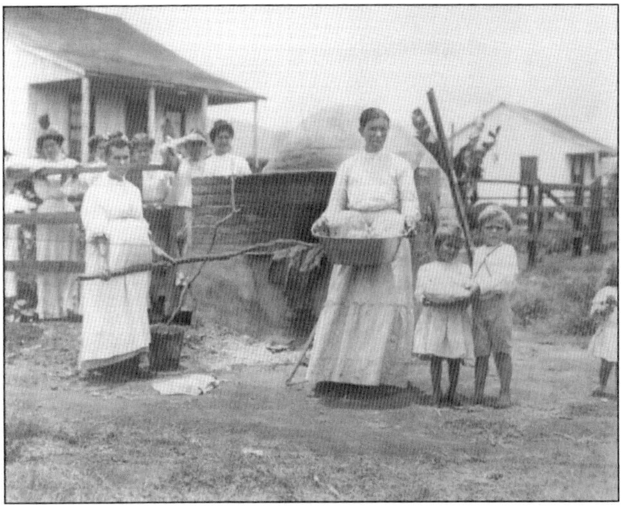
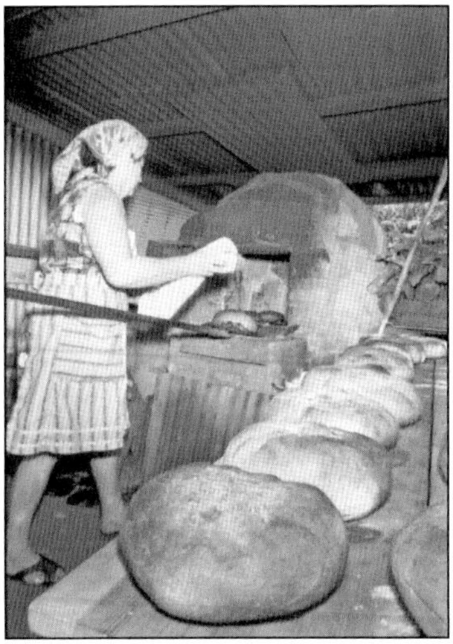

TRADITIONAL BREAD BAKING. Portuguese immigration to Hawaii was from Madeira and the Azores. On the left, children help women bake bread in a traditional Portuguese *forno* (oven). At right, Mary Cordeiro Ferreira does the same in the 1950s at Kalopa. The forno was heated by a wood fire. During the heating, dough was mixed and prepared and allowed to rise. The coals from the fire would then be scraped out of the forno and mopped clean before the bread was put in, so that the stored heat in the stones baked the bread. Out came beautiful brown bread. (Left, HSA; right, Bowen Collection, NHERC.)

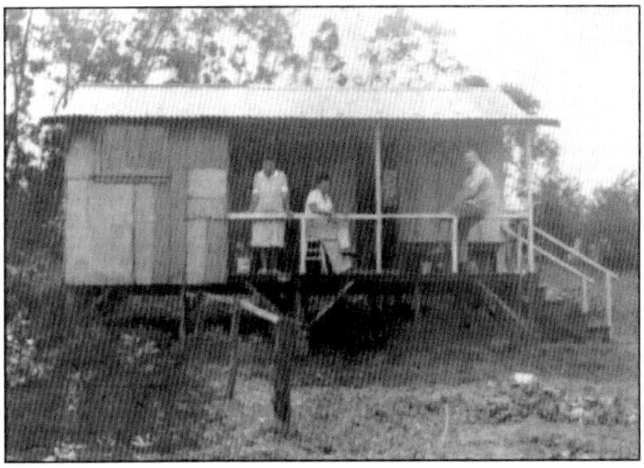
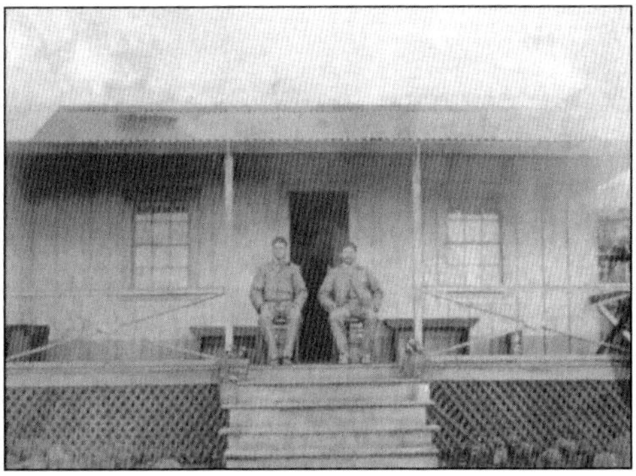

HOMESTEAD AND CAMP HOMES. Most wooden houses featured post and pier foundations. Such structures were easy to assemble, provided reasonable security against flooding, and required little time for grading the land. Two early methods of single wooden-wall construction are illustrated here. At left, mostly vertical planks (and whatever else was available) were erected to keep out the elements. As is easily seen, gaps between the planks rendered this ineffective. At right, battens (smaller boards systematically nailed over the gaps) have improved the integrity of the building. Wooden buildings also featured totan roofs because the metal was easily transported, was easily replaceable, and, as part of a hipped-roof building frame, efficiently diverted rain away from the structure. The construction of the building on the right likely reflects the impacts of plantation era design and construction: increased carpentry skills, use of standardized components, and improved overland transportation for materials acquisition. (Left, Payne Family Collection; right, Becktell Collection, NHERC.)

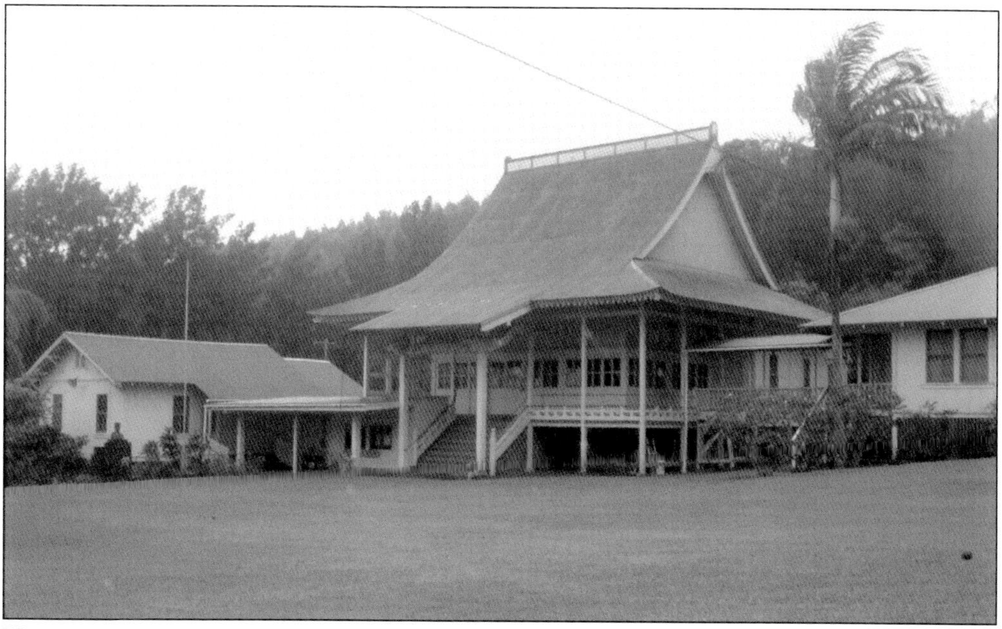

HAMAKUA JODO MISSION. The mission in Paauhau dates from 1898; the original temple building is on the left and a 1910 minister's residence is on the right. The temple in the center, built in the traditional Japanese style around 1910 by well-known carpenter Umekichi Tanaka, includes intricate carvings both in the interior and on the exterior. (CCS.)

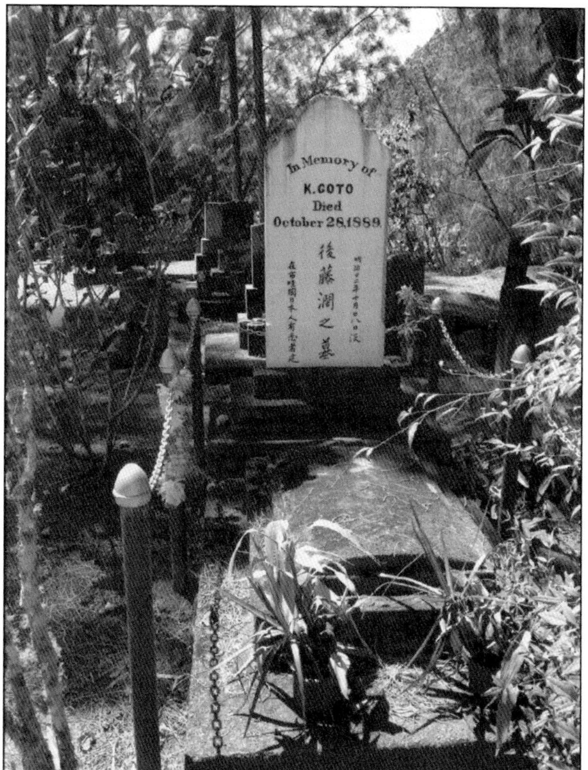

KATSU GOTO RESTING PLACE. Located mauka of the Hamakua Jodo Mission is the grave of Katsu Goto. Goto had arrived with the second group of Japanese immigrants on the ship *City of Tokio* in 1885. He worked on the plantations before becoming an independent merchant, and was an advocate for the rights of Japanese immigrant plantation workers and a victim of racial prejudice. His killing prompted formal inquiries by the imperial Japanese government, an investigation by the Hawaiian royal government, and the conviction of four men. The incident demonstrated to successive Hawaiian governments that overseas powers monitored the treatment of immigrants and that serious abuse could have repercussions. (LR.)

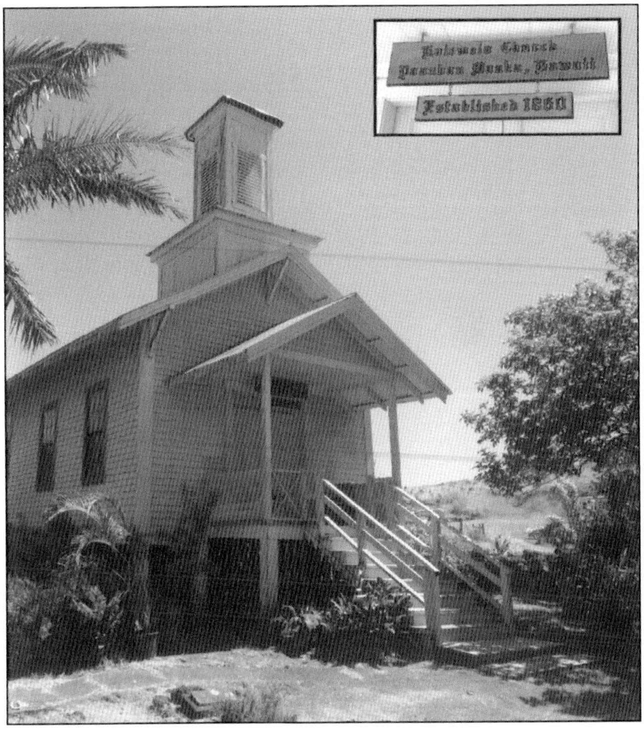

Kamakawiwoole (Kalemela) Church. Charles M. Kamakawiwoole was pastor of this Congregationalist church for 42 years, passing away in 1931. Born in Kohala, he attended Hilo Boarding School and worked at the Nuuanu (Oahu) home of Dr. Gerrit P. Judd before being ordained. As the ethnic composition of the plantation workforce around Paauhau changed over time, his congregation changed; he became known for his choirs of Filipino youth. Reflecting long family ties to the church, most residents of the cemetery carry the Kamakawiwoole name. (RWS.)

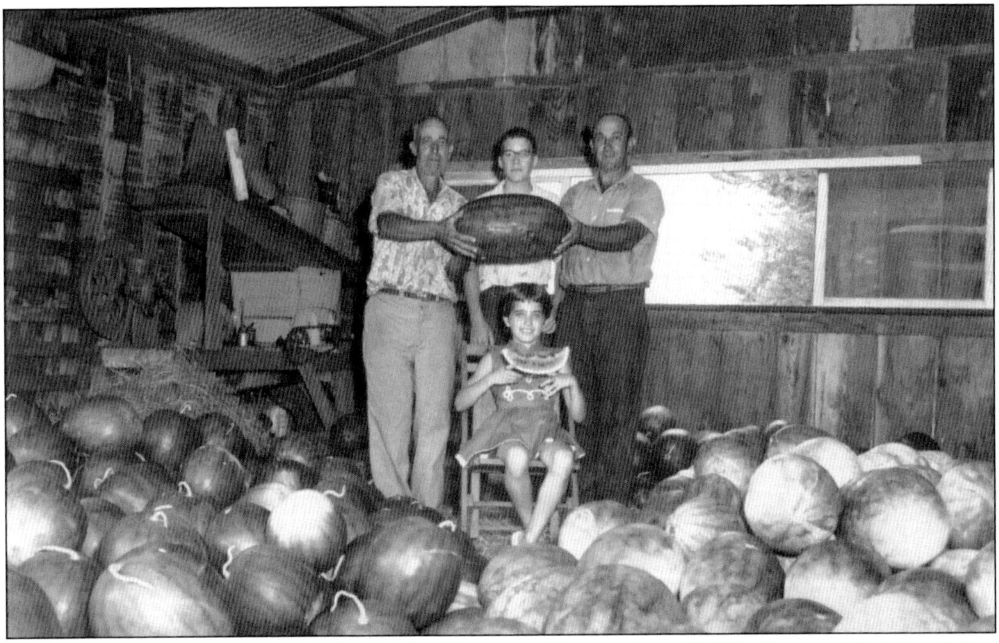

Homestead Agriculture. Predating the Hawaiian Homes Act of 1920, the republic's Land Act of 1895 sought to create a group of small agriculturally productive landowners. Any citizen could lease for purchase or receive long-term leases of government-owned land, subject to occupancy and other provisions. Paauilo, Kaapahu, Kalopa, Kaao, and Ahualoa all had homesteads. Most families entered the program through the lease-to-purchase method and still own the land today. (Larry Ignacio Collection.)

Two

On Mamane Street Makai Side

The original coastal Government Road through Honokaa Town is today called Mamane Street. Mamane, also known as *Sophora chrysophylla*, is a species of flowering plant native to Hawaii generally found at an altitude of 4,000 to 8,000 feet. It can grow as a shrub or tree, reaching a height of up to 49 feet, and produces yellow flowers.

Located on the Hilo side of town, Ohelo Street was an early route to the Paauhau Landing. First manager of the Honokaa Plantation W.H. Rickard helped establish what was then an Anglican cemetery in 1886, in which he is buried (page 83), and the first school in 1889. On Ohelo were also the plantation of Katsu Goto's nemesis, Robert Overend, and the site of Goto's abduction.

Within the civic center are the modest Board of Health buildings (page 28), where scientists waged a nearly five-decade-long battle that eradicated the dreaded bubonic plague in Hamakua. The plague, spread by rodents and their fleas in the cane fields, kills roughly two-thirds of its victims within four days. In Hamakua, the mortality rate was even higher.

Honokaa was technologically innovative. Town booster and "pioneer telephone man" J. Pritchard brought telephone service to Honokaa in 1889 (page 34). Pritchard's company, Hamakua & South Kohala Telephone & Telegraph, was merged in 1913 with the Hilo & Hawaii Telephone & Telegraph Co. and Kona-Kau Telephone & Telegraph Company, forming the Hawaii Telephone Service, another forerunner of Hawaiian Telcom.

Commercial activities in Honokaa developed primarily along Mamane Street between Pakalana and Lehua Streets. Potential development was primarily dictated by the slope of the land. Along the makai side of Mamane, builders had the option of constructing at street level, above, below, and behind their places of business. Basements and partial basements were usually used as storage.

Mamane Street was a lively retail center. While small mom-and-pop operations such as those of the Fujino, Nakashima, Yamatsuka, and Kotake families vied for business with larger family-owned businesses like Ujiki's and Yamato's, the competition was friendly. Proprietors who found themselves unable to meet a customer's needs would regularly recommend another store.

As the second-largest town on the island, Honokaa had the population to support specialty businesses. These included hardware stores, barbers, lawyers, hotels, and theaters. The elaborate Honokaa People's Theatre remains the largest theater on the island.

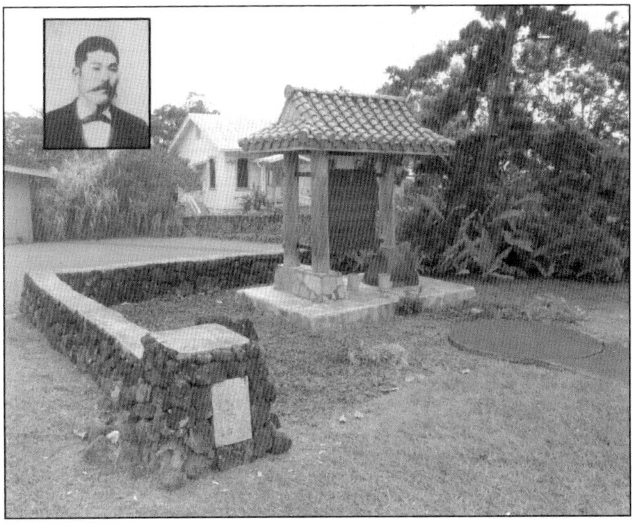

KATSU GOTO MEMORIAL. Goto had attended a secret meeting at night, advising Japanese laborers involved in a labor dispute at nearby Overend Plantation. Previously, the plantation owner had personally threatened Goto. Goto was ambushed on his way home by four men along Ohelo Road fronting the cemetery. Pulled from his horse, he was apparently lynched on a telephone pole at this site directly across from the courthouse. (Jodo Mission; LR). [5]

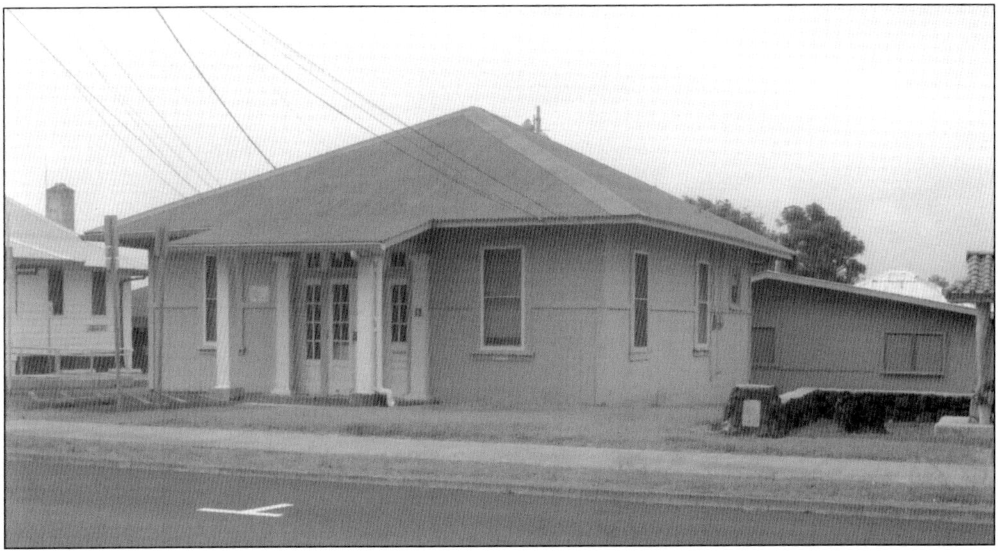

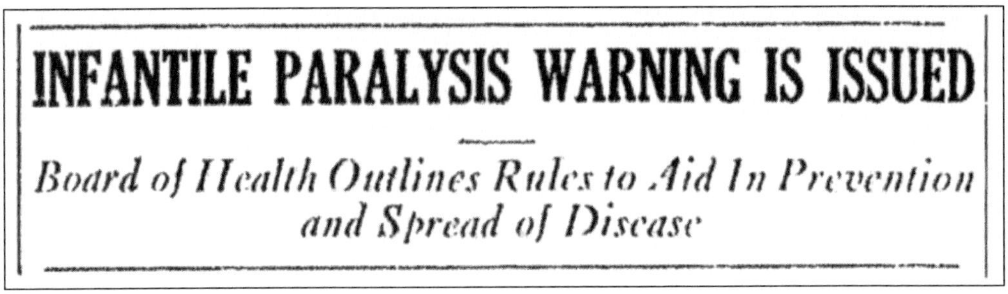

INFANTILE PARALYSIS WARNING IS ISSUED

Board of Health Outlines Rules to Aid In Prevention and Spread of Disease

BOARD OF HEALTH BUILDING. During the territorial period, a multitude of communicable diseases that are considered controlled today threatened the Hamakua community. One was infantile paralysis. Also known as polio, it struck mostly children, although its most famous victim was Pres. Franklin Roosevelt. A victim could end his or her days lying immobile in an iron lung. In 1927, parents were encouraged to isolate their offspring from other children to lessen their chances of catching the disease. (Top, CCS; bottom, HTH.) [6]

Bubonic Plague Threat. Plague reached Honolulu in 1899, Hilo in 1900, and Honokaa in 1910. Fear of plague was so great that sections of both Honolulu and Kahului were deliberately burned to the ground by the government. Once infected, fatality rates were high: in Hamakua, of 112 cases, only one person recovered. Once the method of disease spread was understood, the Board of Health and plantations engaged in ongoing rat (and thus flea) eradication campaigns. The last human case was in 1949, and the last rodent case in 1957. Note the multilingual warning sign. (Hawaii's Plantation Village.)

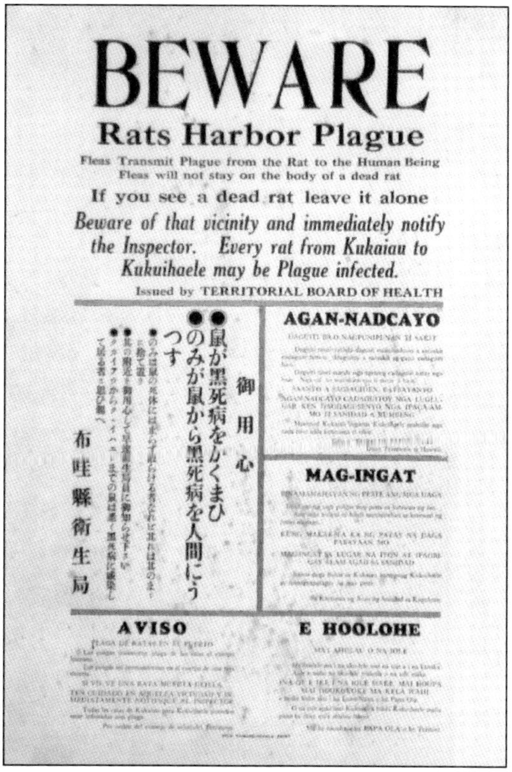

The End. This is the crematorium at the back of the Board of Health facility where the corpses of rats trapped for field studies were disposed of. The plantations had personnel specifically assigned to trap rats; bounties were also offered. (LR.)

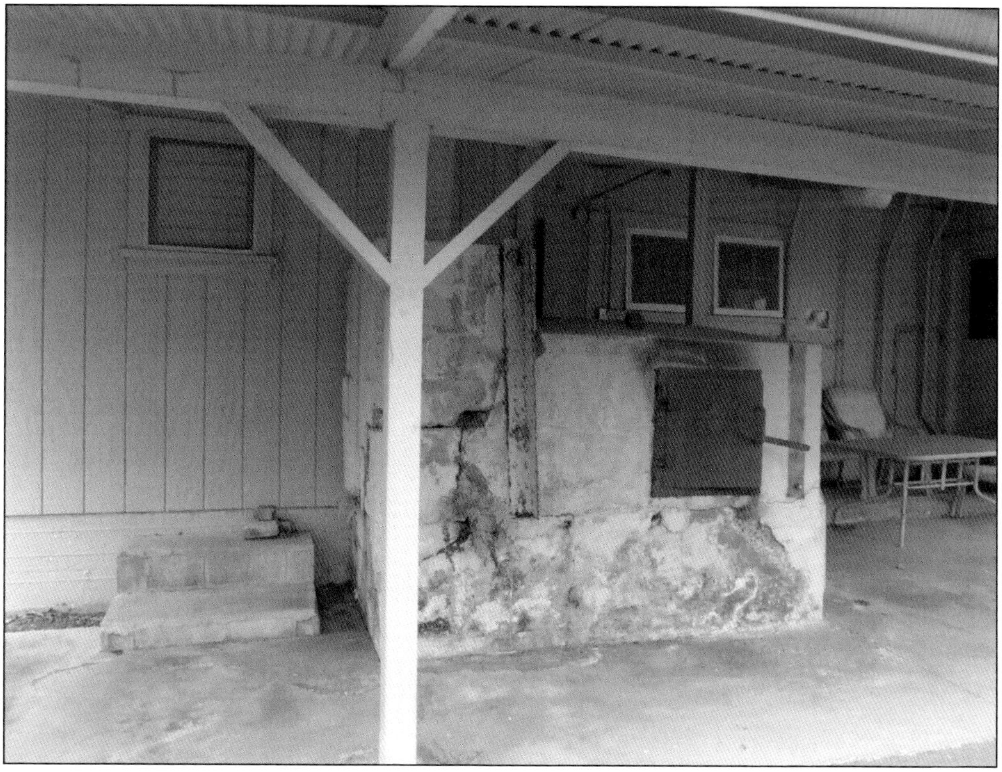

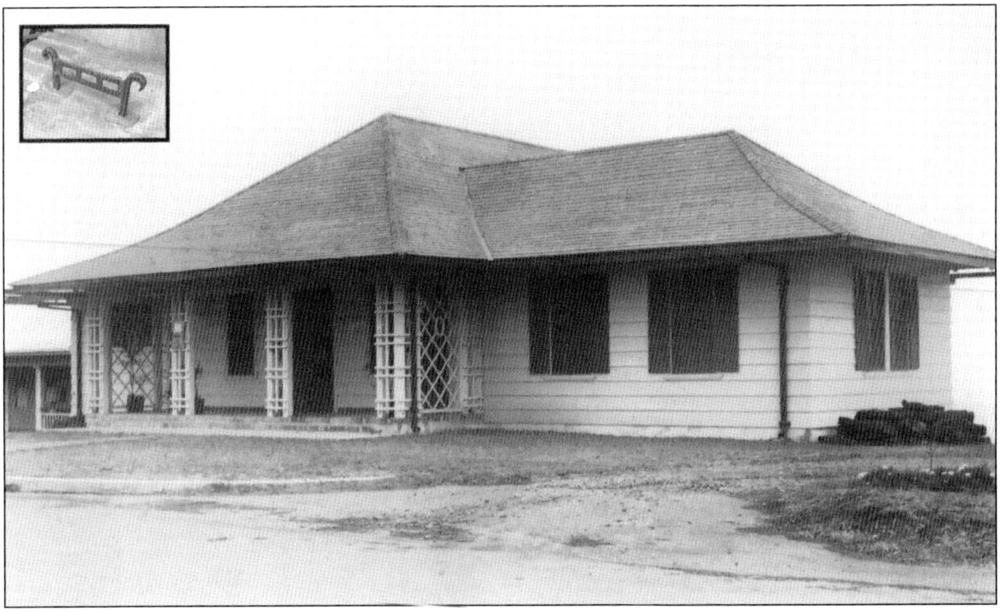

Hawaii Public Library, Honokaa Branch. The present library was a Depression-era federal Works Progress Administration project with the same plan as the library at Kaunakakai, Molokai. The building opened on June 5, 1937. The first librarian was Charlotte MacFarlane and her assistant was Doris Higashi. Design elements include a high, double-hipped roof, large eaves, and a front porch embellished with trellises. Boot scrapers (inset) were added to remove mud from shoes before entering. The second courthouse is visible to the left of the library. (Hawaii Public Library, Honokaa Branch.) [7]

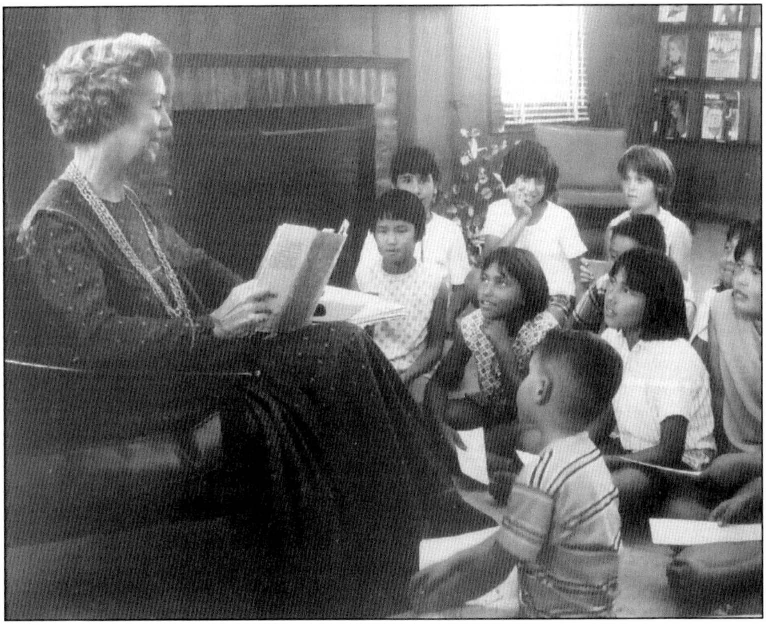

Local Author. Paauilo resident Vivian L. Thompson wrote 24 books for children (including five on Hawaiian folklore) and three plays and taught school. Her titles include *Camp-In-The-Yard* and *The Horse that Liked Sandwiches*. Here she is reading to children in the Honokaa Library during the early 1950s. (HSL.)

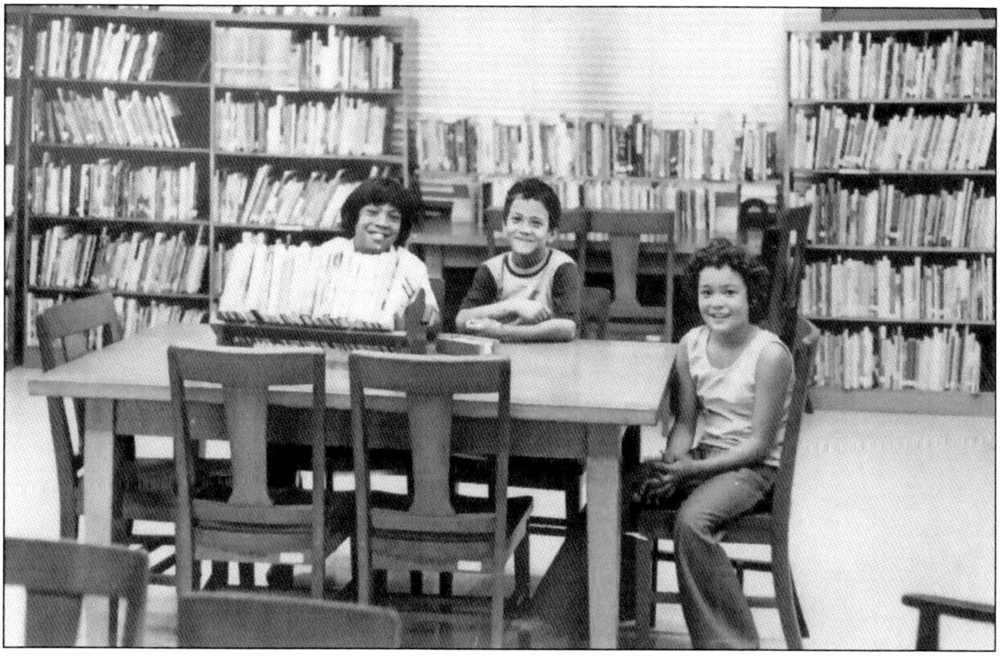

INSIDE THE LIBRARY. The library has 3,040 square feet of space in a cruciform shape. As can be seen here, the facility, located near Honokaa School, is popular with students. The building is literally packed with books, employing high shelves to make the most of the space available. (HSL.)

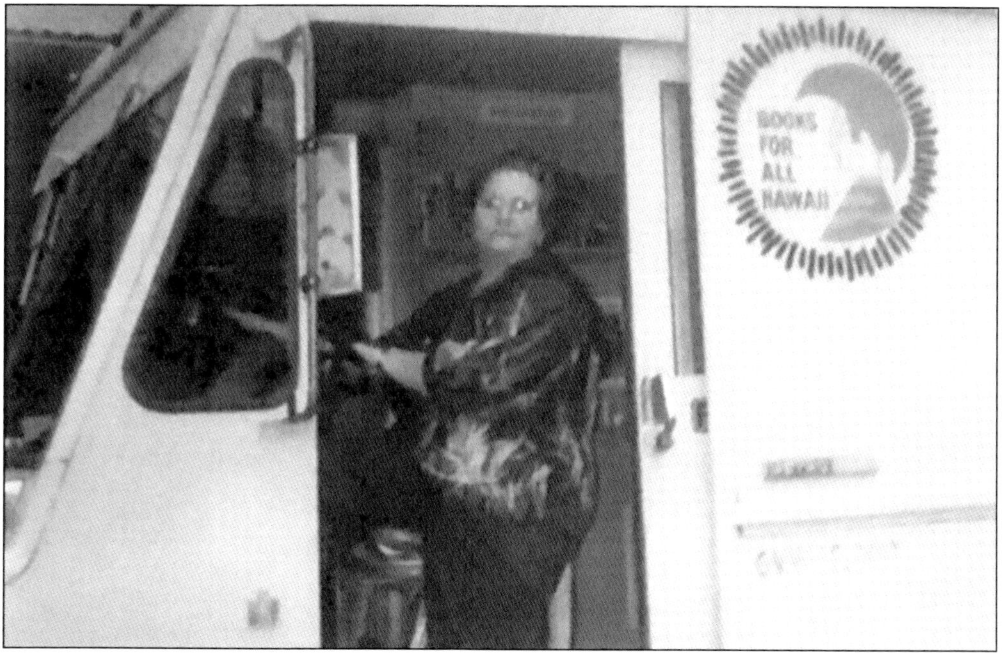

FRIENDLY NEIGHBORHOOD BOOKMOBILE. Bookmobiles have been popular in Hawaii for generations. These "books on wheels" programs are especially important in rural communities during summer months because they encourage children to make good use of their time, facilitate recreational reading, and make additional materials available for summer school projects. Pictured here in 1981 is Gwynne G. Logan, a Waimea area librarian, in the Hamakua Bookmobile. (HSL.)

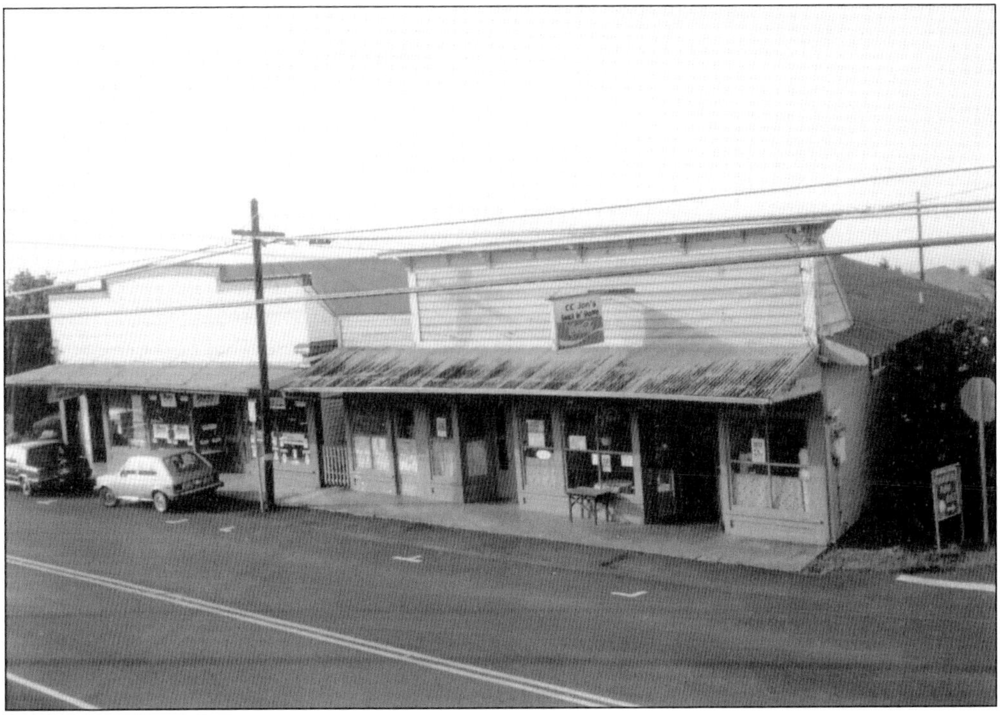

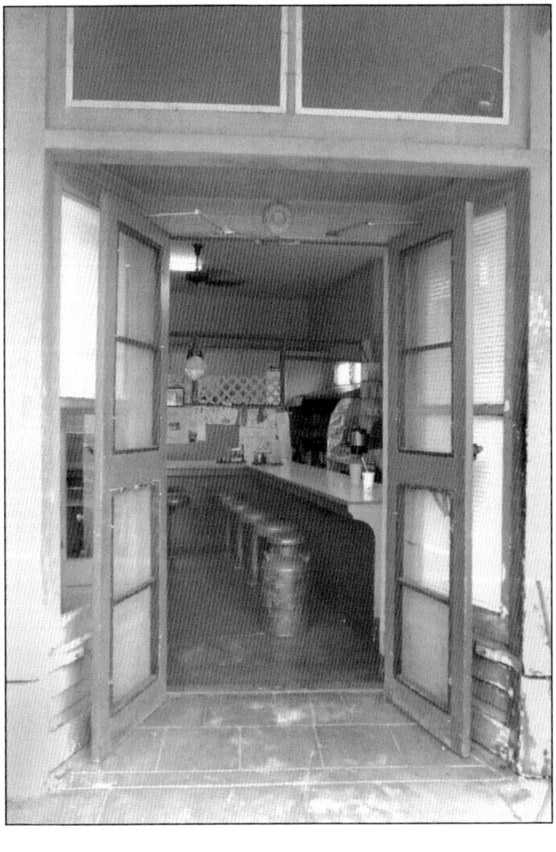

Nakashima (above left) and Fujino Buildings (above right, and left). From 1950 through the 1970s, veteran Teruo Goma ran the Uptown Barbershop, located in the Waipio side of the Nakashima Building. Goma offered a massage with every haircut, always wore white, and could be counted on to attend everyone's funeral. The Hilo side of the Nakashima Building housed the Toshio Nakashima Store, which carried violet candy, black licorice, chewing gum, long john doughnuts, groceries, and laundry detergent. The building is currently home to the Honokaa Youth Center. The Waipio side of the Fujino Building housed Takeko's Beauty Shop. The Hilo side had the Fujino Store, which sold Chinese seeds, candy, and ice shave; the Fujinos were famous for sending an ice cream truck around town on Sundays. For 42 years, the space was the location of CC Jon's Snack Shoppe. Note the fountain-style stools and milk can for sitting at the lunch counter. (Above, Yamato Collection, NHERC; left, LR.) [8, 9]

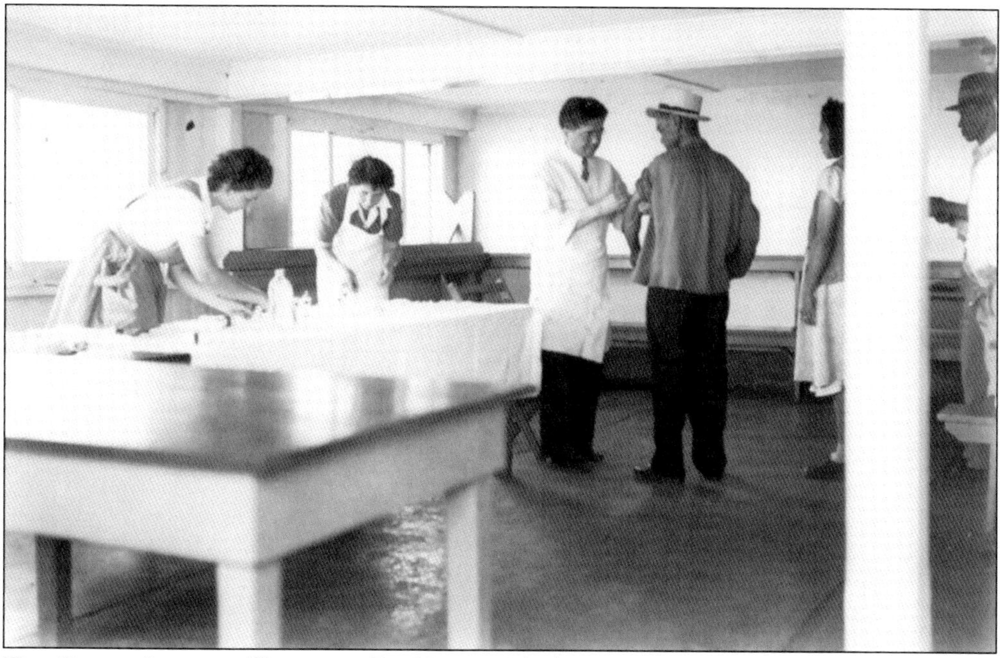

THE OKADA JAPANESE HOSPITAL. Dr. Haruto Okada was born in Paauhau in 1904. In 1937, after medical training in Illinois, he returned to Hamakua to work with Dr. Koshiro Tofukuji at Tofukuji Hospital. Dr. Okada opened his own 12-bed hospital in 1935. All nationalities were welcomed. Note the arched reception window below. The facility contained an operating room, laboratory, x-ray room, and nursery. Part of Dr. Okada's preventive care was to administer shots. The hospital operated until March 1956. (Above, NHERC; below, LR.) [10]

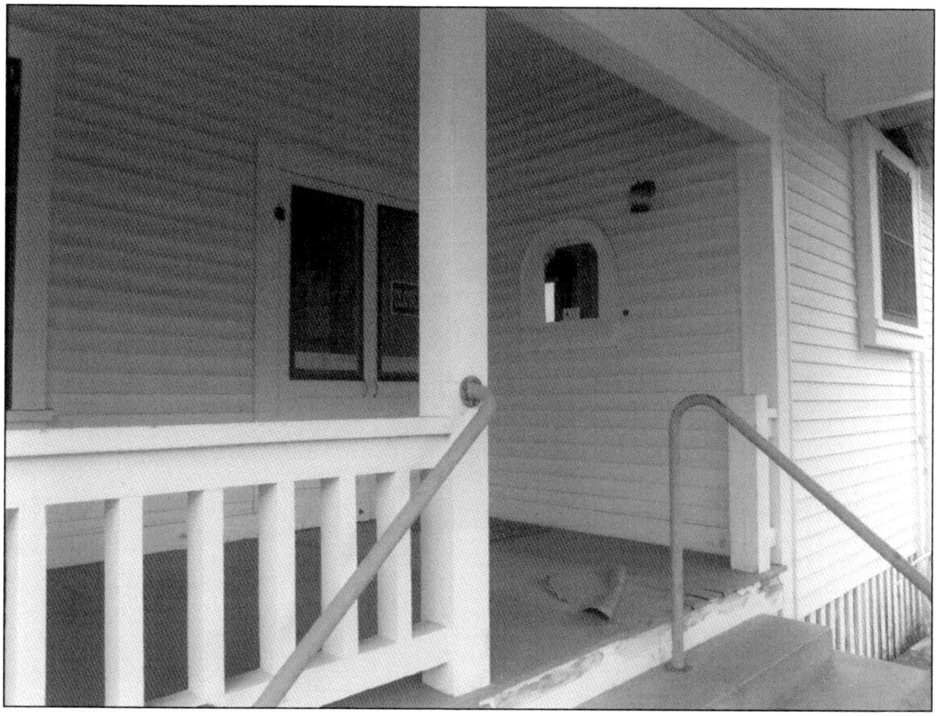

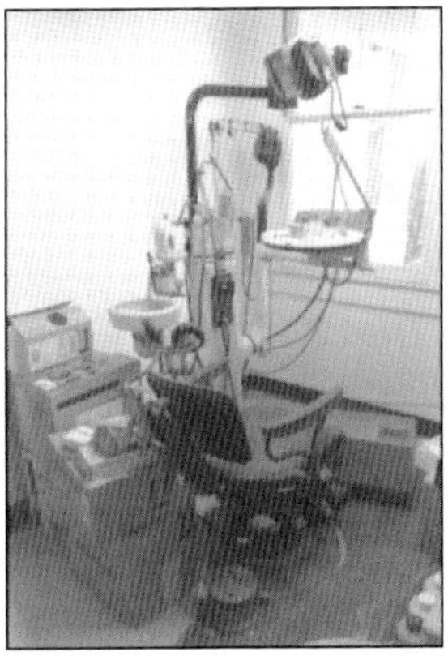

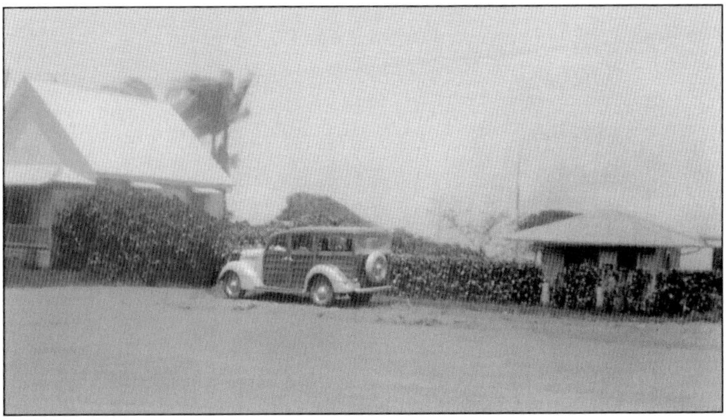

Keeping Tradition. Like his father, Edmund Akioka became a dentist. He employs the traditional honor system for service payments by long time patients. He retains his father's dental equipment on display (pictured); the only difference from previous practice is that the house has been physically separated from the office to prevent patients from wandering into the living area. The exterior photograph shows the small dental office (right) not far from the Hawaii Telephone Service exchange (left, colored white). (Left, LR; right, Ujiki Family Collection.) [11]

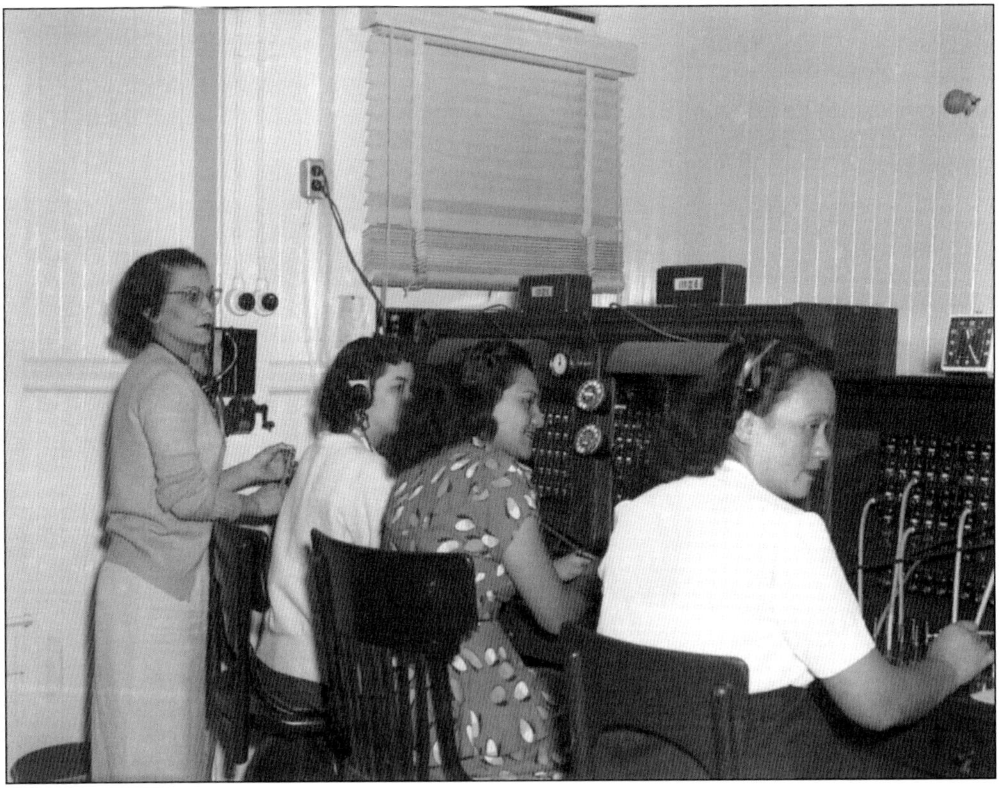

Telephones—The Old-Fashioned Way. Before dial-up systems were introduced in 1957, phone connections were made at telephone exchanges. Anyone wanting to place a call automatically reached the exchange, where the operators connected their calls by placing a cable plug into a specific jack on the switchboard. Knowing one's community telephone operator personally was of benefit in times of emergency or gossip. Company rules originally limited the job to single women. (Christensen Collection, NHERC.) [12]

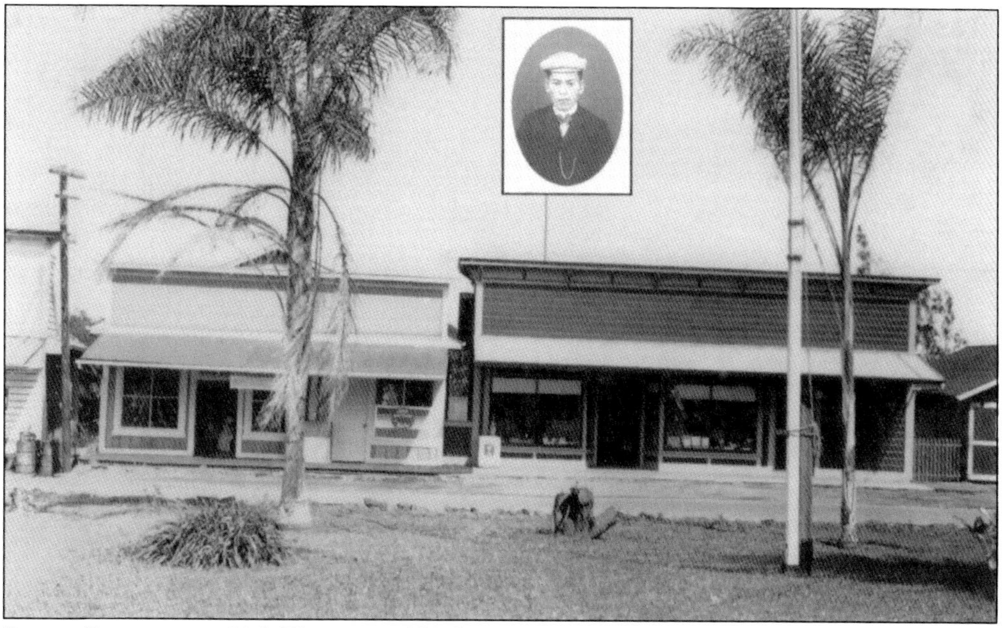

Retail Expansion, 1936. The original Ujiki Store is on the left, and the new store and garage is at right. (Compare this with this book's 1925 cover photograph of the original Ujiki Store.) Masajiro Ujiki, the family patriarch, is pictured as a young man in the inset. (Ujiki Family Collection.) [14]

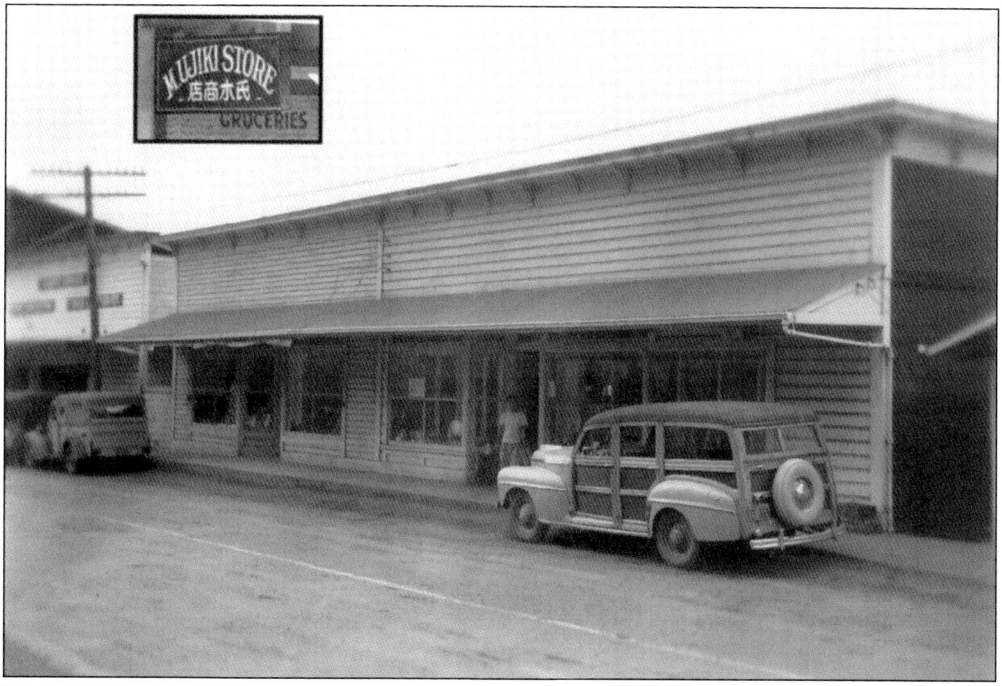

New Store Face, 1942. Despite wartime restrictions on civilian construction, Masajiro Ujiki managed to get materials and permission to combine the original (left) and new stores (right) into one. Included in the remodeling were a recessed entrance bay on the original building and a common parapet throughout. (Ujiki Family Collection.)

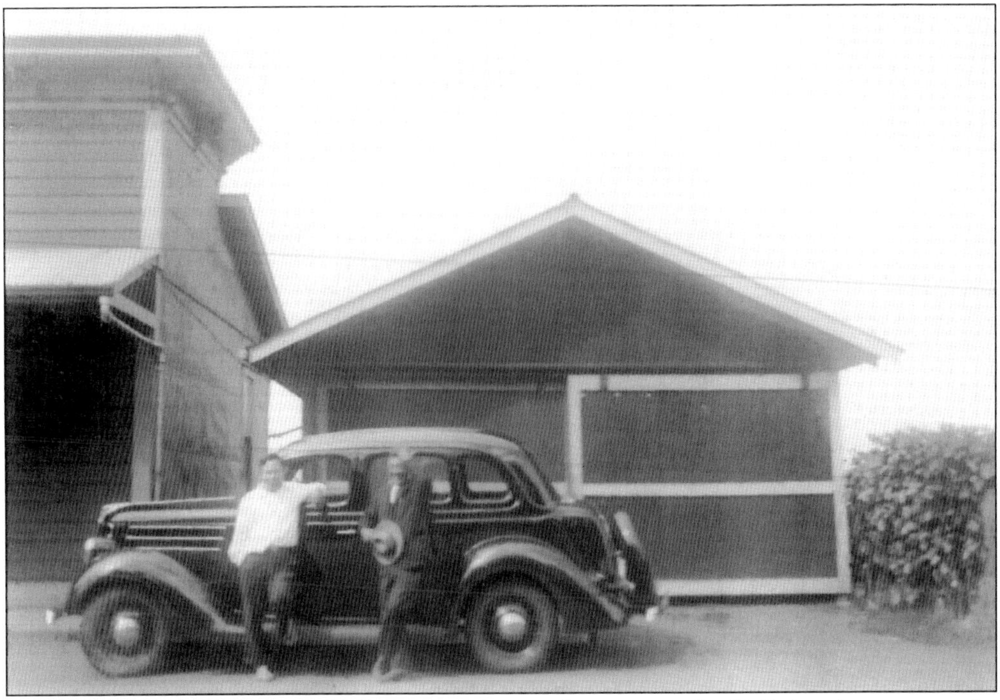

UJIKI "FEED ROOM." Masajiro Ujiki's store continued to prosper. In 1942, he also converted a two-car garage into an additional street-level storage area. The space contained products meant for animal husbandry—hence the name Feed Room. At this time, an original large sliding door was removed and replaced with a single standard door. (Ujiki Family Collection.)

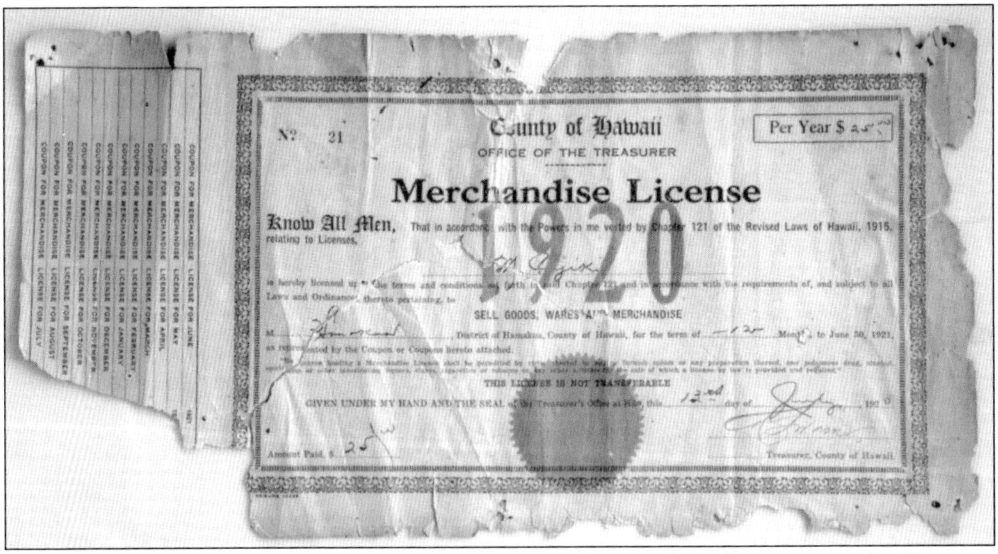

No. 21

County of Hawaii

OFFICE OF THE TREASURER

Per Year $

Merchandise License

1920

Know All Men, That in accordance with the Powers in me vested by Chapter 121 of the Revised Laws of Hawaii, 1915, relating to Licenses,

SELL GOODS, WARES AND MERCHANDISE

THIS LICENSE IS NOT TRANSFERABLE

GIVEN UNDER MY HAND AND THE SEAL of the Treasurer's Office at Hilo, this 13th day of July 1920

Treasurer, County of Hawaii

UJIKI STORE MERCHANT AND LIQUOR LICENSE, 1921. All stores doing businesses in the Territory of Hawaii had to obtain appropriate licenses as well as undergo periodic health inspections. This document authorizes Ujiki "to sell goods, wares, and merchandise." Ujiki Store was known to carry everything. Goot Lun Akioka, the dentist's wife, would shop there, as would the teachers from the Honokaa School teachers' cottages across Mamane Street. (Ujiki Family Collection.)

MASAO UJIKI AND GRANDDAUGHTER SARAH, LATE 1980S. Four generations of Ujikis have lived on the 100-year-old property. As was the practice in many such small businesses run by immigrants, all family members (and often those who married into the family) were expected to contribute to the enterprise; simultaneously, the business was looked at as a vehicle by which subsequent generations, through education, could rise economically into the professional classes. In the case of the Ujikis, of the three surviving children of Masajiro and Momoyo, son Masao stayed with the store, Takeshi returned to the store after being away at school, and daughter Misao also went away to school before becoming an educator. Masao's children went to mainland colleges: Clyde became an educator, Gerald a surgeon, and Karen a pediatrician. Included in the next generation, Karen's daughter Sarah (pictured) became a podiatrist. (Photograph by Brian Breakstone.)

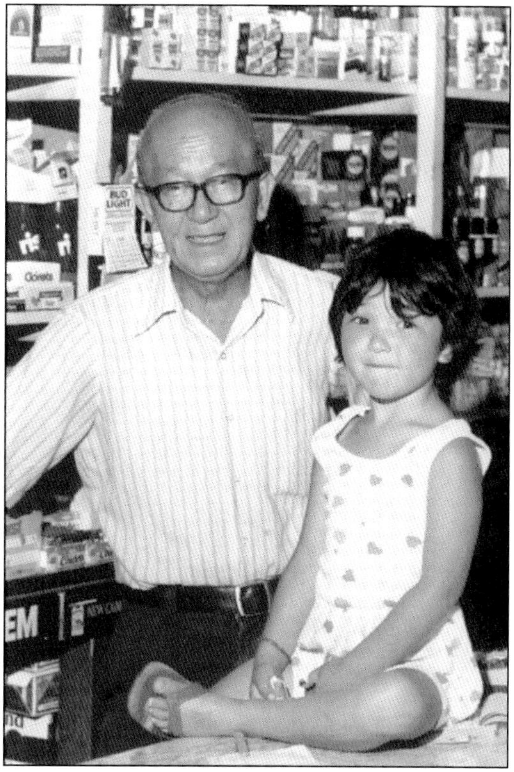

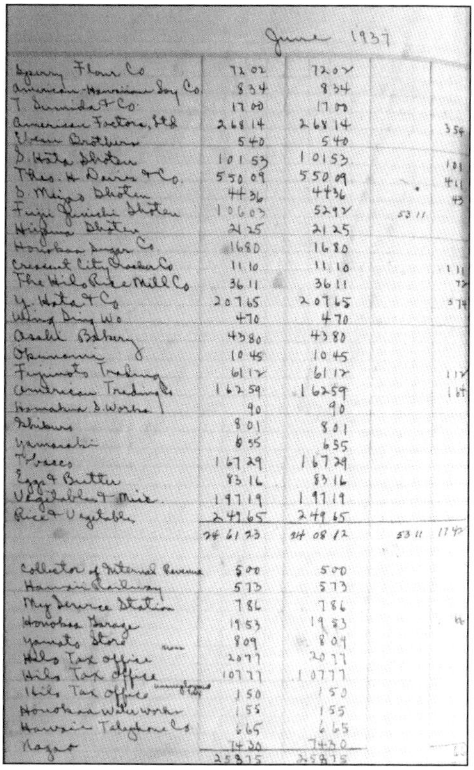

June 1937

Sperry Flour Co	72 02	72 02		
American-Hawaiian Soy Co.	8 34	8 34		
T. Sumida & Co.	17 00	17 00		
American Factors, Ltd	268 14	268 14		3 54
[illegible] Brothers	5 40	5 40		
S. Hata Shoten	101 53	101 53		1 01
Theo. H. Davies & Co.	550 09	550 09		4 11
S. Meijo Shoten	44 36	44 36		43
Fuji Junichi Shoten	106 03	52 92	53 11	
[illegible] Shoten	21 25	21 25		
Honokaa Sugar Co	16 80	16 80		
Crescent City Soda Co	11 10	11 10		1 11
The Hilo Rice Mill Co	36 11	36 11		72
Y. Hata & Co	207 65	207 65		5 74
Wing Sing Wo	4 70	4 70		
Asahi Bakery	43 80	43 80		
Okumura	10 45	10 45		
Fujimoto Trading	61 12	61 12		1 12
American Trading Co	162 59	162 59		1 64
Hamakua S. Works	90	90		
Shibuya	8 01	8 01		
Yamasaki	6 55	6 55		
Tobacco	167 29	167 29		
Eggs & Butter	83 16	83 16		
Vegetables & Mix	197 19	197 19		
Rice & Vegetables	249 65	249 65		
	24 61 23	24 08 12	53 11	17 42
Collector of Internal Revenue	5 00	5 00		
Hawaii Railway	5 73	5 73		
[illegible] Service Station	7 86	7 86		
Honokaa Garage	19 53	19 53		[illegible]
Yamato Store	8 09	8 09		
Hilo Tax office	20 77	20 77		
Hilo Tax office	107 77	107 77		
Hilo Tax office unemployment	1 50	1 50		
Honokaa Waterworks	1 55	1 55		
Hawaii Telephone Co	6 65	6 65		
Nagao	74 30	74 30		
	258 75	258 75		

UJIKI STORE LEDGER, 1937. Before computers, businesses used ledger books to balance their accounts. This page from the Ujiki Store ledger from June 1937 illustrates business relationships with many other small local Hamakua and Hawaii island companies, including Hilo Rice Mill Company, Asahi Bakery, Hamakua Soda Works, Wing Sing Wo, and S. Hata Shoten; important local heavyweights such as Honokaa Sugar Company; and territory-wide sugar and retail factors such as Theo. H. Davies and Company. Accurate accounting was very important. Working capital was always limited, inventory needed to be monitored, product orders had to be made long in advance through a complicated distribution network mostly from Oahu, and the local system of providing credit to long term customers could create a liquidity crunch. Other insights from this document include the types of products involved (tobacco, eggs, butter, and vegetables) and how decades of inflation have devalued the dollar (90¢ owed to Hamakua Soda Works). Some things also never change, as entries include the Collector of Internal Revenue and Hilo Tax Office. (Ujiki Family Collection.)

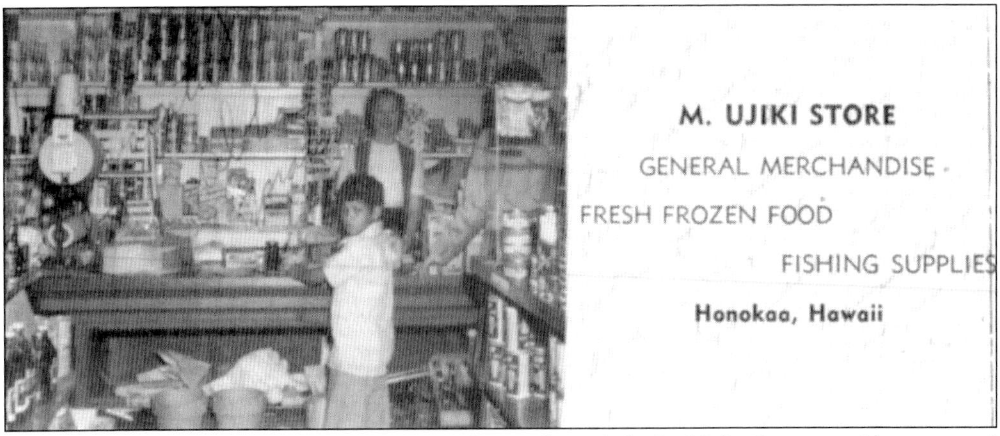

Reaching Out to Youthful Customers. Opened in 1915, the Ujiki Store steadily increased its product offerings to meet the demands of Honokaa and Hamakua residents. The 1920 *City Directory, Island of Hawaii*, listed Ujiki as a purveyor of general merchandise, groceries, dry goods, hats, and notions; the 1923 *City Directory* mentioned groceries, general merchandise, dry goods, toilet articles, confectioneries, tobacco, and cold drinks. This advertisement, from the 1950 Honokaa High School yearbook, *Ka Nani O Honokaa*, helps to illustrate that the Ujikis had developed the most extensive inventory of goods in town. The store was fortunate because its location was close to the Hilo approach to town, the government office complex, and Honokaa School. Undoubtedly, students were a significant customer base. (HHSY.)

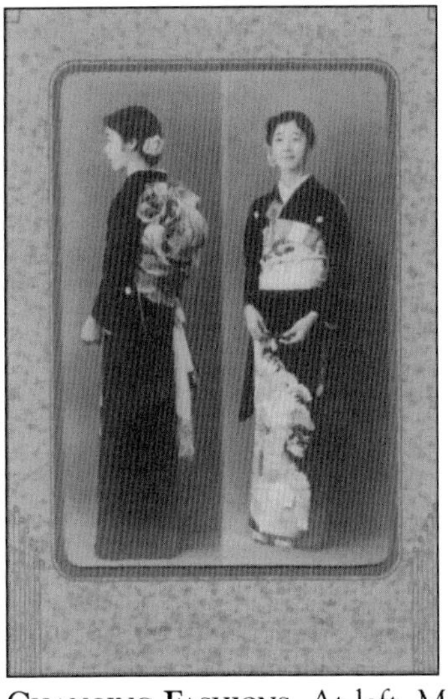

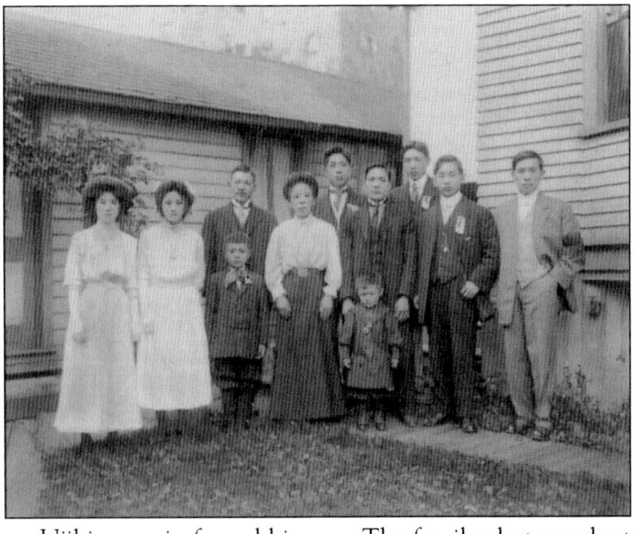

Changing Fashions. At left, Masaye Ujiki poses in formal kimono. The family photograph at right, taken in the backyard of the Ujiki compound, features the clothing and hairstyles worn in the 1910s, including combed hair and long white skirts of the young women; collars, vests, and pocketwatches for the men; and a sailor suit for the youngest child. The prosperity enjoyed by the Ujikis is evident. (Both, Ujiki Family Collection.)

The Ujiki Children Pose in the Photographer's Prop, 1914. Every ethnic group, every generation, adores its children. In this case, the photographer set up his camera at the Ujiki store (or another store), hung a black curtain, and wheeled the "boat" into place. Note the edge of the totan awning above and the boardwalk for the store below. The little son has dropped his milk bottle on the boards below, where it lies in photographic eternity. Meanwhile, his older sister has listened to directions and faces the camera. Note the Japanese and American flags on the boat. (Ujiki Family Collection.)

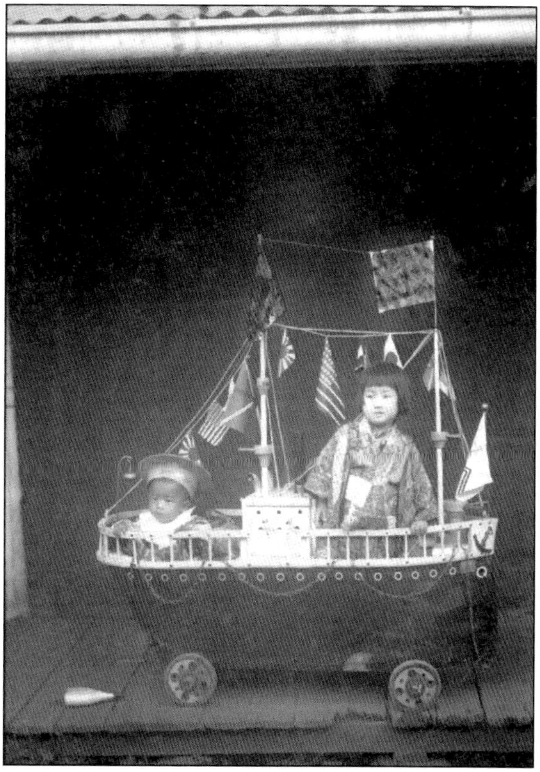

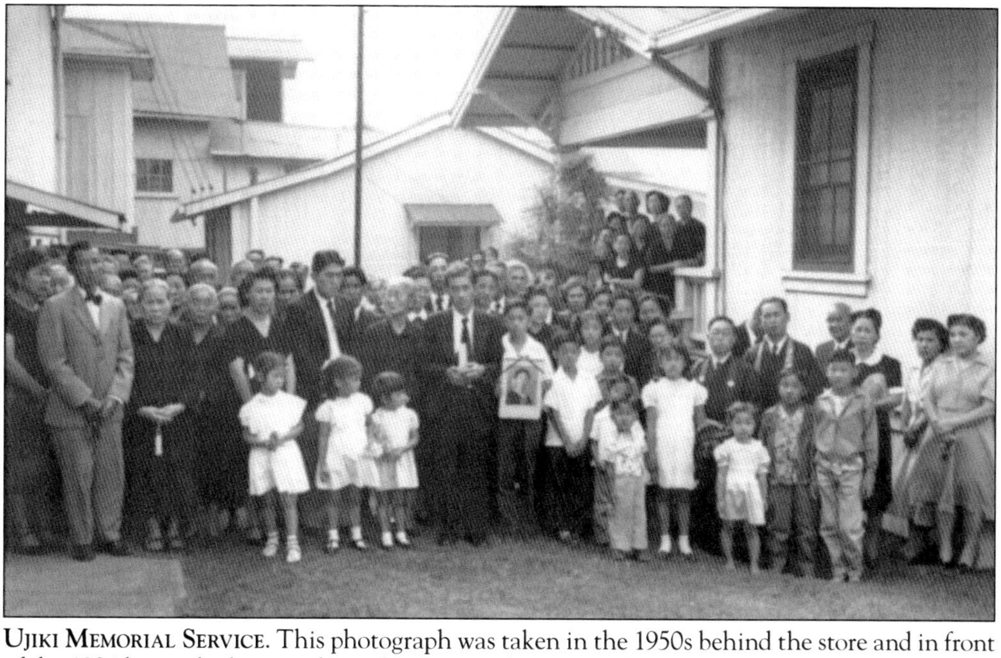

Ujiki Memorial Service. This photograph was taken in the 1950s behind the store and in front of the 1934 house, looking in the makai-Waipio direction. The immediate family members carry the photograph of the deceased, Masao's wife, Masaye Ujiki, and the wooden *ihai*, upon which the posthumous name given by a Buddhist priest has been written. The Hongwanji Reverend Tsugi is the left-most priest standing at right center. (Ujiki Family Collection.)

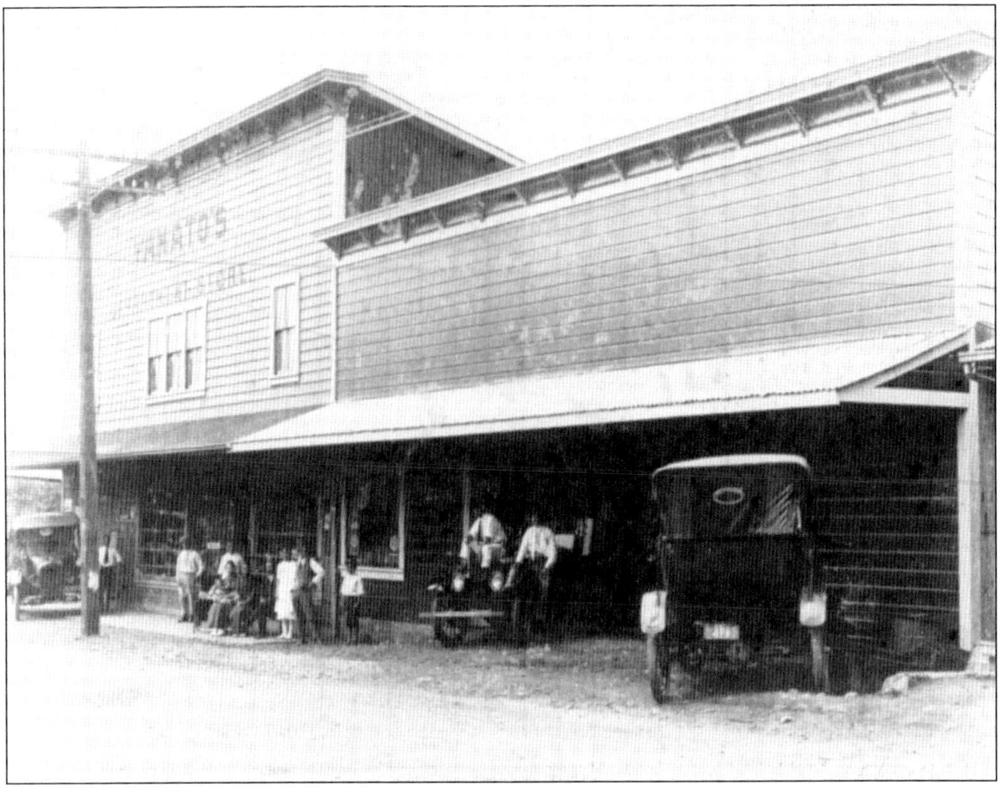

The Yamato Department Store and Garage, 1920s. Like many family operations, the store sold a multitude of items, including groceries, liquor, magazines, and comics and provided delivery service. The first floor was a store, warehouse, garage, and light-testing booth, while the second floor had rooms for rent. The family dwelling, automobile storage, and more rooms for rent were makai in detached single-story buildings. The garage featured gas pumps and a pit for under-car repair service. Waste oil was placed on Rickard Place for dust control. (Ruis/Botelho Family Collection, NHERC.) [15]

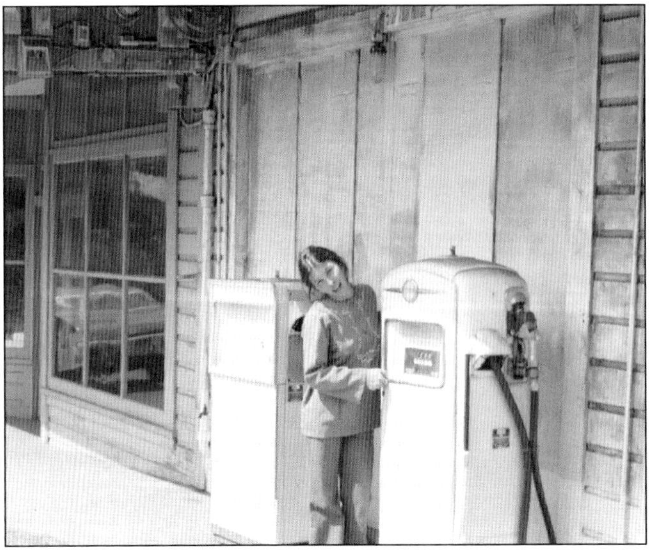

Curbside Gas Pumps. Introduced at the beginning of the 20th century, curbside gas pumps became recognized as a hazard capable of burning pedestrians and buildings alike should vehicles traveling the adjacent street strike them. Municipal and state laws eventually required separate on-property traffic islands where vehicles would approach at slower speeds. Berni Ruis poses between the last of the storefront gas pumps at Yamato Store. (Ruis/Botelho Family Collection.)

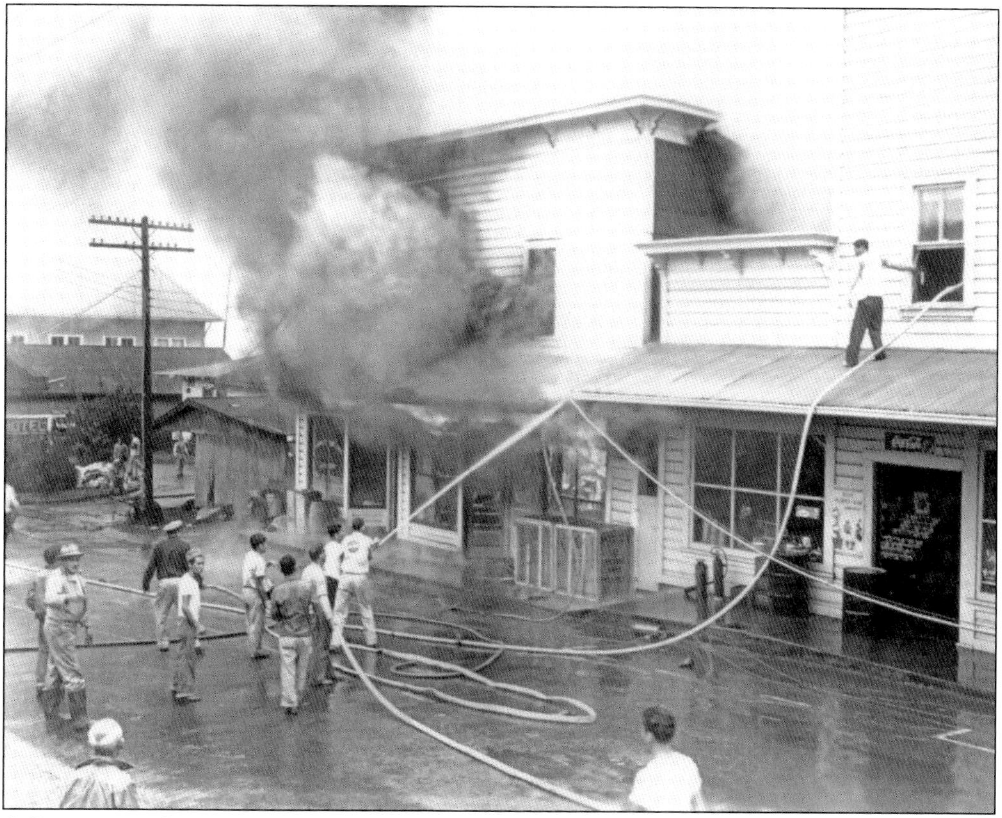

A Family and Community Disaster. A child playing with matches started a fire that destroyed the Tanaka family laundry business and threatened other closely packed wood-framed buildings. Fortunately, the fire station was nearby, giving firefighters the opportunity to limit the damage to one property. The instigator of the fire, soon nicknamed "Firebug," still carries that moniker. (Ruis/Botelho Family Collection.) [16]

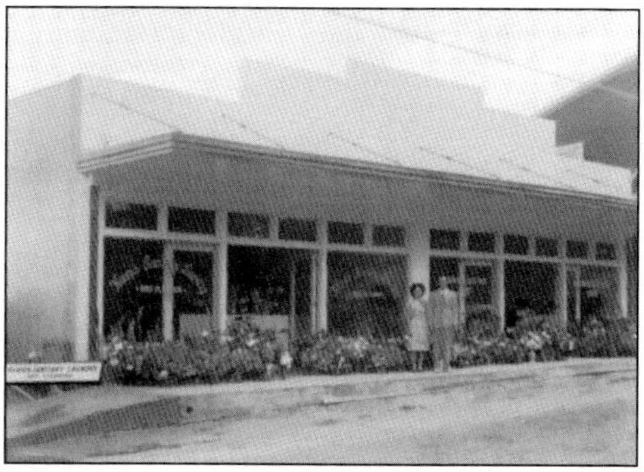

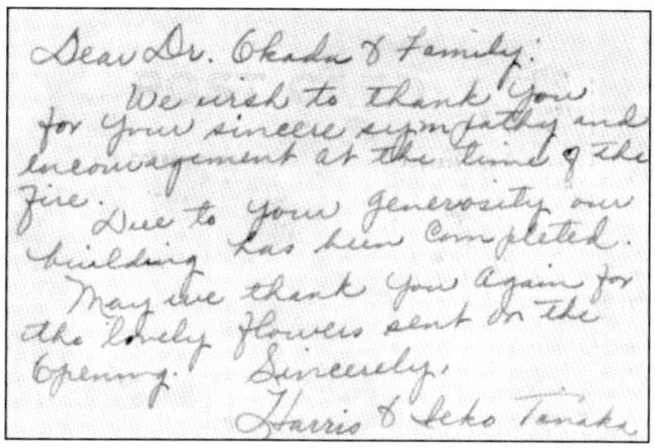

Dear Dr. Okada & Family:
We wish to thank you for your sincere sympathy and encouragement at the time of the fire.
Due to your generosity our building has been completed.
May we thank you again for the lovely flowers sent on the opening.
Sincerely,
Harris & Ieko Tanaka

Perseverance and Community Cohesion. A postcard shows Harris and Ieko Tanaka standing proudly on opening day in front of their new Harris Sanitary Laundry building. The fire could have ruined the Tanakas, but through their own hard work and financial and other assistance from their neighbors, they began again. The thank-you note written on the reverse side of the postcard speaks volumes about the sense of community in Honokaa. (Earl Tanaka Collection.)

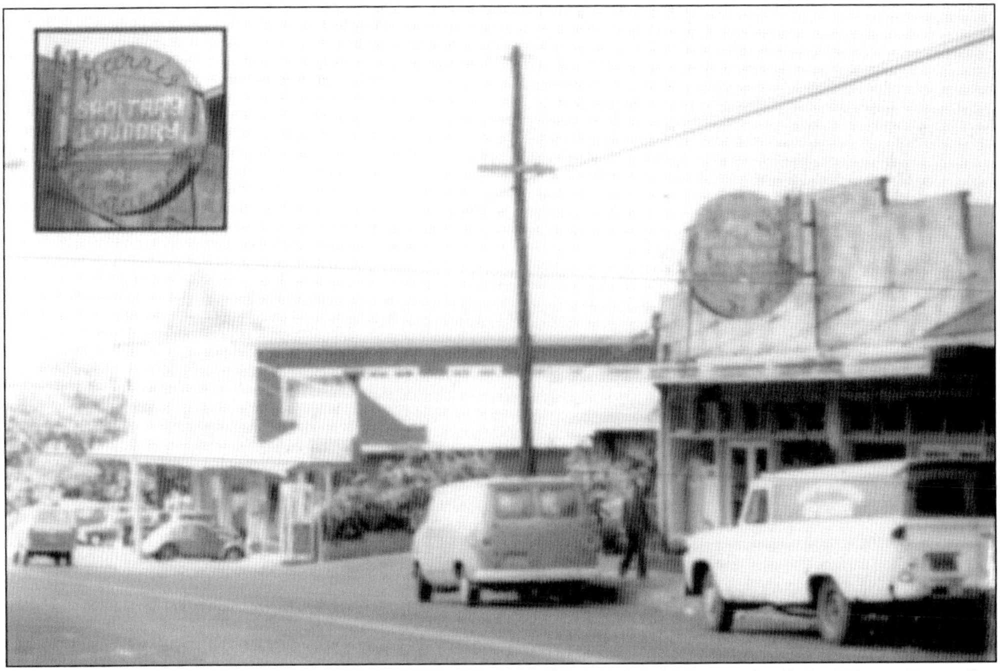

Harris Sanitary Laundry. The red-and-white truck at right distinguished the Harris Laundry from those in other towns with different colors. Before the days of permanent-press garments, Tanaka was successful in gaining numerous high-volume uniform cleaning and detailing contracts at Camp Tarawa and other military establishments. The view shows Mamane Street looking toward Waipio. (Ruis/Botelho Family Collection, NHERC.)

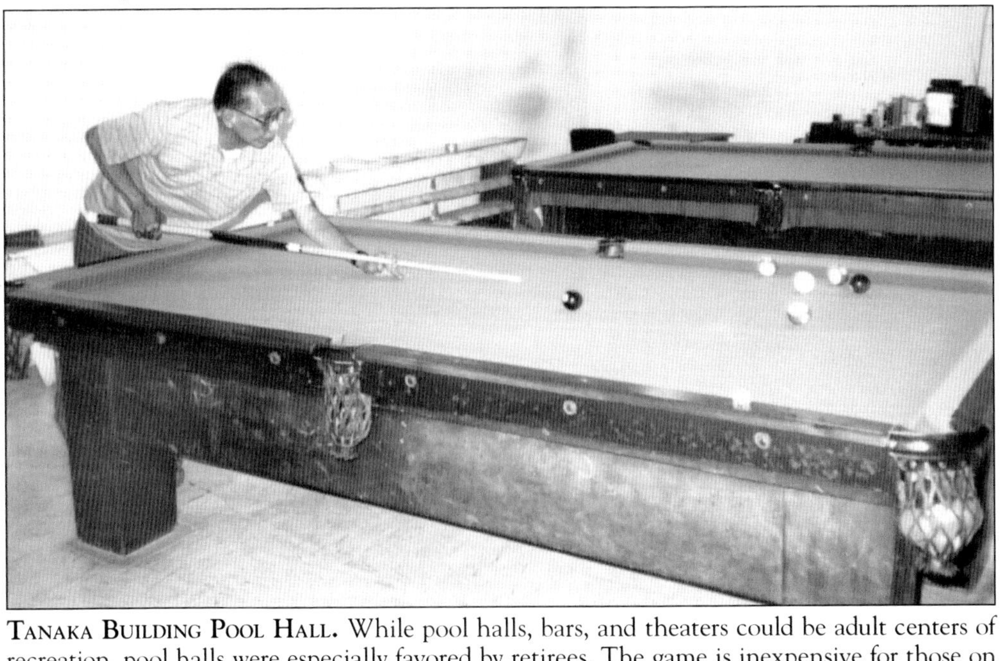

Tanaka Building Pool Hall. While pool halls, bars, and theaters could be adult centers of recreation, pool halls were especially favored by retirees. The game is inexpensive for those on limited incomes, is not physically demanding, and lasts longer than movies. (Yamato Collection, NHERC).

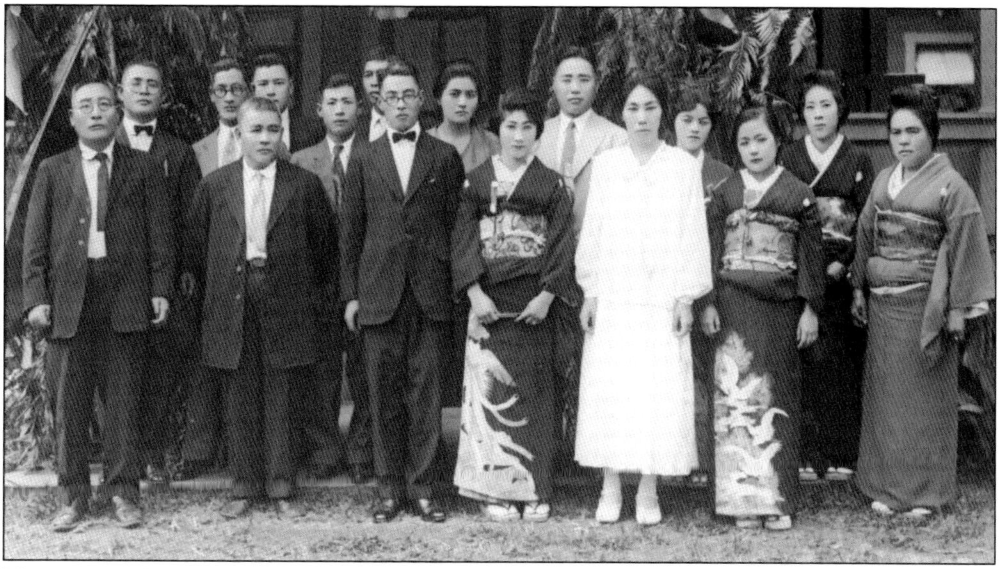

VICTOR AND TOMIKO MORITA WEDDING CELEBRATION. Most of the women are wearing formal Japanese kimono. Kimono, meaning "thing to wear," are T-shaped, straight-lined robes worn with the hem at the ankle and feature attached collars and long, wide sleeves. Kimono are wrapped around the body and secured by an *obi* (sash) tied at the back. Such garments disappeared from the public streets immediately after December 7, 1941. (Morita Family Collection.) [17]

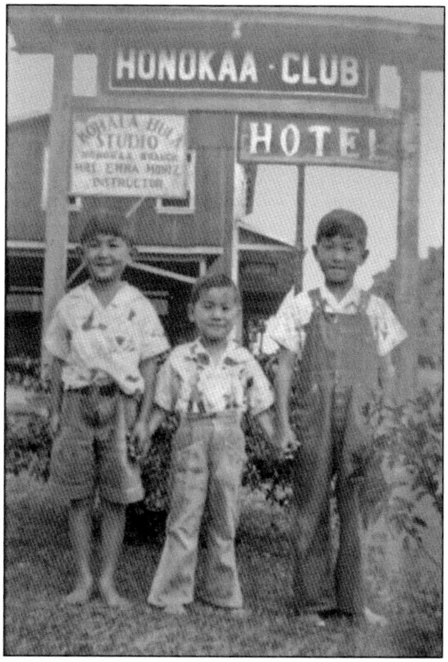

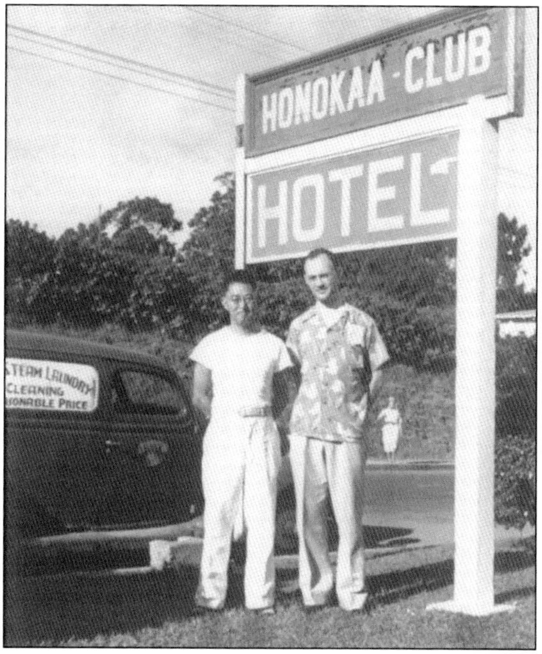

A FAVORITE PLACE TO TAKE PHOTOGRAPHS. At left, from left to right, Alex, Robert, and Henry Morita, sons of the owner, stand in front of Hotel Honokaa Club sign around 1938. Victor Morita (left) and a guest were similarly photographed in the late 1940s. (Also advertised was "Kohala Hula Studio, Honokaa Branch, Mrs. Emma Moniz, Instructor.") The hotel received its full name, Hotel Honokaa Club, purportedly because patrons wanted the moniker to reflect both a place to stay and a place to play. (Morita Family Collection.)

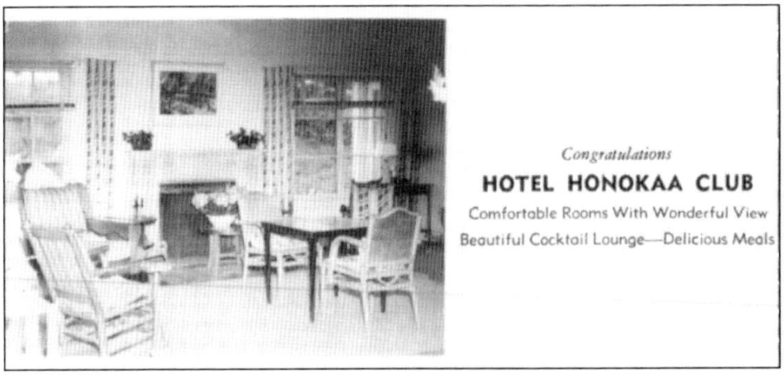

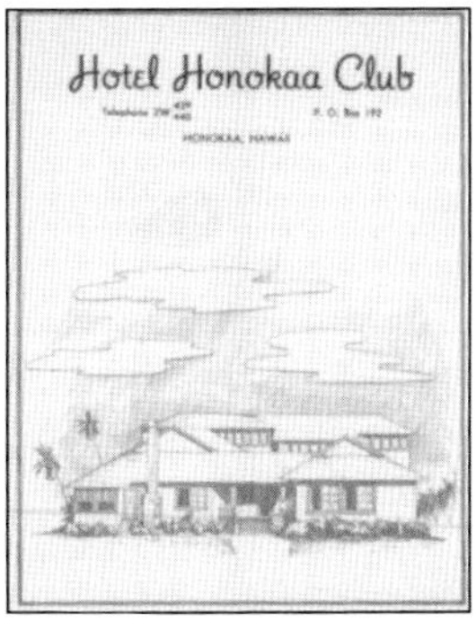

ADVERTISEMENTS AND MENUS. Traditionally, each year, the student staff of the high school's *Ka Nani O Honokaa* yearbook solicits local businesses to purchase advertisements. The businesses hope this will be reciprocated through purchases by friends and relatives attending the graduation. This advertisement from 1950 suggests the comfort offered to potential guests of Hotel Honokaa Club. Also shown is a menu from the club, which included *teishoku* dinners (a set meal on a tray), sizzling steak, or lobster dinners. (Left, HHSY; right, NHERC.)

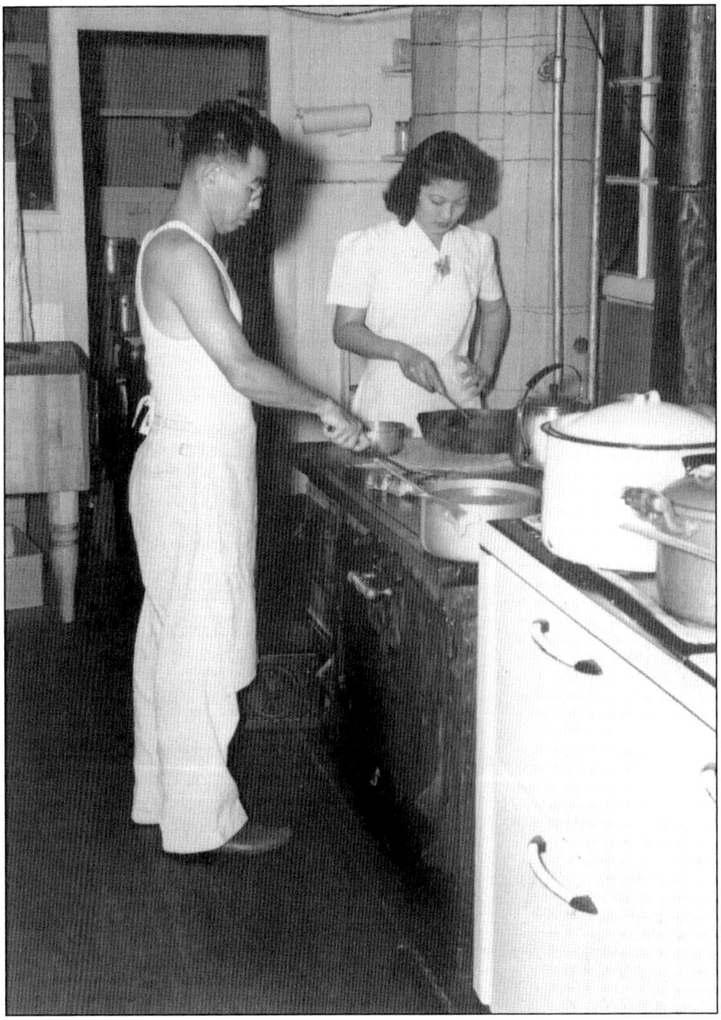

VICTOR PREPARING FOOD IN KITCHEN WITH HOTEL WAITRESS. While the appliances have changed, the room remains the same. Throughout the years, the Hotel Honokaa Club continued to be the social capital of Honokaa, famous for its steak dinners and wedding *luau*. Locals like "Hunter" Cardoza (named for his hobby) were waiters there. The club retains its charm as a living example of pre–chain hotel local accommodation and a place for the community to socialize. (Morita Family Collection.)

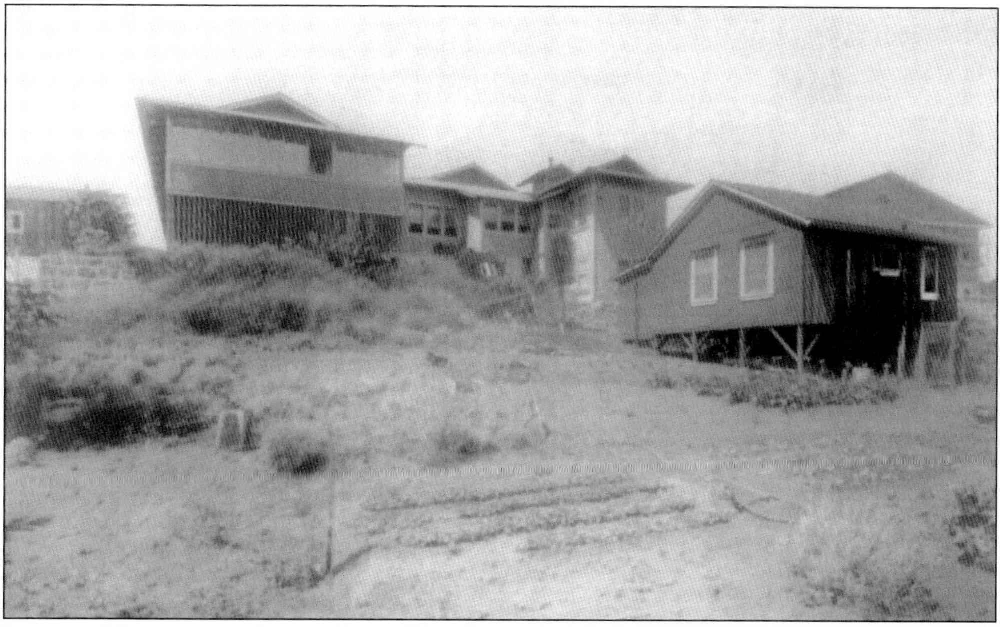

Looking Mauka from Awong Road (Koa Street), pre-1948. The end of wartime restrictions on private construction, combined with the need for upgraded overnight accommodations, led to additional development along the makai side of the Hotel Honokaa Club. The 1948 two-story addition closed the original U-shaped building, retaining ventilation through a central atrium. (Earl Tanaka Collection.)

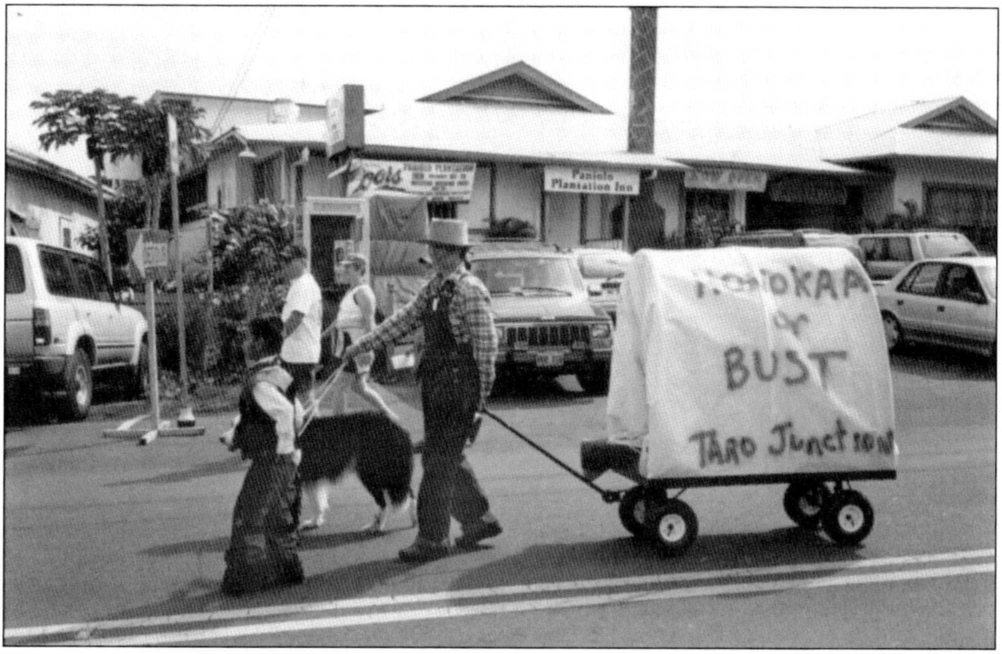

Western Days Parade on Mamane Street. Festivals and parades are a very long-standing tradition along Mamane Street. Examples of such festivities are Festival of the Holy Ghost, Western Days, Plantation Days, International Peace Festival, and Rizal Festival Parade. Note the covered wagon in keeping with the Western theme. (Yamato Collection, NHERC.)

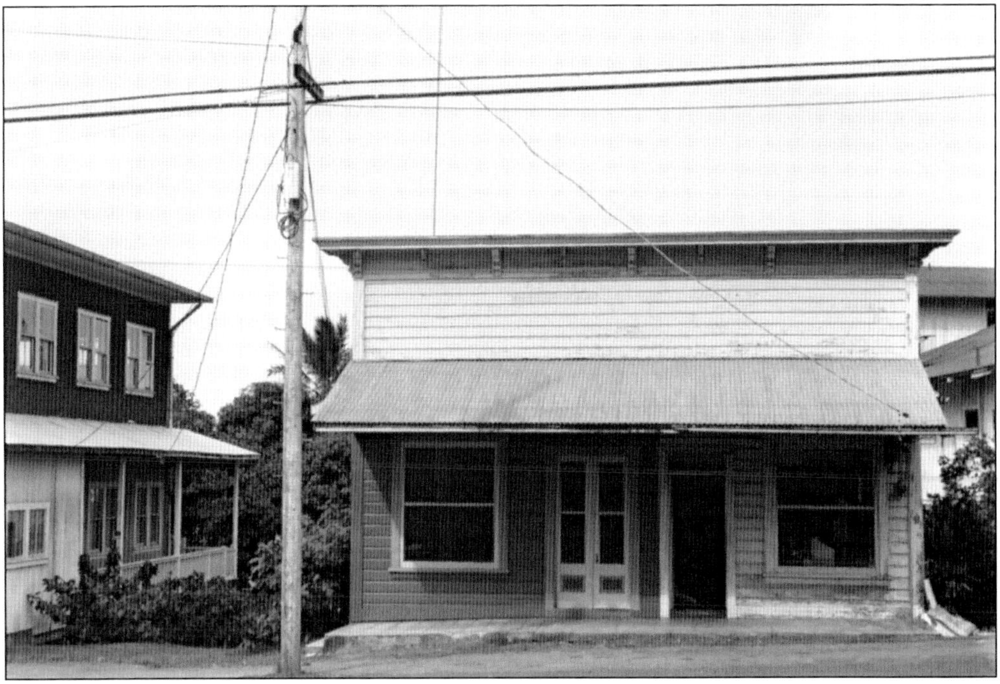

ORIGINAL BANK OF HAWAII BUILDING. The First Bank of Hilo was one of the first to offer business loans in Honokaa, beginning in 1910. First Bank eventually sold its loan portfolio to the Bank of Hawaii (BOH); in 1927, BOH planned a new concrete building. Manuel Botelho purchased the original structure and moved it to its current site. Tenants since the move have included the US Soil Conservation Service, Edith Fujimoto Dress Shop, and Miura Tailor Shop. (Ruis/Botelho Family Collection). [18]

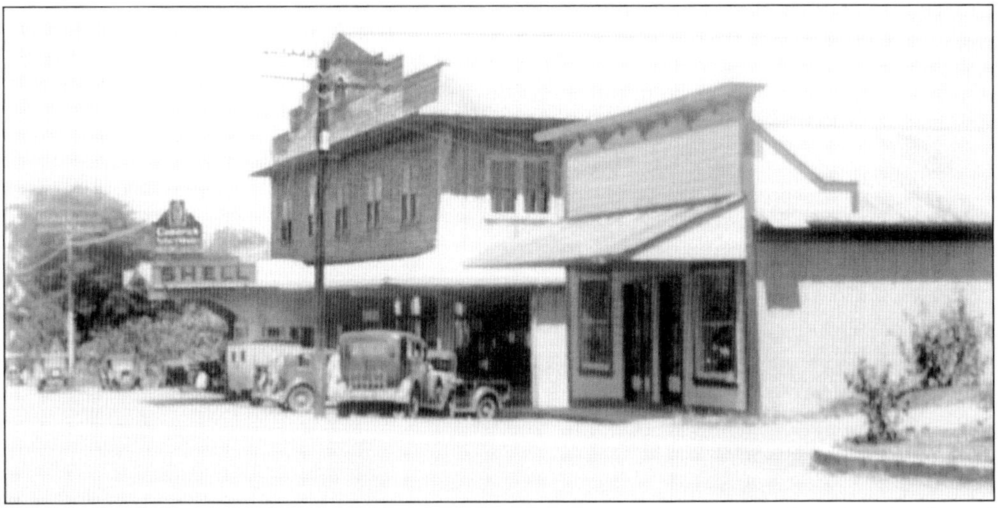

BOTELHO BUILDING. Manuel S. Botelho came to Hawaii as an infant, attended public schools, and went to law school in Indiana. He opened a garage near the Kuramitsu property before purchasing land on the Hilo side of town in anticipation of the railroad's arrival. His two-story building has held a garage, automobile dealership, dance hall, beauty salon, electric repair, appliance, florist and meats stores, a post office, and the draft board. Botelho also was a Hamakua District Court judge. (Ujiki Family Collection.) [19]

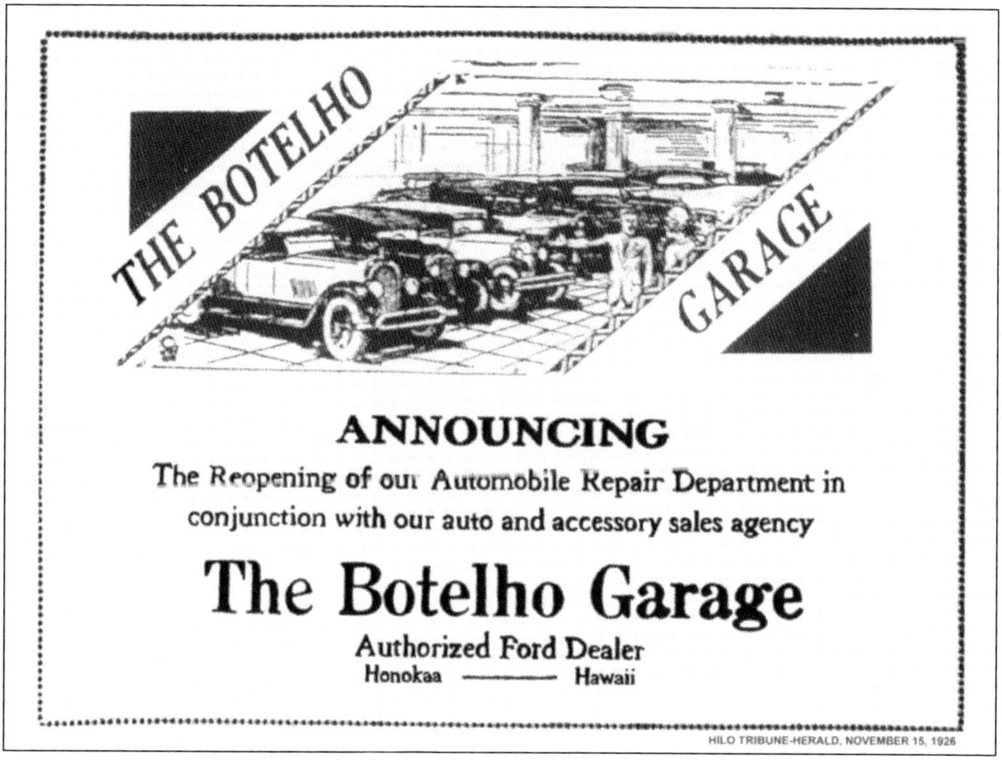

AUTO DEALERSHIP AND REPAIR CENTER, 1926. At the beginning of the 20th century, when the public began depending on automotive transportation, vehicle owners were not guaranteed automobile services. (Newspapers, for example, published the locations of gasoline stations.) The difficulty of finding parts for different makes of vehicles gave Manuel Botelho the insight to open both a Ford automobile dealership and repair facility. (HTH.)

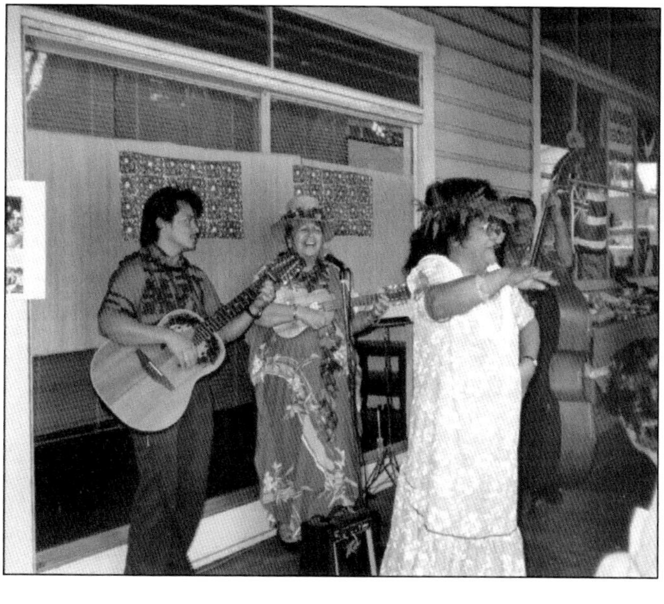

BOTELHO BUILDING STREETSIDE ENTERTAINMENT. Honokaa has a long history of activities held along Mamane Street, beginning with horse racing and then including paniolo, war victory, and school homecoming parades, Hawaiian music and hula at store openings, farmer's markets, folk and jazz festivals at the People's Theatre, and in more recent years, the Peace Festival and First Friday celebrations. (Yamato Collection, NHERC.)

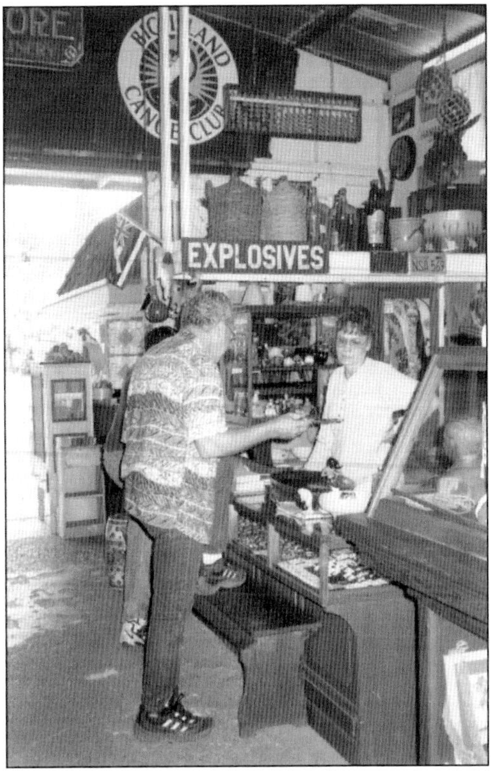

Former Botelho Auto Repair. Local lawyer M.S. Botelho branched out into the automobile businesses in 1912, foreseeing prosperity buoyed by the general public's increasing love affair with cars. His garage was originally behind the present Honokaa Marketplace. In 1927 he built the new Botelho Building, which included both the garage and an automobile dealership. One great thing about such well-built older buildings is that they can be reused as retail space for entirely different businesses. Grace Walker, known to everyone as Aunty Grace, has been selling antiques, books, clothing, and other used items since 1986 in the old automobile repair space. Her shop contains a fascinating collection of business signs from local family retail operations that have long since closed. (Yamato Collection, NHERC.)

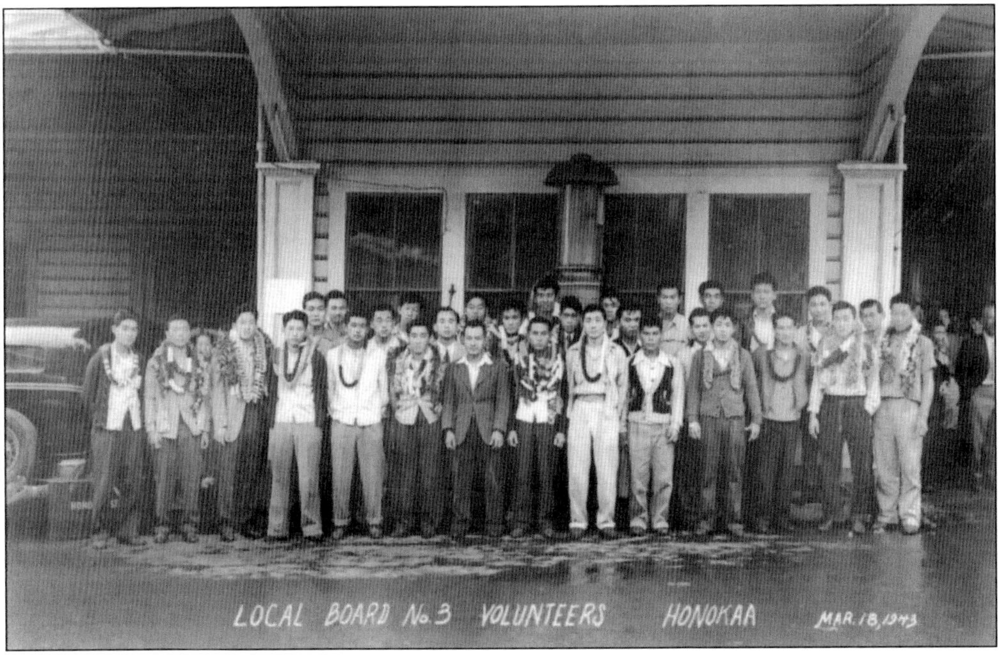

Volunteers for the War Effort. Standing in front of the Botelho Building, volunteers prepare for their induction into the armed services on March 18, 1943. Family members wait on the right. The Botelho Building contained both the local draft board downstairs and the USO dance hall upstairs. (Ujiki Family Collection.)

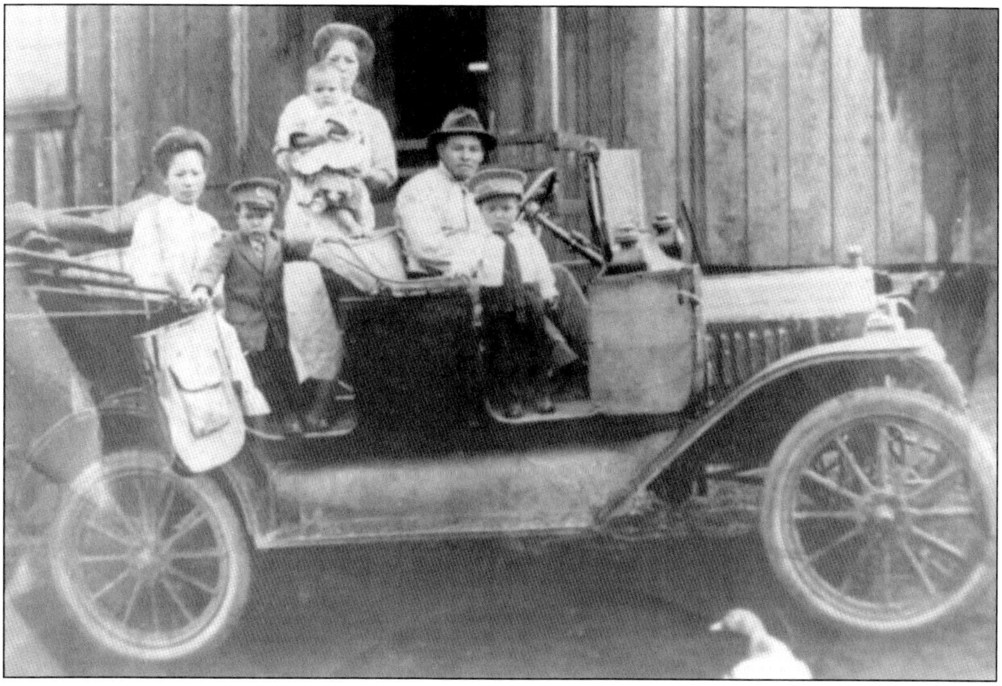

PAPA KUWAYE'S TAXI. Not many families had cars around 1910, so Mr. Kuwaye's touring car was ideal for taking people around Honokaa and to Hilo. During the late 1930s, his son Eddie took over the Kuwaye Bros. transport business, gathering passengers from Haina to Paauhau in a sedan to then catch his big bus in Honokaa. Eddie would distribute film canisters from the Hamakua theaters along the way, and people would also ask him to acquire items in Hilo. Pictured here around 1917 are, from left to right, Hige Kuwaye Obasan (Papa's sister-in-law), Ryoei, Mama holding Jimmy, Eddie, and Papa in the driver's seat. (Kuwaye Toyama Family Collection.)

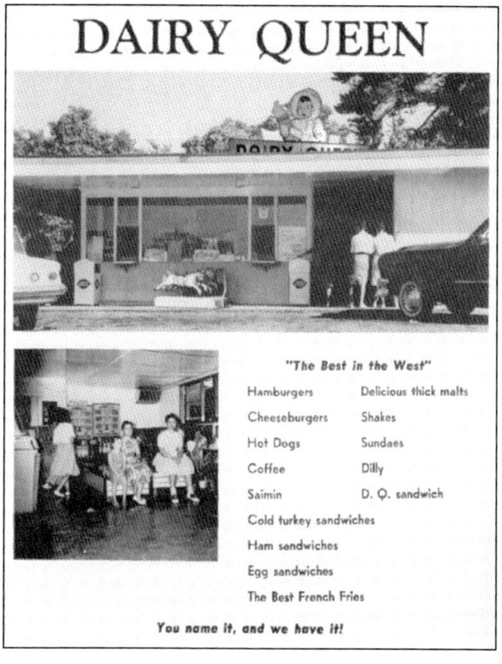

DAIRY QUEEN. The first Diary Queen opened in Illinois in 1950 with its soft-serve ice cream, and the company has expanded through the franchise system since. The local franchise has been owned at various times by Melvin Ah Ching and Violet and Antone Ramos. Families would place coins in the "riding horsey" for *keiki* (children's) rides out front, and teenagers would mini-bowl inside. Makai of the building was the earlier site of J.J. Andrade Meat Market. Presently, the site is occupied by Blane's Drive Inn. This advertisement is from the 1962 *Ka Nani O Honokaa* yearbook. (HHSY.) [20]

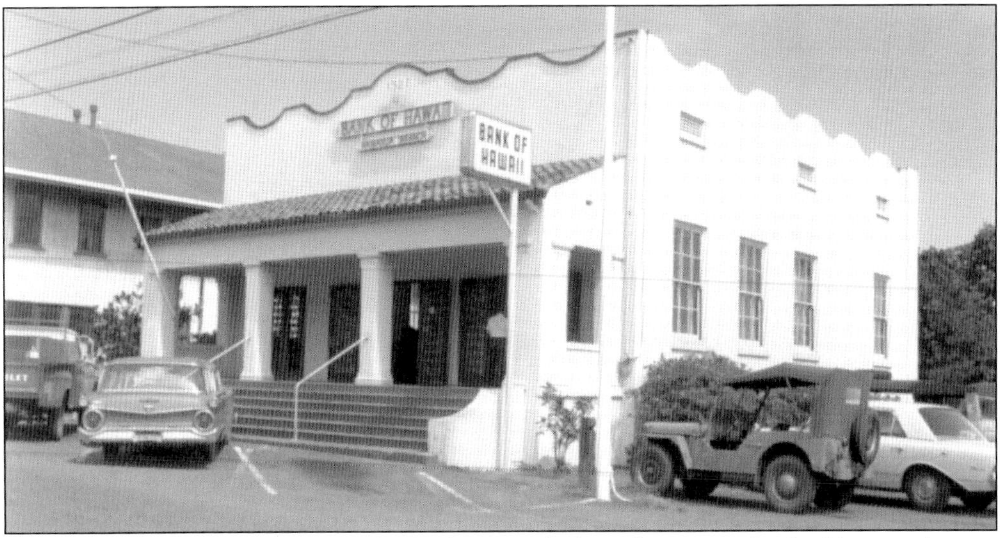

Bank of Hawaii. In 1910, First Bank of Hilo opened a branch in a wooden building on this site in Honokaa. In 1921, Bank of Hawaii acquired the First Hilo branch. Longtime manager Francis R. Fraser was known to provide loans to local entrepreneurs both through the bank and out of his own pocket. The present building was constructed in 1927 and reflects the California/Mediterranean architecture popular in public buildings of that era. (SHPD.) [21]

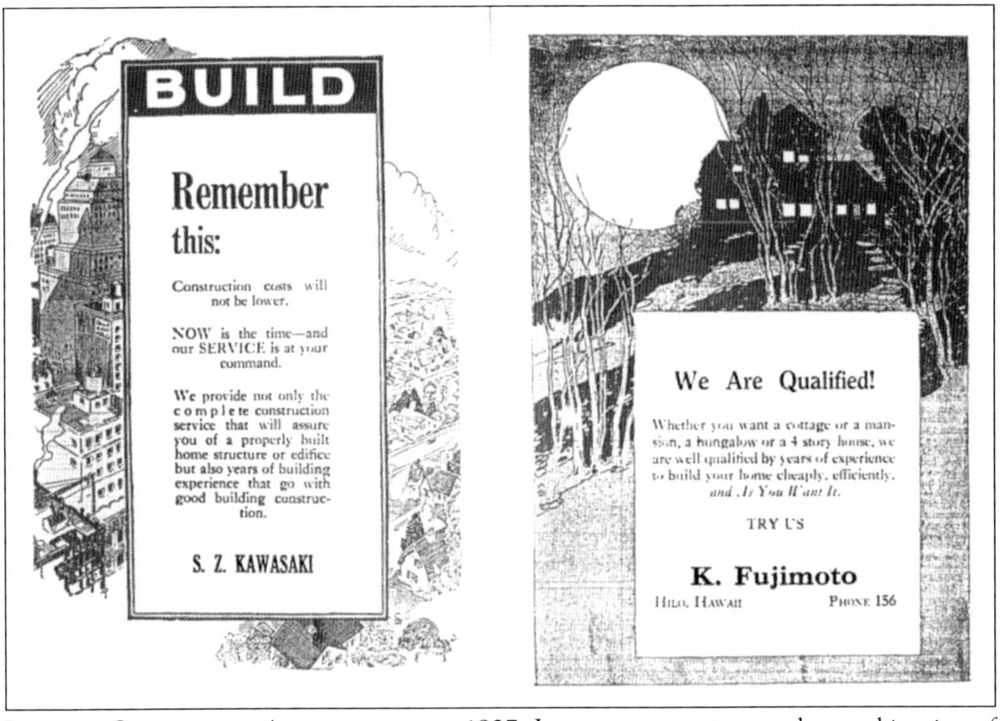

Japanese Contractor Advertisements, 1927. Japanese carpenters used a combination of tools they brought from the old country and tools imported from the mainland to construct plantation-style camp housing, gymnasiums, and mill structures. When their contracts were up, large numbers of these men organized their own companies, moved to Honokaa and other towns, and competed for more general business. (HTH.)

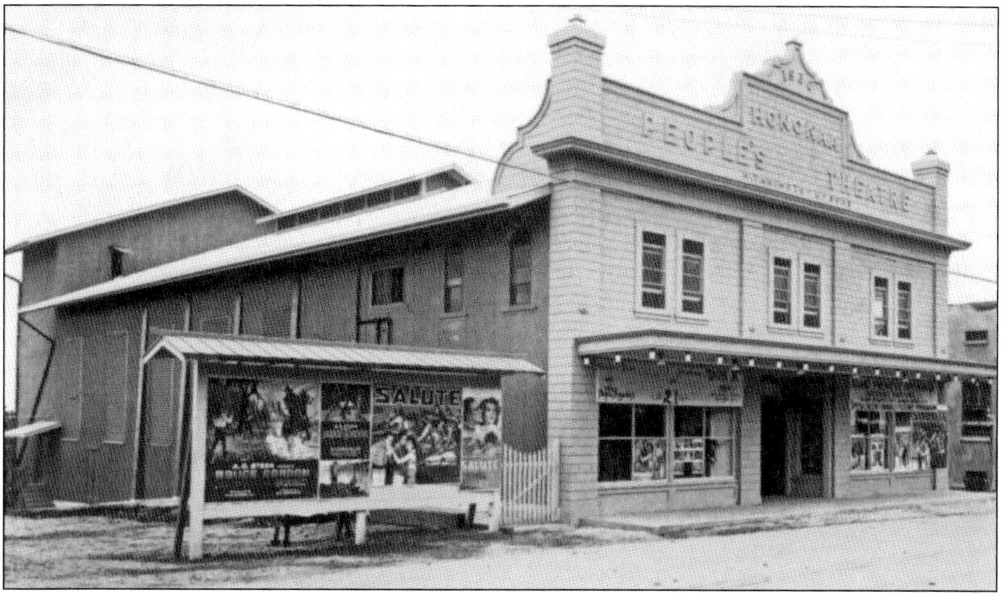

HONOKAA PEOPLE'S THEATRE, C. 1930. This early photograph shows the original parapet detailing, reflecting the elaborate architecture of picture palaces in an era when many patrons went to the movies to escape the harsh economic reality of the Great Depression. The paneling that provided the gentle curves and the rounded finials on the end columns has since been removed. The date of construction has been relocated below the town's name. (Ruis/Botelho Collection, NHERC.) [22]

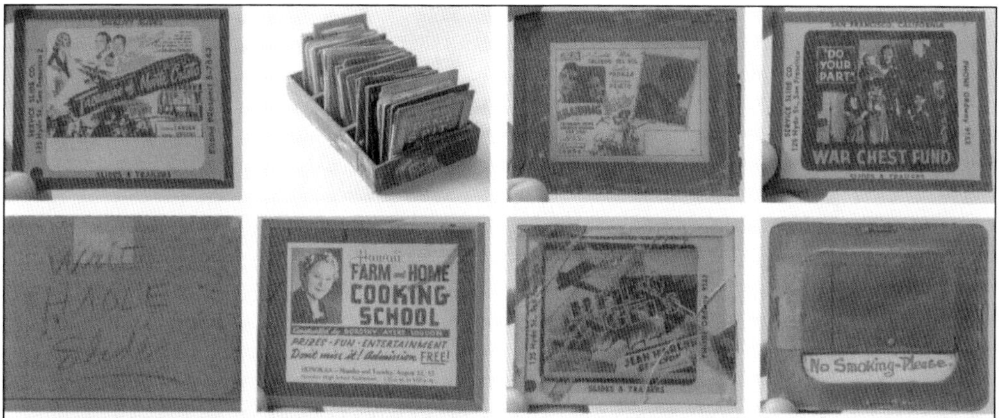

LANTERN SLIDES AT THE THEATER. Lantern slides were developed before movies actually moved. A series of slides were the main attraction, as an announcer would act as a storyteller, providing context and color. After the arrival of motion pictures, lantern slides were relegated to support roles, used by theaters for advertisements (mostly to encourage patrons to visit the candy counter), public-service announcements, and declaring the rules of behavior. (HPT.)

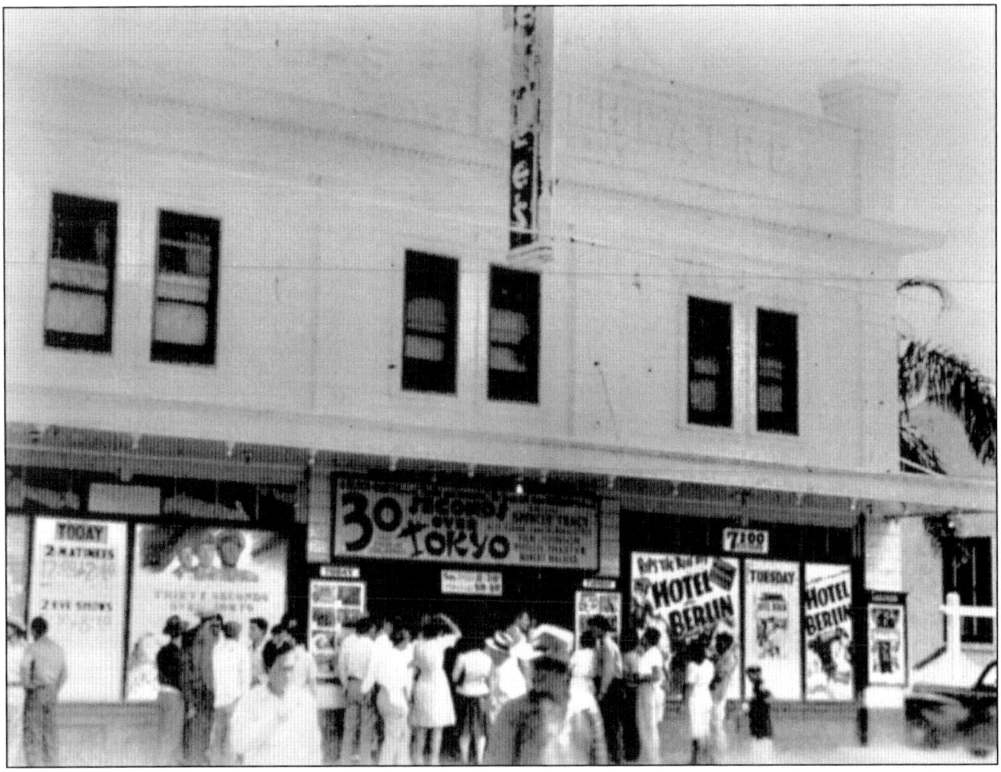

30 SECONDS OVER TOKYO, C. 1945. Movies provided much escapist entertainment. Programs regularly included two movies, a cartoon, and newsreel, with the films separated by an intermission; this allowed patrons to stock up on candies and popcorn and stop for a *lua* (bathroom) break without missing out on anything. Here, movie patrons have lined up to view war-related features. As a teenager, Ed Castillo's theater job was to ring a hand-held "Santa Claus" bell through the town to announce the movies of the night, return to the theater in time to put on records before the movie, and then pull the curtain. Note the neon sign above the pedestrian awning. (HPT.)

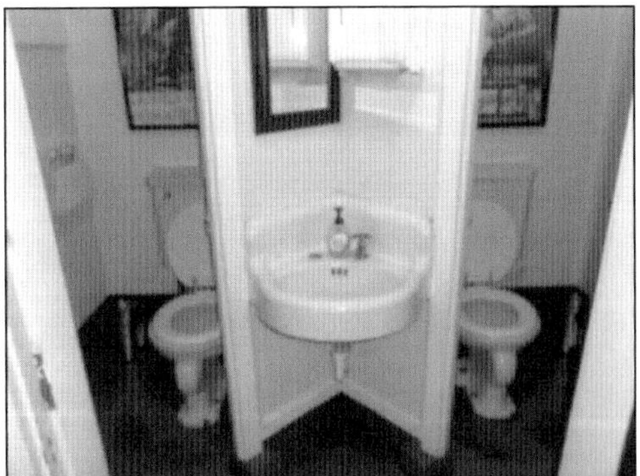

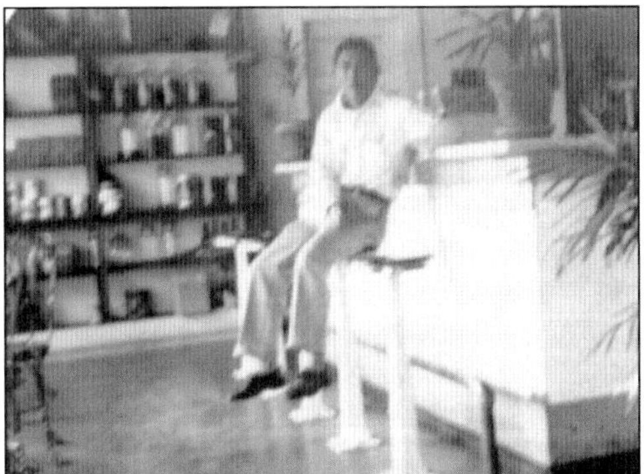

INSIDE THE THEATER. Space in commercial buildings was often at a premium. In the women's restroom, carpenters used ingenuity to fit a sink by beveling into the stall space. Counter operations for sales of theater munchies outgrew the original lobby space. Jiro Kawatachi (at right) operated both the theater and sweet shop across the street. But the era of Jiro ended when Peggy Tanimoto's son paid $61 (today over $150) at Ikeuchi's for a gallon of paint on the theater account, angering Jiro. (Left, LR; right, Kawatachi Family Collection.)

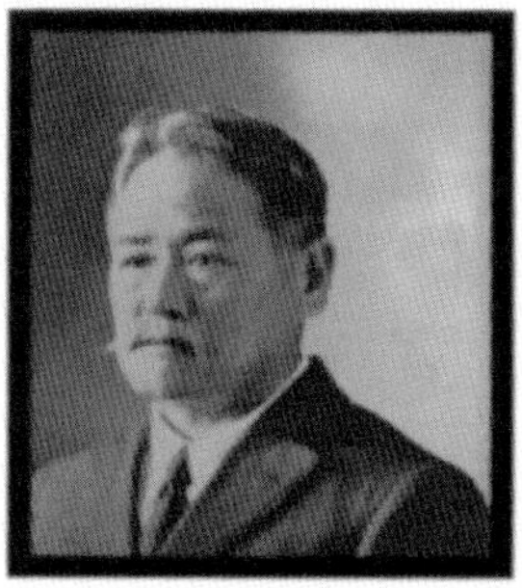

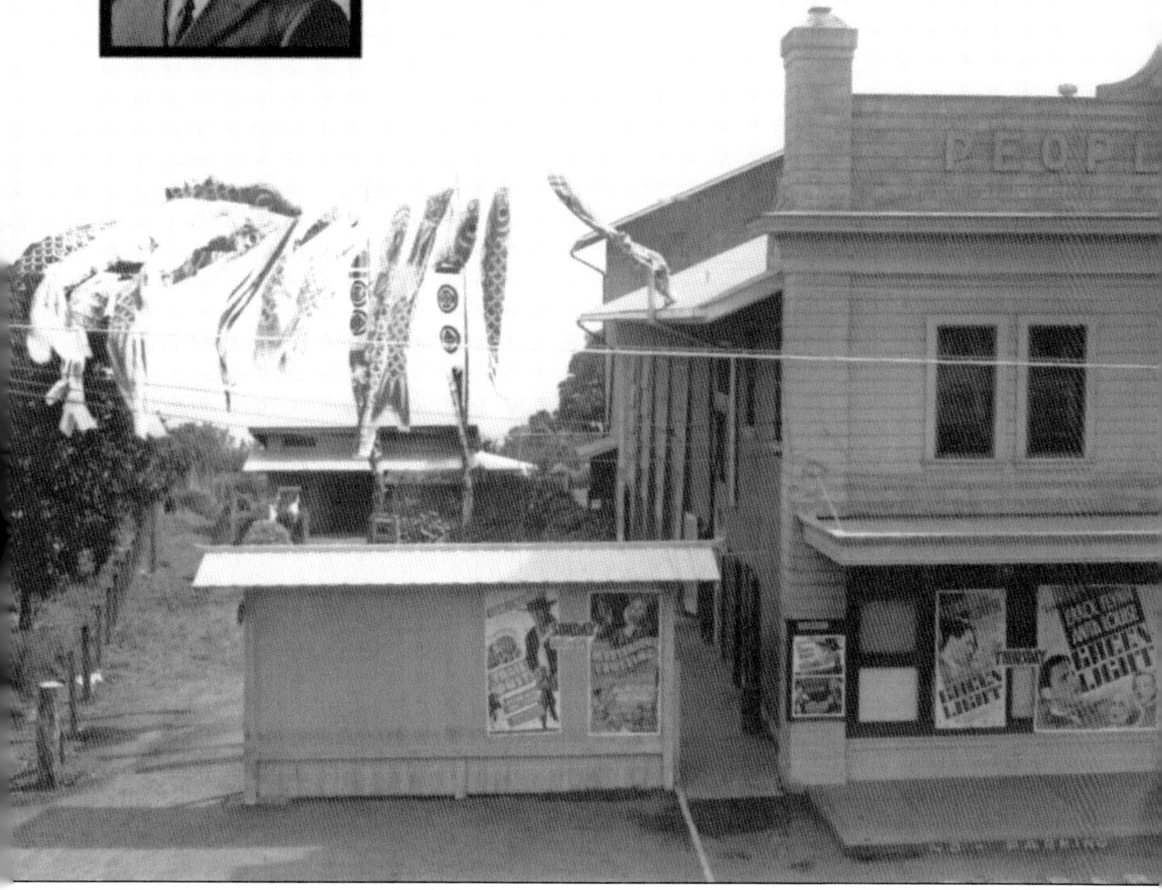

Boys' Day at the Theatre, c. 1937. Like parents everywhere, Japanese families have traditions focusing on their children. March 3 is Girls' Day, known as Hinamatsuri, (also called Doll's Day). For Girls' Day, platforms are covered with red material and used to display as many as seven levels of ornamental dolls, representing (in order of importance) the emperor and empress, attendants, and musicians in traditional court dress. Boys' Day, or Tango no Sekku, is May 5. For Boys' Day, families raise overhead symbolic *koi* (carp)-shaped flags and streamers. Chinese legend, influential in Japan for centuries, states that a carp swims upstream to become a dragon. The ability of carp to swim against the current and over waterfalls also symbolizes health and strength. The movement of the streamers in the wind represents the flow of water. In this photograph, Honokaa People's Theatre founder Hatsuzo Tanimoto (inset) has placed numerous carp and streamers in the Hamakua trade winds to recognize his sons Yoshio, Zenichi, Tetsue, Yoshimi, Teruo, and Takaichi. The photograph shows that Hatsuzo exuberantly flew more koi than he had sons. (Ruis/Botelho Collection, NHERC.)

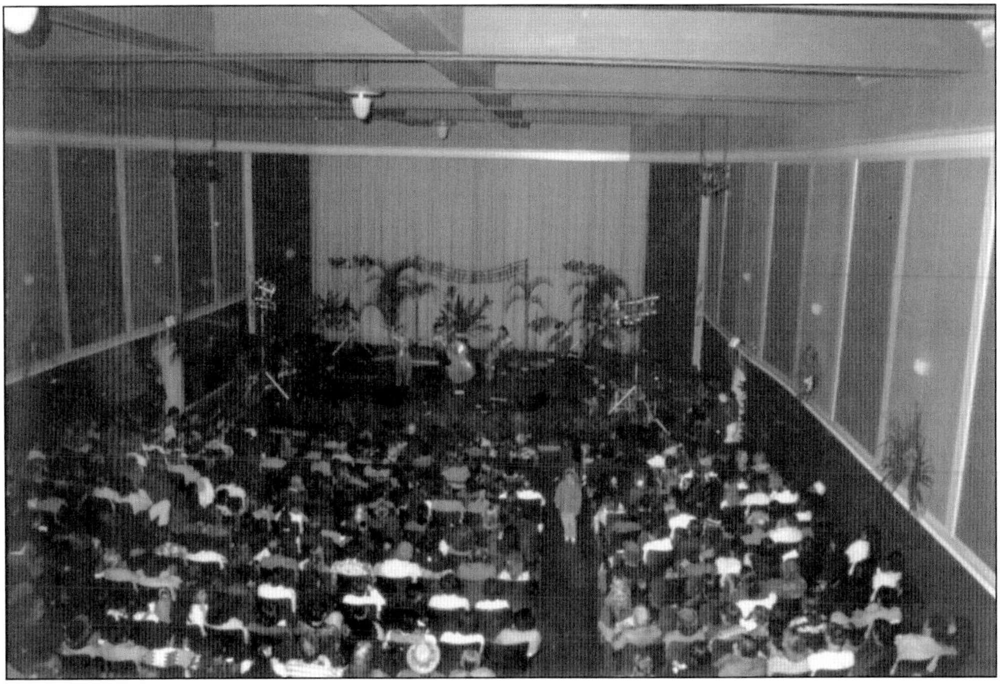

Honokaa People's Theatre Live Performances. While the Tanimotos had produced live children's programs on Saturday mornings before films were shown, owner Dr. Tawn Keeney greatly expanded live entertainment at the People's Theatre. By removing a section of front-row seats, he accommodated live hula productions. Other venues have included Hawaiian, folk, and jazz music performances. (Yamato Collection, NHERC.)

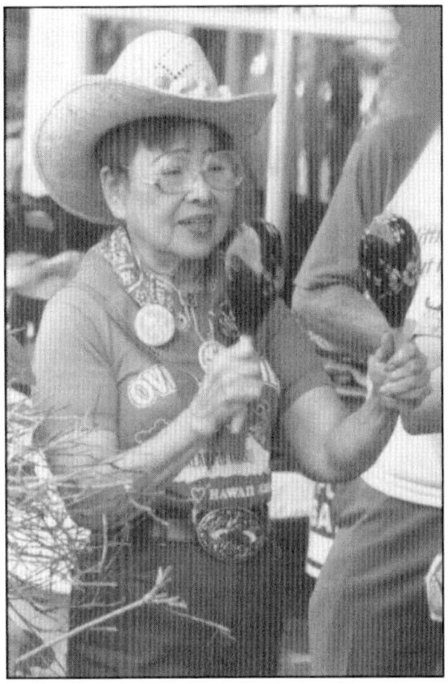

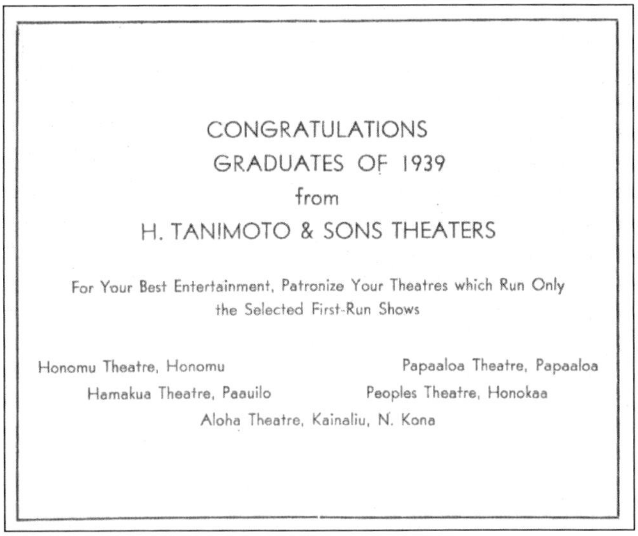

CONGRATULATIONS
GRADUATES OF 1939
from
H. TANIMOTO & SONS THEATERS

For Your Best Entertainment, Patronize Your Theatres which Run Only the Selected First-Run Shows

Honomu Theatre, Honomu
Papaaloa Theatre, Papaaloa
Hamakua Theatre, Paauilo
Peoples Theatre, Honokaa
Aloha Theatre, Kainaliu, N. Kona

Peggy Tanimoto. Peggy Tanimoto was a beloved personage of Honokaa for many years. She and her husband, Christian, owned the People's Theatre and had a theatrical bent of their own. Peggy participated in numerous community plays, parades, and other activities. At left, she is dressed in Western attire and is playing the maracas during an event on Mamane Street. At right is an advertisement from the 1939 *Ka Nani O Honokaa* yearbook. (Left, Yamato Collection, NHERC; right, HHSY.)

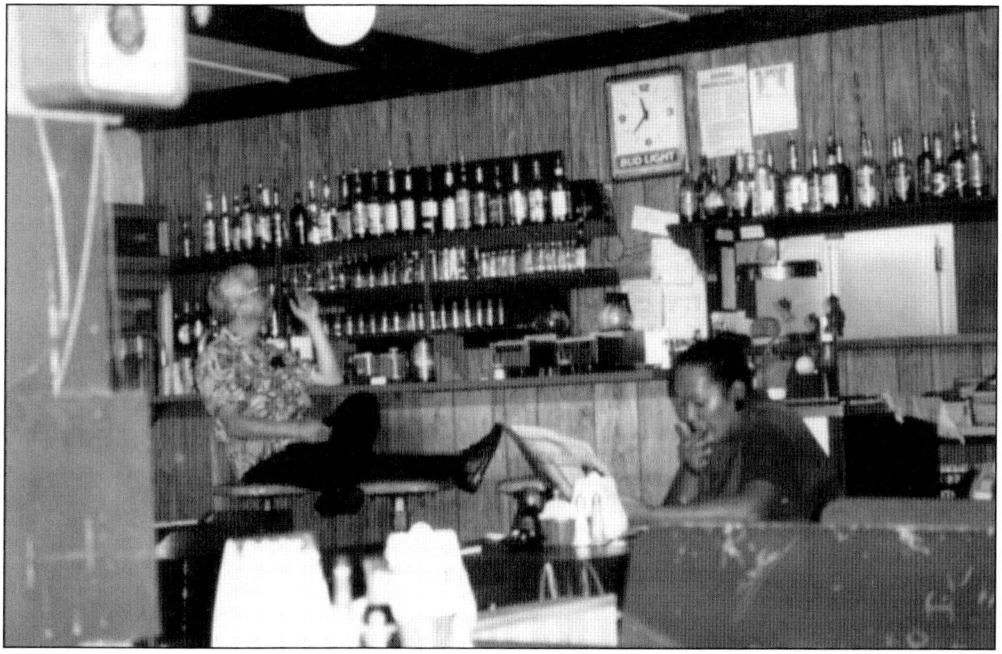

HERB'S PLACE. Named for Herb Hirayama, this establishment was known for its fresh salad bar and excellent homemade salad dressing. Another business occupant was known as Bar 9. Tsutomu "Racehorse" Onomura and George Vierra were the developers of this area. Onomura died in 1996, and the building no longer exists. (Yamato Collection, NHERC.) [23]

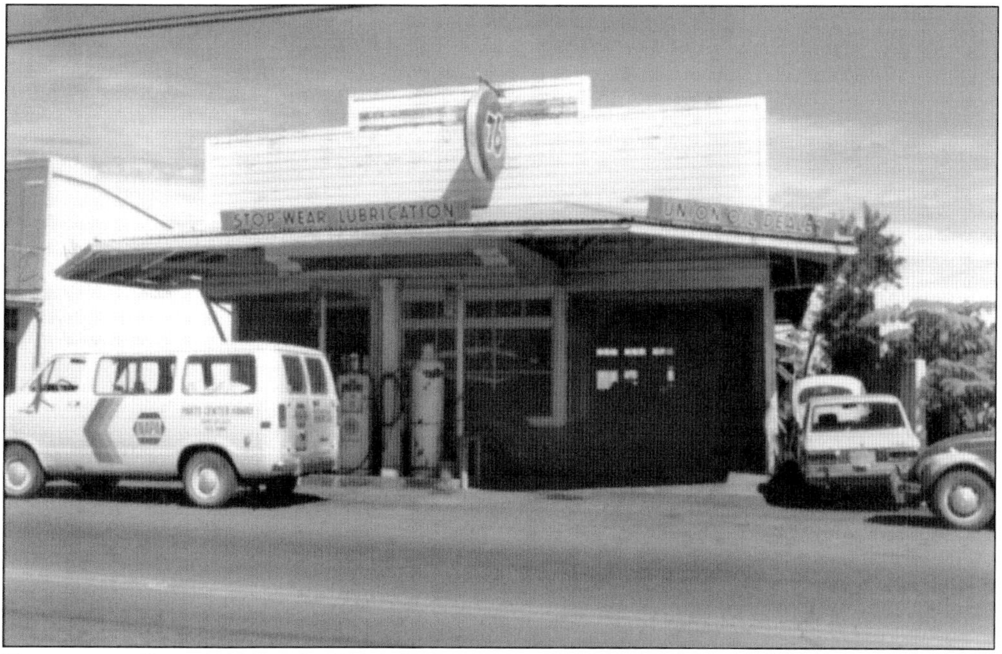

KURAMITSU GARAGE. This building first appears on 1914 maps as a Japanese theater. Local tradition says that it was also where local Japanese marriages were arranged. Its longest use was as a gas station, as seen here, known variously as the Kuramitsu, Honokaa, and Paiva Garage. (Paiva Family Collection.) [24]

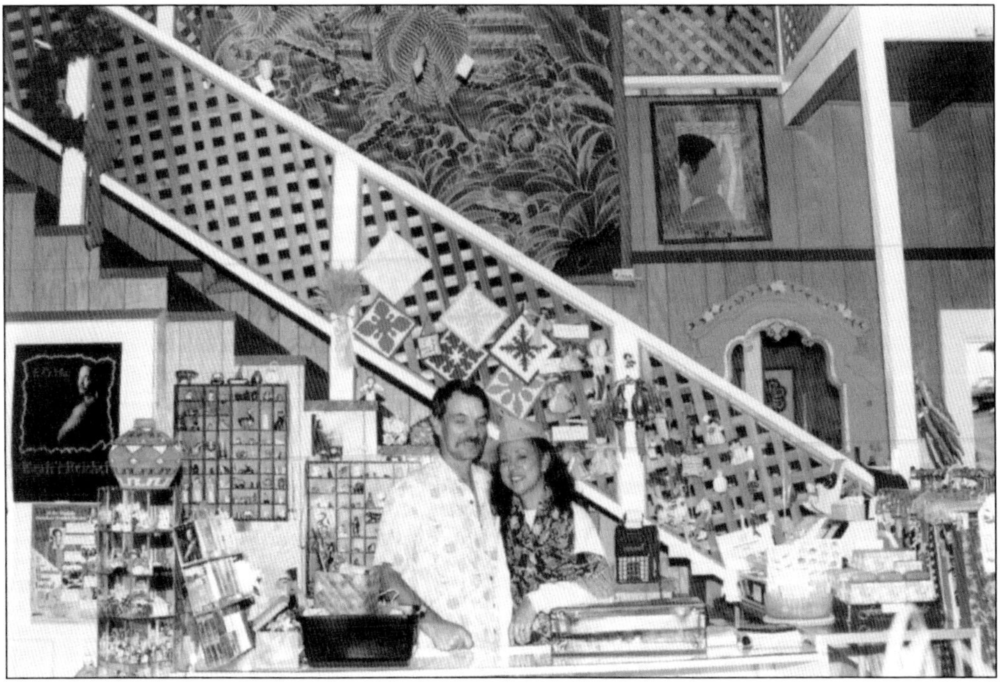

Rehabilitated Kuramitsu Garage Interior. In 1994, owners Sheila and William Chambers renovated the Kuramitsu/Paiva Garage into a retail store. During the work, they found that the complex actually consisted of two buildings, with the second constructed at an angle to the first. In the basement, they also located evidence of a gasoline engine and cables that provided electrical power to film projectors when the building was a Japanese theater. (Yamato Collection, NHERC.)

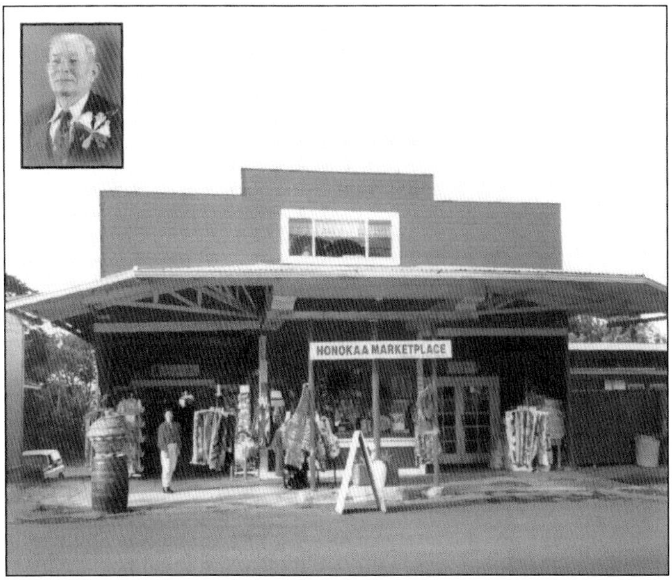

Adaptive Reuse. Elements of the old gas station can still be seen due to the decision to retain the extensive front canopy built for the Kuramitsu Garage. The canopy provides shelter for pedestrians interested in both the products of the store and views up and down Mamane Street. The shop is dedicated to the memory of entrepreneur Alfred J. Nobriga (inset), who operated a transportation company, dairy, and ranch. (Yamato Collection, NHERC.).

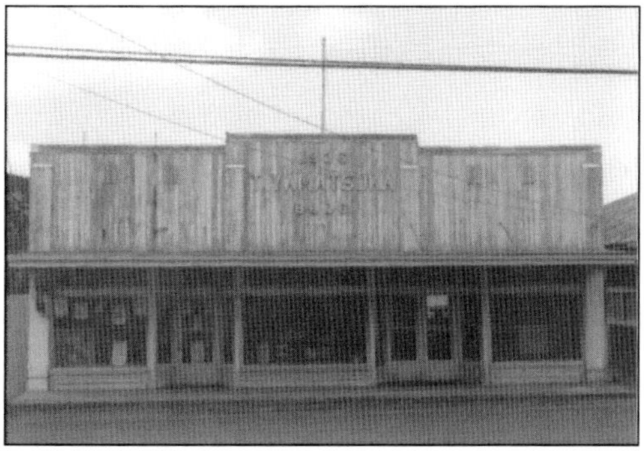

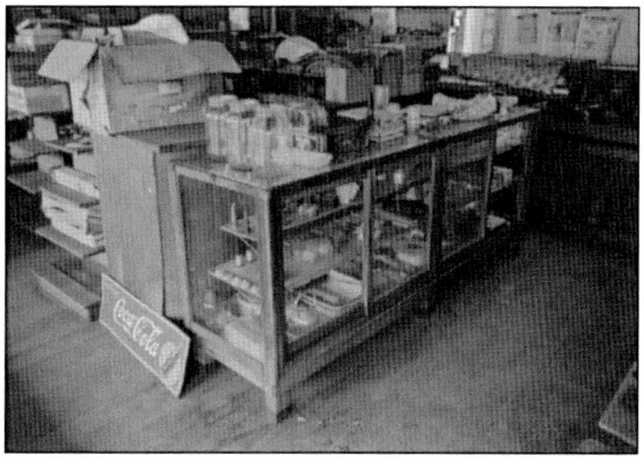

YAMATSUKA BUILDING. Teiji Yamatsuka, the original owner, once worked at the Hamakua Shokwai across the street, rising to vice president. He then became independent, opening this general dry goods store in 1936. In 1948 he went into real estate, acquiring much of the land makai of the Andrade Building and on the Hilo side of Lehua from the Honokaa Sugar Company before subdividing it. Twenty-one years older than his wife, Tamayo, he died in 1952, leaving his widow to run the store alone for many years. (Left, photograph by Berni Ruis; right, photograph © Franco Salmoiraghi.) [25]

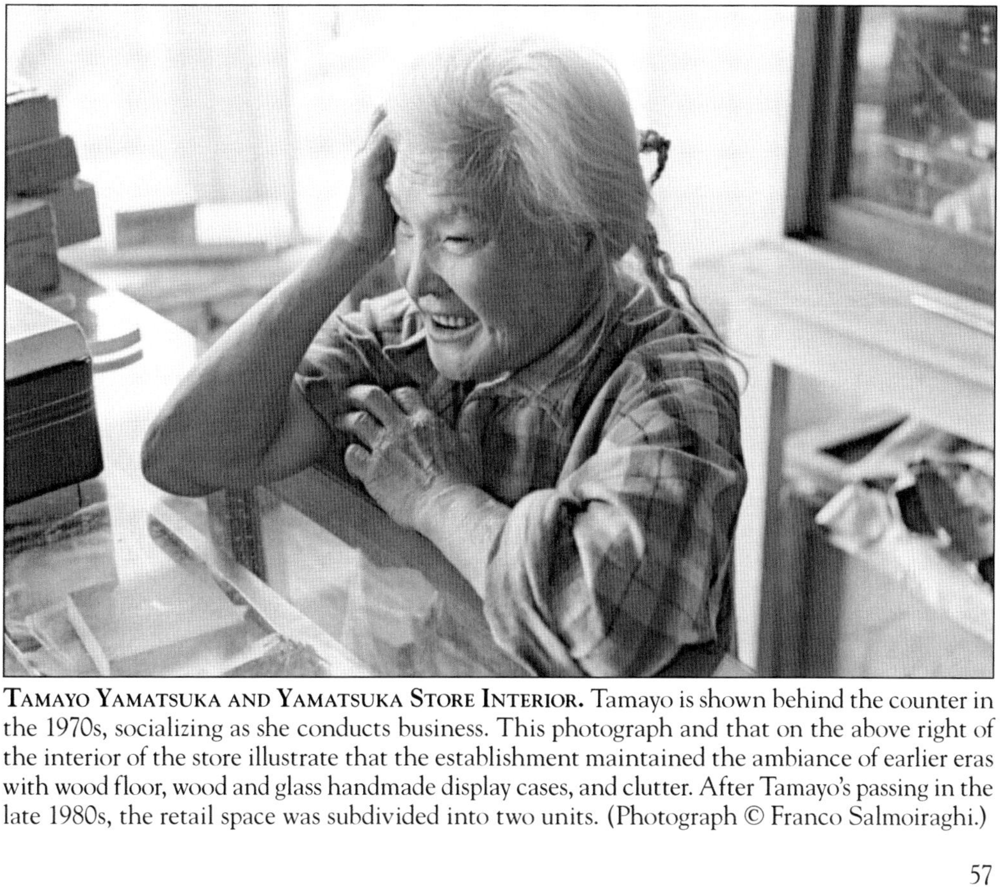

TAMAYO YAMATSUKA AND YAMATSUKA STORE INTERIOR. Tamayo is shown behind the counter in the 1970s, socializing as she conducts business. This photograph and that on the above right of the interior of the store illustrate that the establishment maintained the ambiance of earlier eras with wood floor, wood and glass handmade display cases, and clutter. After Tamayo's passing in the late 1980s, the retail space was subdivided into two units. (Photograph © Franco Salmoiraghi.)

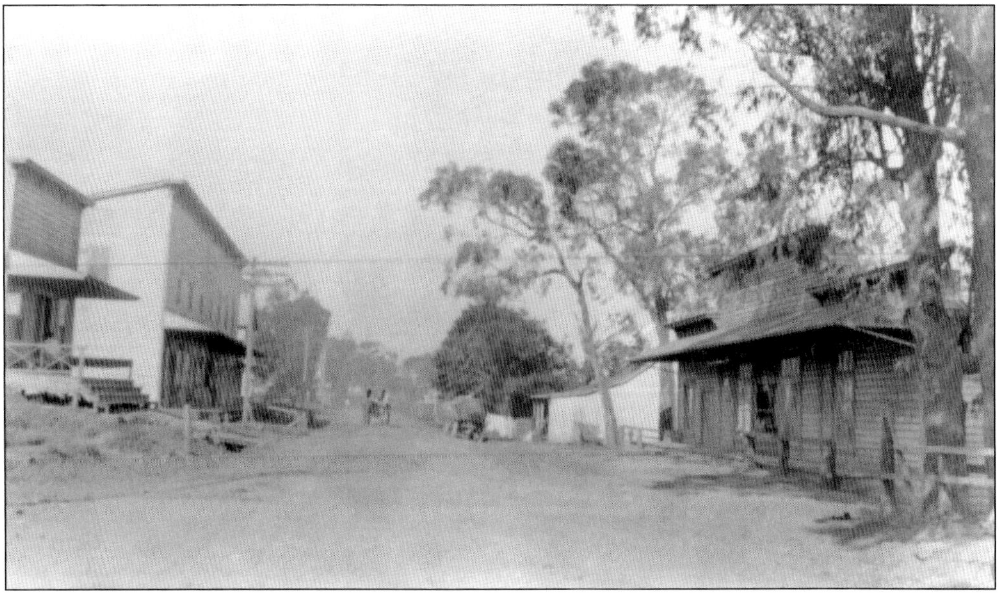

GOVERNMENT ROAD, C. 1912. Looking in the Waipio direction, notice the horse-drawn wagon in the center, the dirt street, and trees along the makai side of the road. The present-day Credit Union (Holmes/Lawson/Awong Store) is on the immediate right and the Holmes/Rice Building is at left. The former A.S. Cleghorn/J.R. Mills store site is out of view at far left. (LM.)

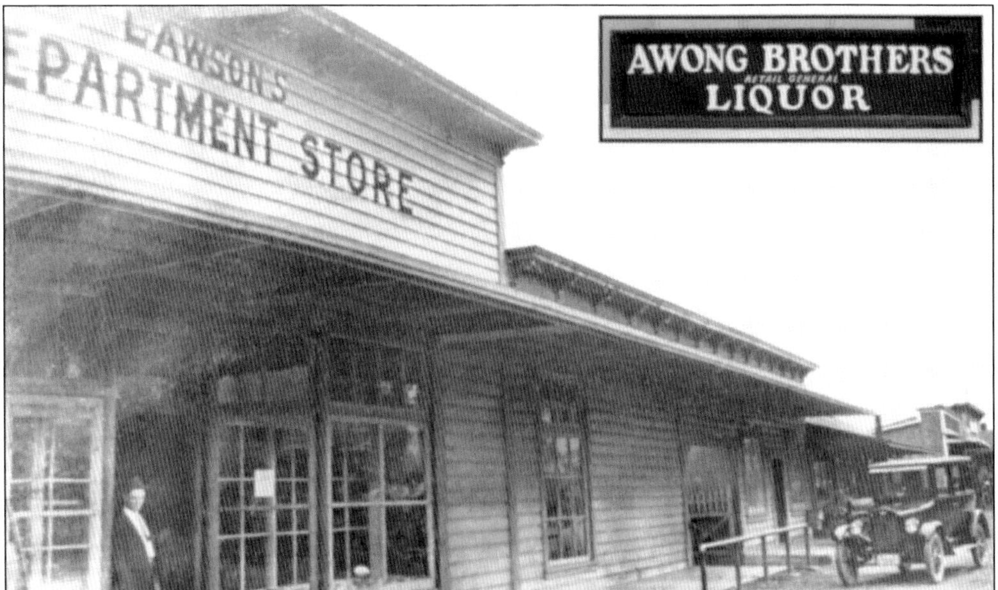

MOVING THROUGH TIME. The present Credit Union Building has had many lives. Started in 1882 by W.H. Holmes, three Holmes brothers operated a general store until A.L. Moses acquired it in 1919. William Lawson became owner in 1921. The Hilo side once housed a stable and later the John Mendes Saloon. Alfred Awong became the owner in 1947. The establishment carried produce, meat, clothing, shoes, and fabric; goods were delivered. The credit union acquired the property in 1968. (Ruis/Botelho Family Collection; insert, NHERC.) [27]

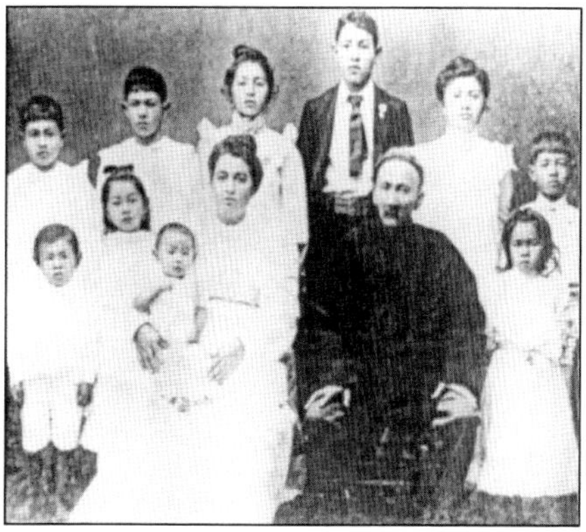

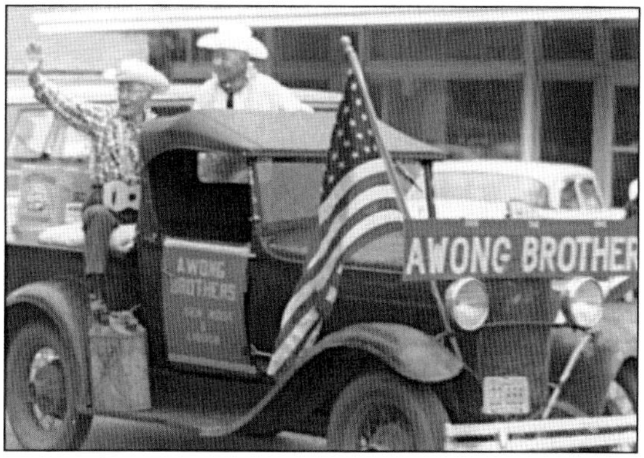

Original Awong Family, c. 1906. The Awong family is a typical Hawaii amalgamation of cultures, in this case Chinese and Portuguese. Family members at left are, from left to right, (first row) George, Nellie, baby William, Jacintha, patriarch Au Yan or Yap, and Annie; (second row) Alfred, Antone, Emilia, Henry, Mary, and John. At right, the Awong brothers enthusiastically contributed to the parade at festival time. (Left, Awong Family Collection; right, Yamato Collection, NHERC.)

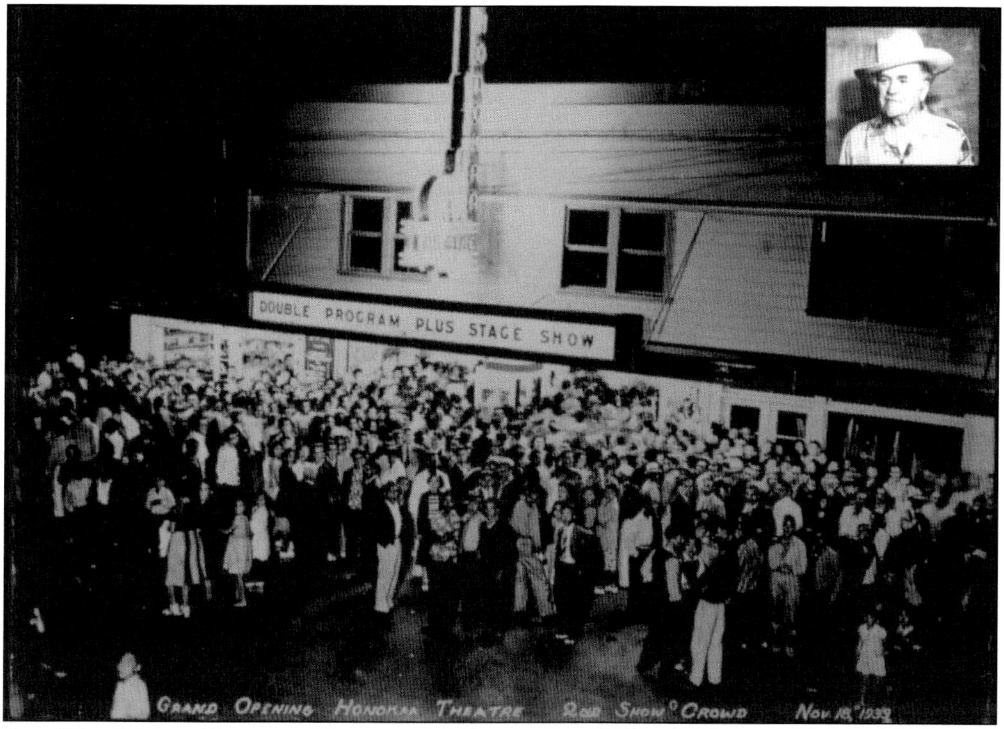

The "Doc" Hill Honokaa Theatre Opening, 1939. William "Doc" Hill arrived on the Big Island in 1913, making a name for himself as an itinerant eyeglass salesman (hence "Doc"). An entrepreneur, Hill ultimately had interests in real estate, automobile dealership and repair, print shops, jewelry stores, mortuaries, drugstores, the electric utility, nine theaters, and soda companies. Hill was a territorial and later state senator. His Honokaa Theatre was unofficially known as the "Republican theater," while People's was the "Democratic theater." (Courtesy of Katherine Mendes Hooper and Peter Tomich; inset, William "Doc" Hill.) [28]

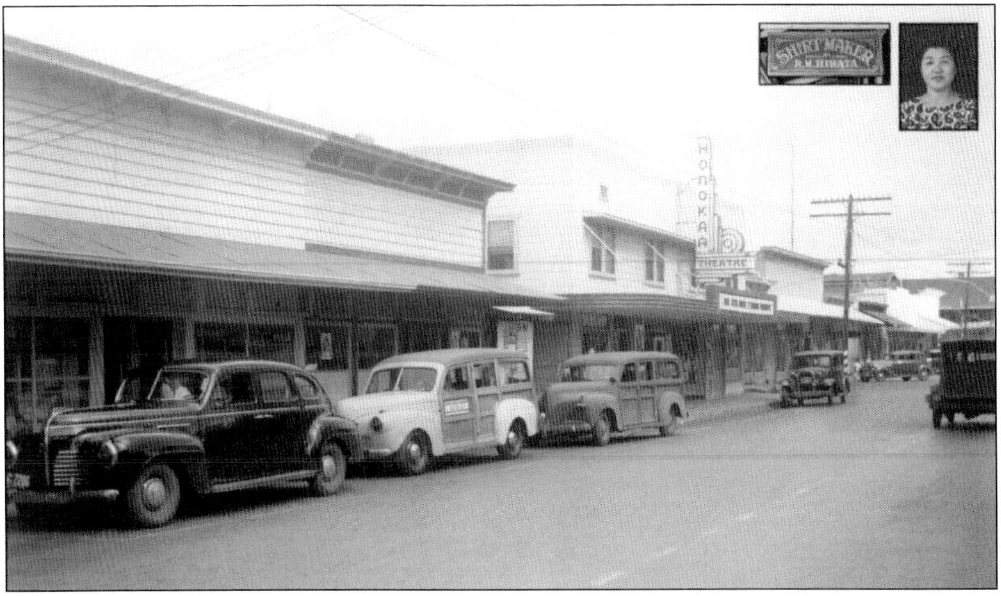

Hirata Building. During World War II, thousands of Marines were based near Waimea, preparing for or recovering from battles at Tarawa, Iwo Jima, and the planned invasion of Japan. The USO provided programs, services, and live entertainment. Here, a USO convoy, with mandated blacked-out headlights, awaits. After the war, well-known local seamstress Ruth Hirata had her shop here. She was an early creator of "Aloha" shirts. Her colorful long-sleeved shirts became popular with local entertainers. (Gary Cockrell Collection; insets, SHPD; NHERC.) [29]

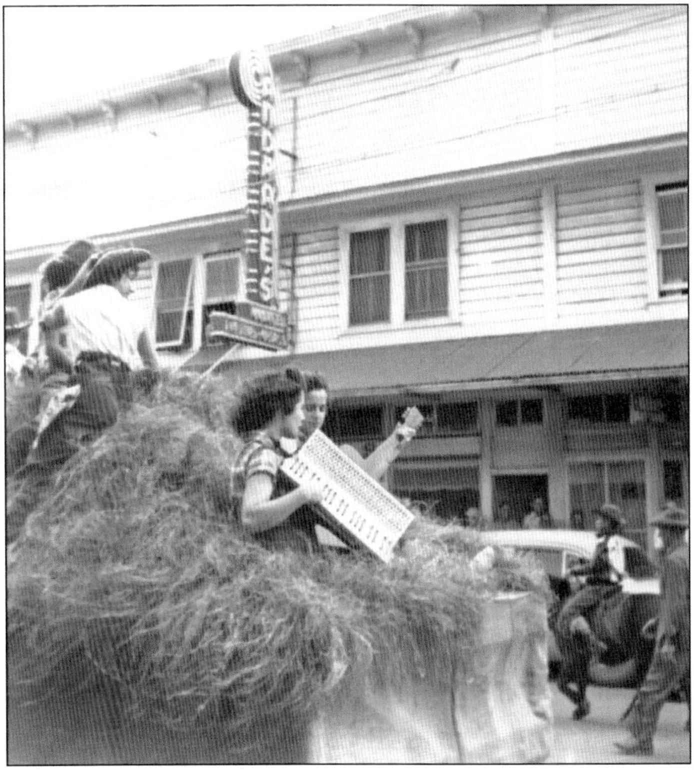

Western Days Tradition. While horse racing and similar activities have moved "up makua" to the Rose Andrade Correia Stadium, parades similar to the one pictured here continue during Western Week as a tradition on Mamane Street. The girls on a hay float in front of the Andrade Building (note the neon sign) are, from left to right, (bottom) Elain Adrian and Eleanor Adrian; (middle) Marian Adrian; (left background) Maxine Souza and Rowena Souza. (Corrine Kealoha Collection.) [31]

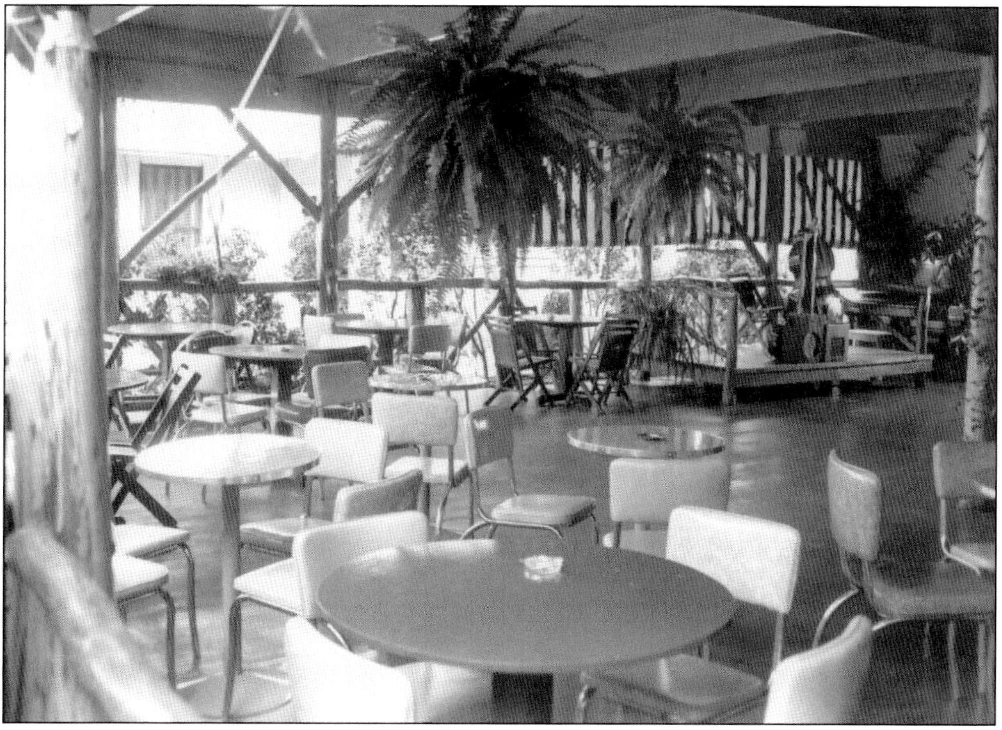

Andrade Building. Local entrepreneur John Jose Andrade owned a cattle ranch, slaughter house, and meat market. In 1924, he erected this structure on the makai side of Mamane Street. The building featured commercial activities on the first level and, unlikely as it might seem, both hotel rooms and a dance floor on the second. During World War II, Andrade's thrived, and business at the improvised officers' club was so busy that waitresses were forced to line up glasses along the bar and pour liquor down the line, only to start again when they finished. After the war, Andrade's Café became the Honokaa Café. The Ohia Lanai (birthplace of the Hawaii Saddle Club), a laundromat, and the Fernandez tailor shop also operated downstairs. Cowboys attending the rodeo would stay upstairs at the Andrade Hotel, sometimes as many as eight or nine to a room. (Both, Andrade Collection, NHERC.)

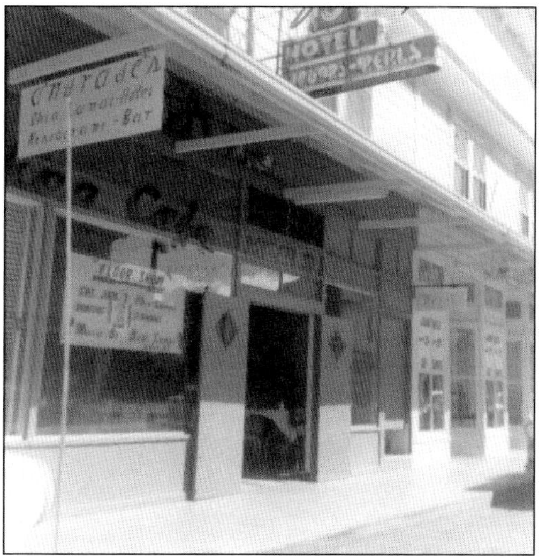

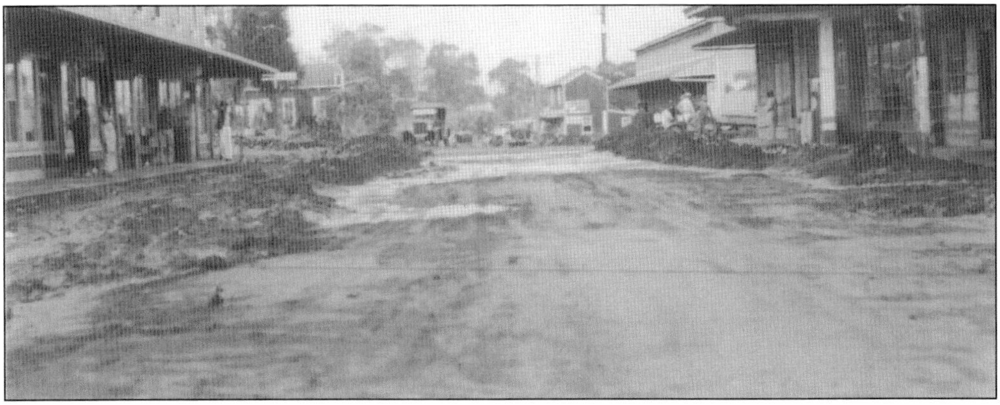

Flood on Mamane Street. Honokaa's commercial buildings, built up to the street, mask the fact that the town is built on a steep hillside. In 1932, sustained rains brought water and mud from the sugar cane fields above, covering Mamane Street with debris. This is the Mamane-Lehua intersection, looking makai-Waipio. On the left is the Ferreira Building and on the right the Ikeuchi Hardware and Andrade (then with gas pump) Buildings. (Private donor.)

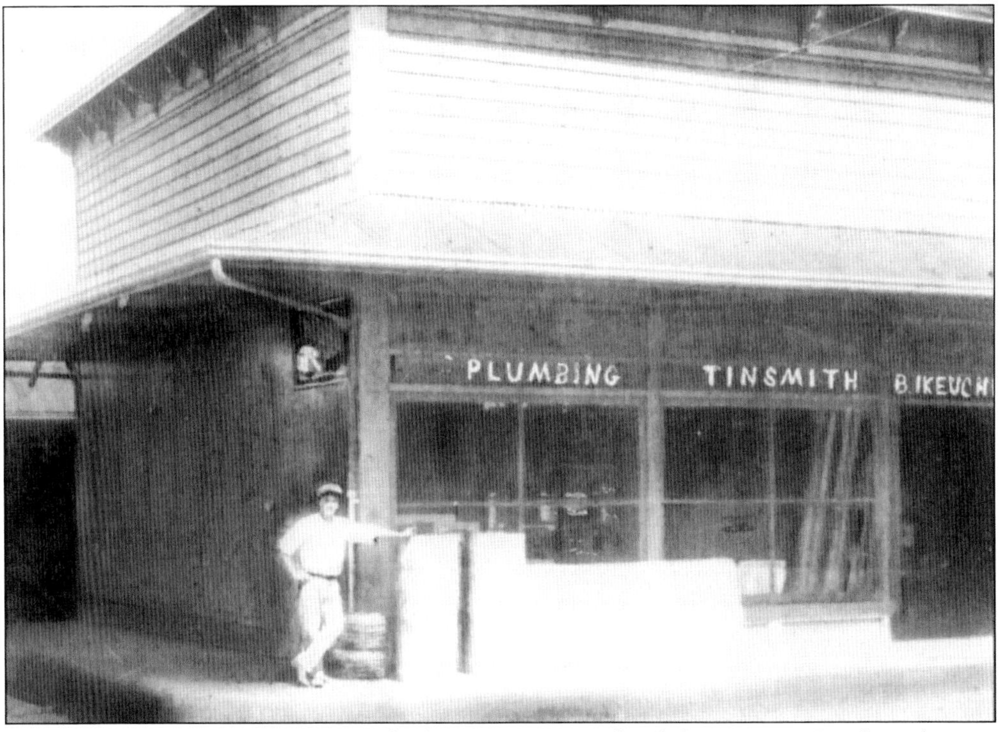

B. Ikeuchi and Sons Hardware. The longest-operating family business in Honokaa, this was originally the site of the Kwong Yee Chong Store. In 1926, Bunso Ikeuchi bought "all goods, wares, merchandise, stock in trade furniture and fixtures" from the Lam Chew Estate. Later that year, he purchased the property from Keahonui Rickard. Here, the photographer has hand-written product advertisements (plumbing, tinsmith) and the owner's name, B. Ikeuchi, directly on the image. (Ikeuchi Family Collection.) [32]

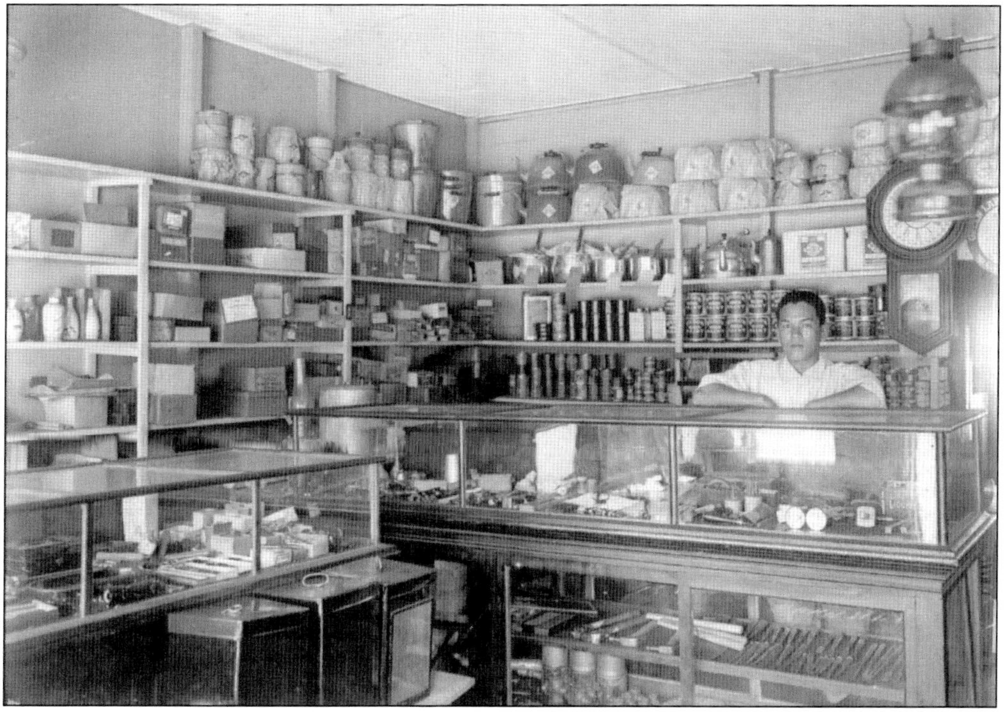

Interiors of Ikeuchi Hardware Stores. Successful retail specialization miles out in the country requires knowing one's customers' needs, maintaining a large inventory, having mechanical skills, and providing personal service and credit. Above, an early photograph of the first store (located immediately Waipio-side of the Yamatsuka Store site), includes jars, pots, kettles, metal containers, valves, paint, and hammers. (Note the lamp at upper right, prior to electricity coming to town in the 1920s.) The photograph at right, taken in 2015, includes various axes, poles and pipes, as well as a hand-made wooden cabinet with drawers for different sizes of nuts and bolts. (Above, (Ikeuchi Family Collection; right, LR.)

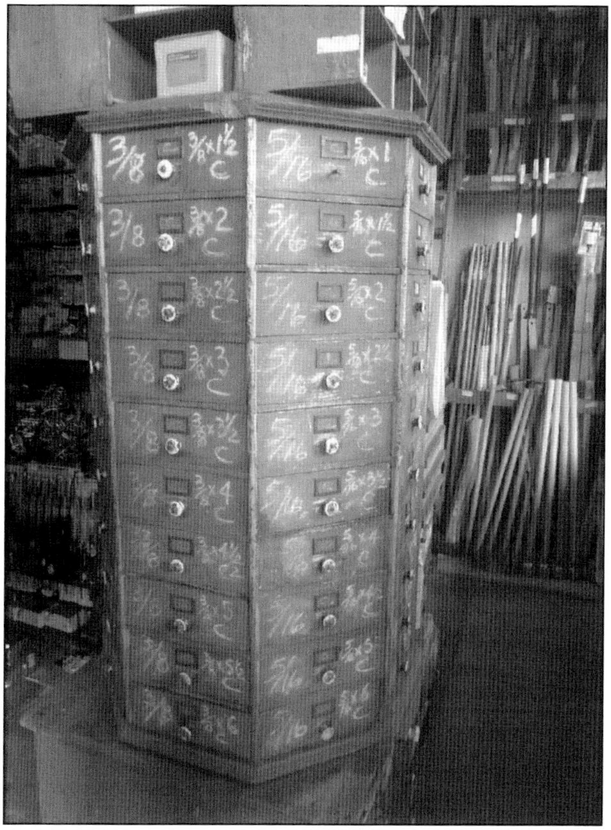

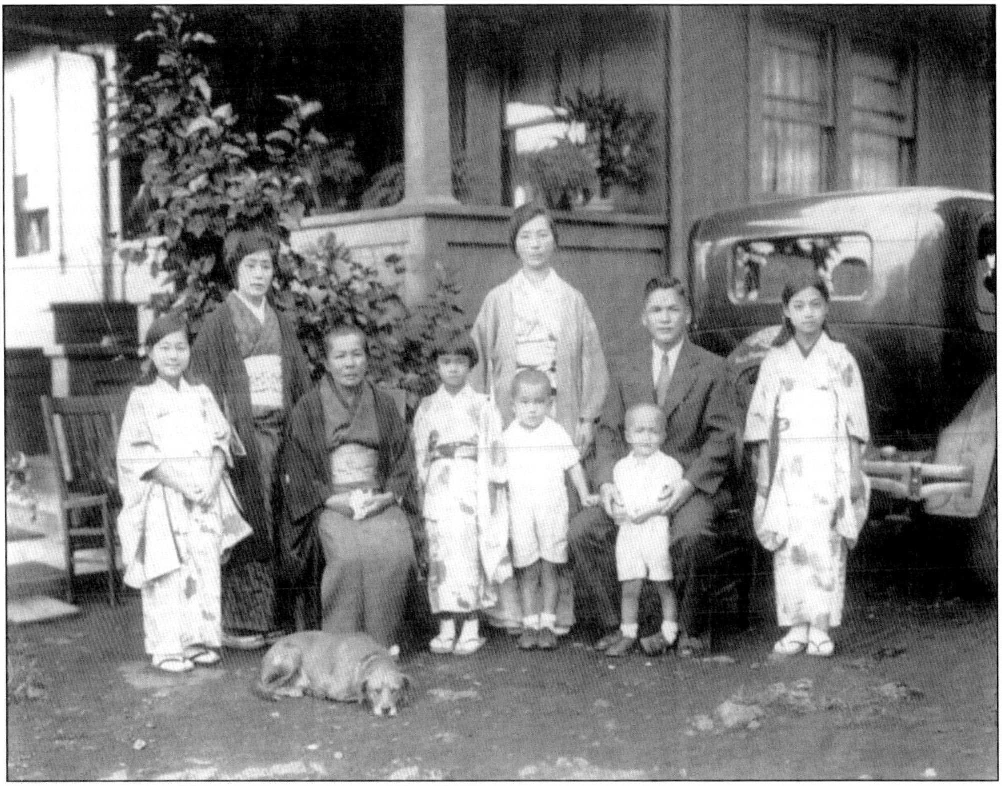

The Extended Bunso Ikeuchi Family at Home. In this photograph taken behind the store on Lehua Street, the women retain traditional attire while the males have adopted Western clothing. Pictured are, from left to right, (first row) Yasuko Taketa, Bunso's niece; Kuyo Yamane Ikeuchi, Bunso's mother, seated; Taeko Ikeuchi, Bunso's second daughter; Harold (Hideo) Ikeuchi, Bunso's oldest son; Walter Ikeuchi, second son and future father of Alan and Susan, presently the two family owners; and Yaeko Ikeuchi, oldest daughter; (second row) Saki Taketa, Yasuko's mother and Bunso's sister; Misuyo Takeuchi, Bunso's wife; and Bunso Ikeuchi, seated. (Ikeuchi Family Collection.)

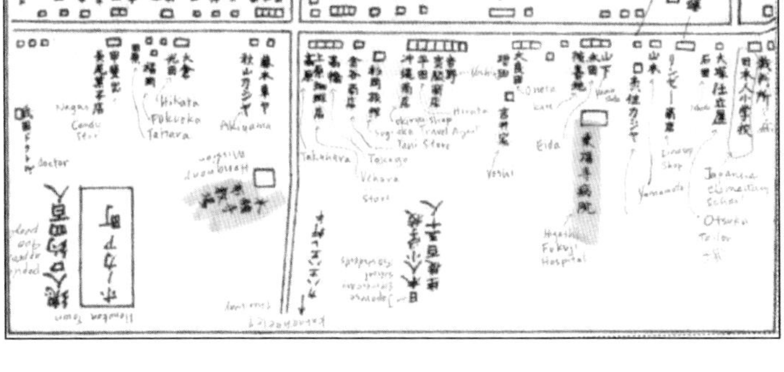

Haina–Government Road–Lehua–Mamane Intersection, 1914. This map, by Japanese national Nekketsu Takei, shows the proliferation of Japanese retailing activities that had occurred after plantation labor contracts ended and hundreds of emancipated people sought both goods and employment opportunities in Honokaa. (*Hawaii Ichiran.*)

Three

On Mamane Street Mauka Side

The Hilo-mauka corner of Mamane and Lehua Streets has a complex history, as do many properties located at important crossroads. The property was once leased to Archibald Cleghorn, (father of Princess Kaiulani), who had a chain of stores in Waipio, Honokaa, Paauilo, and Honolulu's Fort Street. The property was subsequently leased to J.R. Mills, a local landowner, community leader, and postmaster before his indictment and conviction in the death of retail competitor Katsu Goto (pages 25, 28). Carpenter Kiyoichi Irie apparently demolished the Cleghorn Store structure in the 1920s and erected the present edifice, which is named after Antone Luce Ferreira, who acquired it from Irie in 1933. The building became famous as the site of the Long Soup Corner eatery during World War II (page 67).

Due to topography, constructing any building along the mauka side of Mamane required excavation. The amount of digging needed, combined with the size of the owner's financial resources, dictated the shape of the building. The Sakata Building, for example, is an early long single-story structure built up from the street. The Rice/Holmes, Souza, and Jesus Building owners chose to build upward two stories rather than deep. Sometimes this has functioned well, as in the case of the Jesus Building, where the second story is at ground level in the back; the opposite is true with the Hasegawa Building, which is actually a multilevel structure.

The Sakata Building lot, in addition to being the site of the Tofukuji Hospital, is the likely location of the original George Hardy homestead. Born in 1822 as William Bickle Smith, he served in the British navy before changing his name and joining the American navy. He participated in the 1846 Mexican War siege of Tampico, visited Hawaii in 1850, and returned in 1851. Hardy was awarded Grant 1073 on the mauka side of the Government Road, and his land rental and sales agreements directed development in that section of Honokaa.

Honokaa School contains the original jail, Lyceum, and courthouse sites. (The Lyceum was the 19th-century social center of Honokaa.) Beginning in 1924, when portions of the present property were given by Honokaa Sugar for an expanded school, the grounds were terraced to accommodate a series of new buildings that illustrate territorial-era public educational institution architecture.

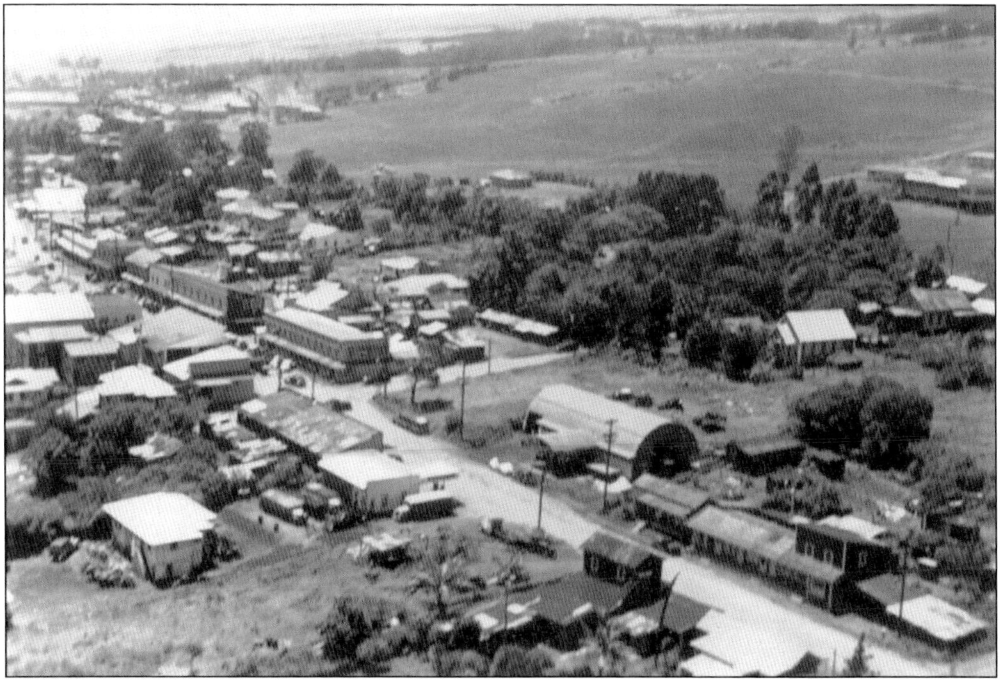

FERREIRA BUILDING AND THE MAMANE-LEHUA INTERSECTION. Antone Luce Ferreira was a homesteader and store owner from Kalopa before making the gutsy move to purchase the present Ferreira Building on the busiest corner in Honokaa. For most of its history, his building has been a small-business incubator. In 1974, Paul and Anita DeDominico (whose family once owned Rice-A-Roni and Ghirardelli Chocolate), bought the Hawaiian Holiday Macadamia Nut Company from Theo H. Davies. The Ferreira Building is pictured here around 1978, when the DeDominicos leased the structure, containing commercial displays on the lower floor and offices above. The inset shows the concrete cylinder that local police stood on when directing traffic at the hectic intersection in front of the building. (Above, Christensen Collection, NHERC; below, SHPD; inset, LR.) [33]

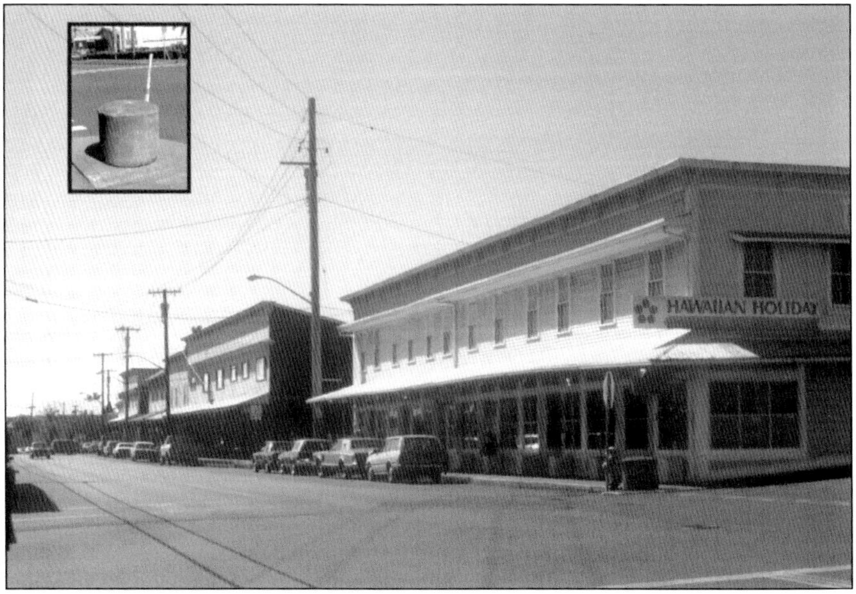

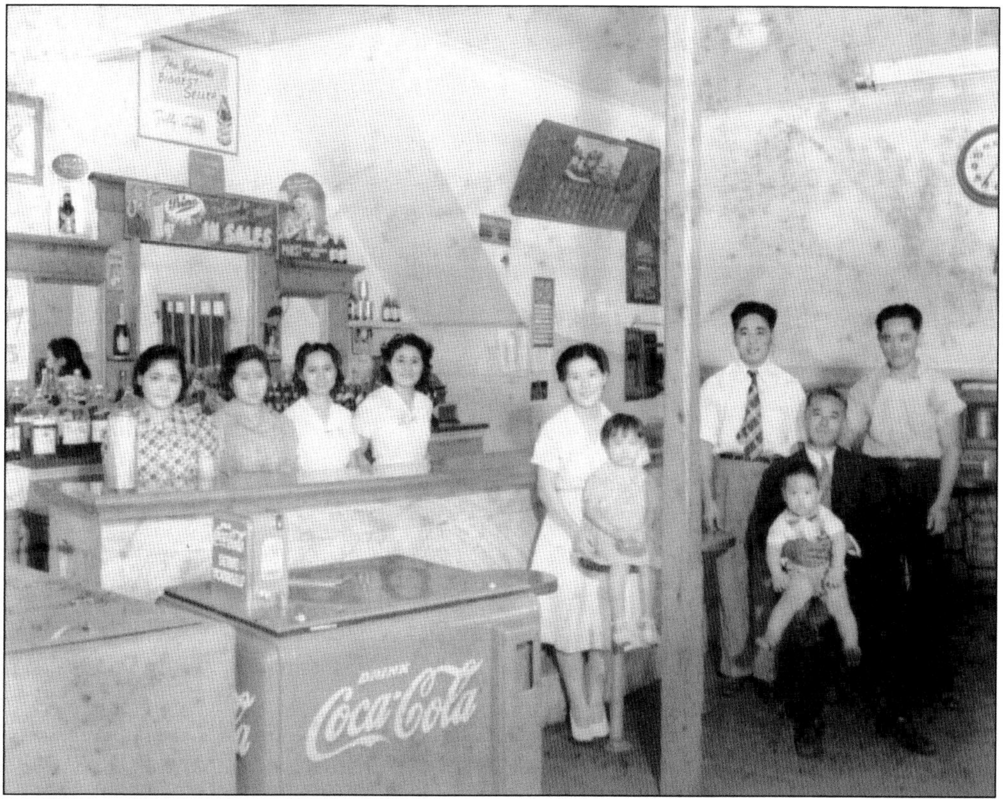

Paradise Restaurant. In 1938, Tomisei Kaneshiro, who had taught himself English through a correspondence course and then worked at Hamakua Shokwai, opened the Paradise Restaurant at the Ferreira Building's Waipio corner. The restaurant proved popular with the Marines during World War II, who, because they had difficulty pronouncing "saimin," described the fare as "long soup." The site became known as Long Soup Corner. Note the Coca-Cola bottle dispenser in the foreground. The design required patrons to reach into ice water to retrieve their drinks, an additional cooling thrill for hot customers in the days before air conditioning. (T. Kaneshiro Family Collection.)

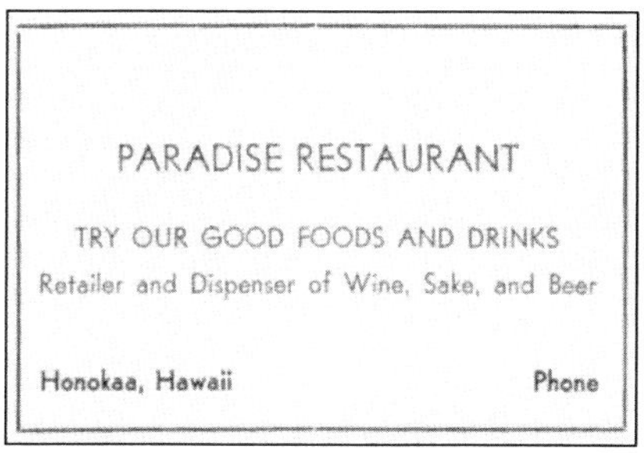

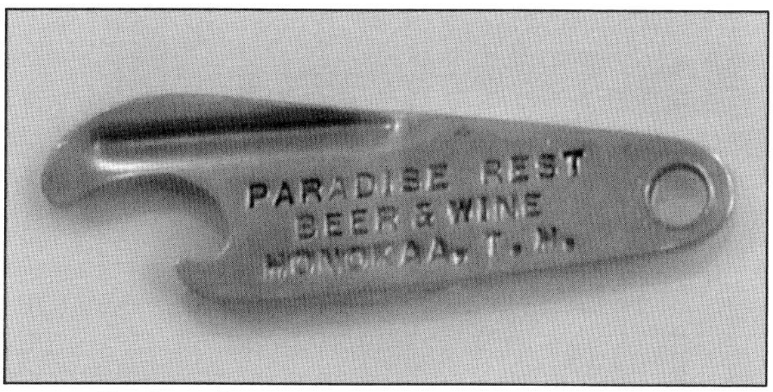

Advertising. Small-business owners historically found it necessary to advertise to gain new customers, but most could only afford limited publicity. Billboards (even on the sides of buildings) were illegal after 1927. Instead, advertising went onto tangible things such as wall calendars, yearbooks that would be saved (as in the 1939 *Ka Nana O Honokaa* yearbook advertisement at left), bottle openers that could be used over and over again, matchbook covers, and neon signs. (Left, HHSY; right, Larry Ignacio Collection.)

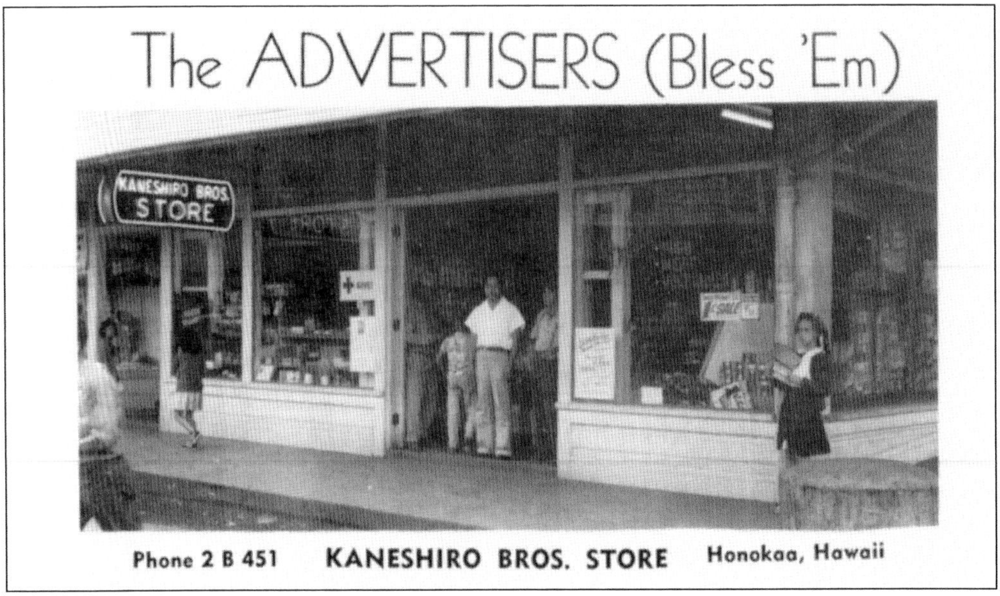

T. Kaneshiro Store by Day. In 1940, Tomisei Kaneshiro's elder brother Tomimasa began T. Kaneshiro Store, a general-merchandise firm, adjacent to his brother's restaurant in the Ferreira Building. In 1948, the restaurant was closed, the dividing wall between shops removed, and the space reworked to accommodate groceries, fish, and meat. Tomisei became the butcher, learning the art through a correspondence course. Other items for sale included hardware, shoes, Oriental goods, dry goods, and fabrics. This is a 1950 *Ka Nani O Honokaa* yearbook advertisement. (HHSY.)

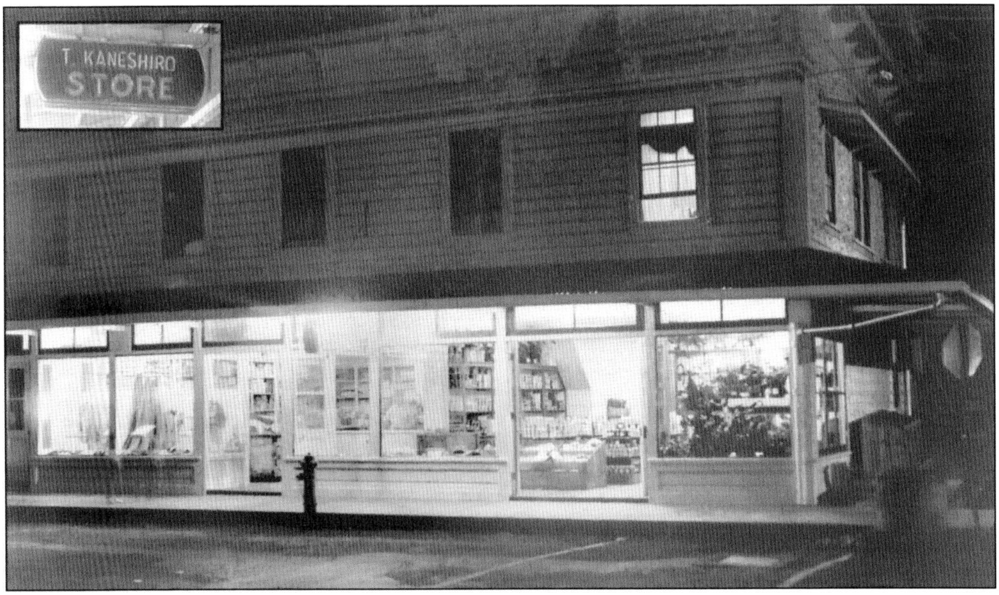

T. Kaneshiro Store by Night. Personal service and long hours were marketing tools regularly employed. Tomisei's son Roland remembers, "In the old days, when I was a teen-ager working for my Dad, we delivered the customer's groceries, carried them into the house, put the perishables away in the refrigerator, and set everything else on the table. It was an honor system." This photograph shows the store in the late evening. Notice the blurred "ghost" figures of two children and the shopkeeper. (T. Kaneshiro Family Collection.)

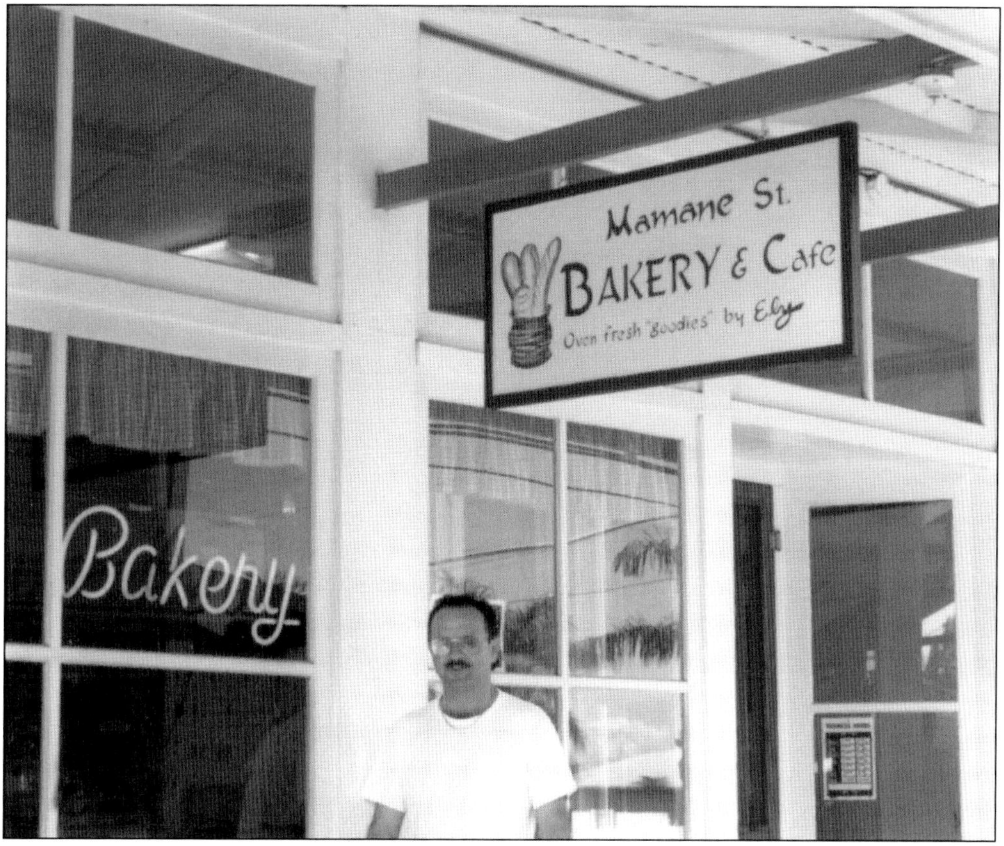

Neighborhood Bakery. Also located in the Ferreira Building from approximately 1992 to 2008, the Mamane Street Bakery and Café produced cakes, pies, doughnuts, and breads, mostly for other businesses such as the airlines and supermarkets. Its proprietor was Eliahu Pessah. The bakery has now moved up the mountain to Waimea. (Yamato Collection, NHERC.)

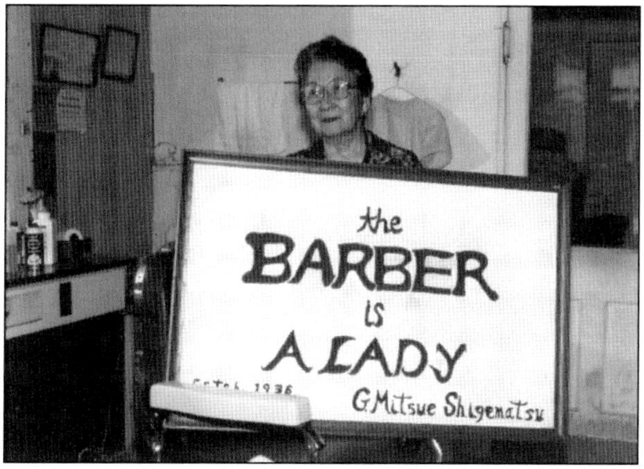

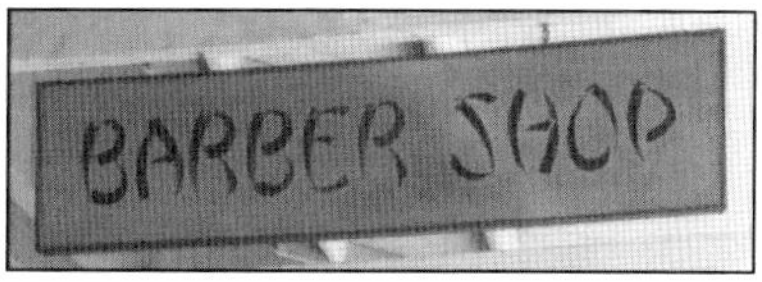

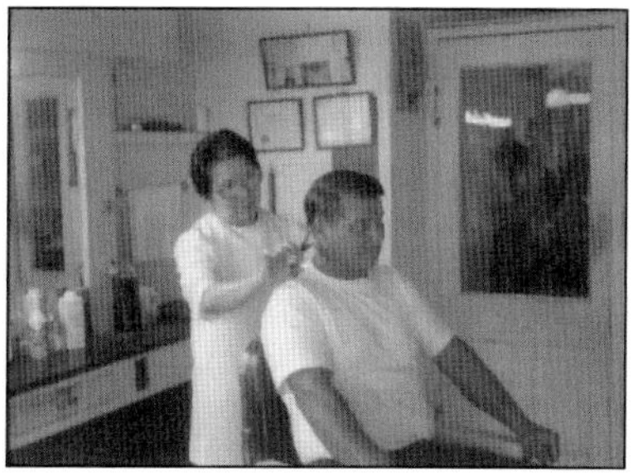

Lady Barber, Established 1936. Grace Mitsue Shigematsu and her husband, Shoichi, cut hair in the third shop from the Waipio side of the Ferreira Building for many years. In 1978, due to the acquisition of a master lease to the Ferreira Building by the Hawaiian Holiday Macadamia Nut Company, she moved to the Holmes Building. The space is now occupied by Larry Ignacio's Plantation Days Museum. (All, Yamato Collection, NHERC.)

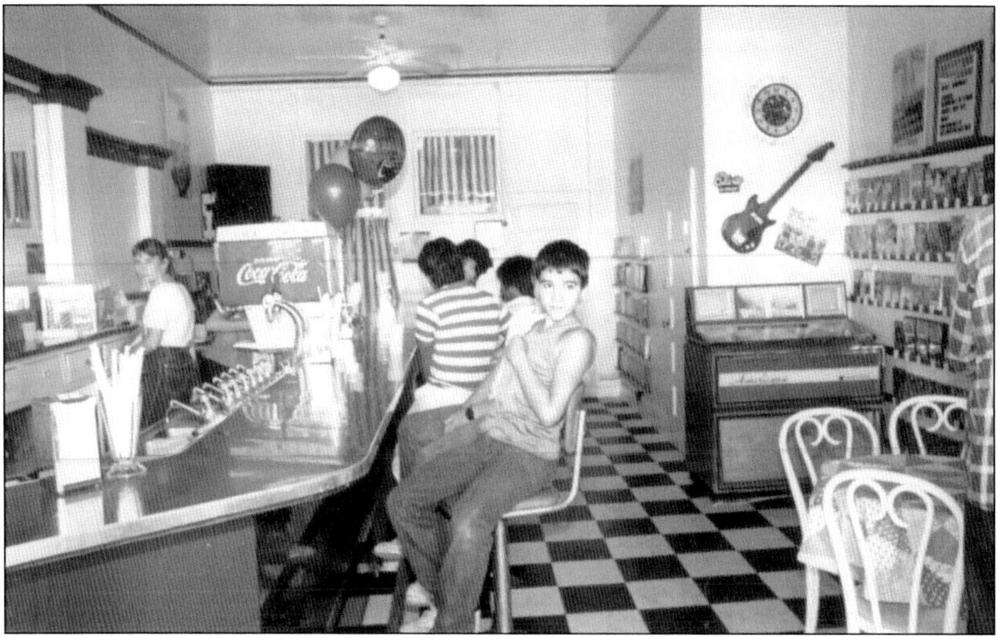

TANAKA FOUNTAIN, HAMAKUA FOUNTAIN. Located in the Ferreira Building, as seen in the above photograph, this establishment was the essential old-style soda fountain. Its decor from the postwar period included alternating colored floor tiles, swivel seats, a long counter with Coca-Cola and nickel-plated syrup dispensers, a jukebox, and oiled table cloths. (Yamato Collection, NHERC.)

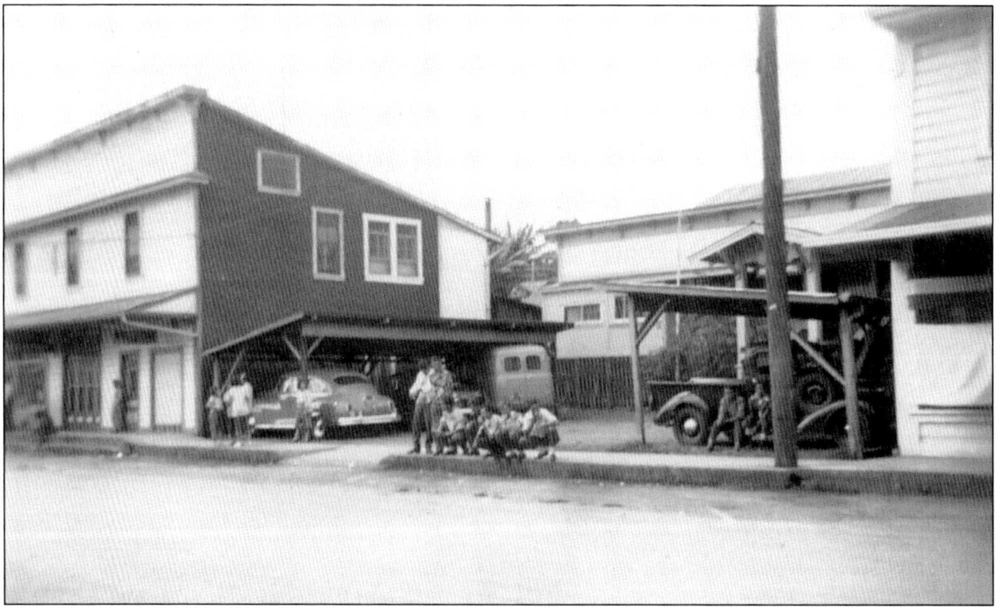

JAPANESE HOTEL. This was the site of Katsu Goto's 1889 leased store. The 1914 *Hawaii Ichiran* map shows numerous Japanese-operated businesses added to the downtown section of Honokaa. By 1925, the property seen here was Japanese owned. Henry Teruo Nakamura acquired it in 1932; his mother was running a hotel there by 1935. Census records show former commercial fisherman Kiedo Oshima running the hotel in 1940 with his wife as housekeeper. True to the automobile age, the front of the hotel had a parking lot. (Kenny Becktell Collection, NHERC.) [34]

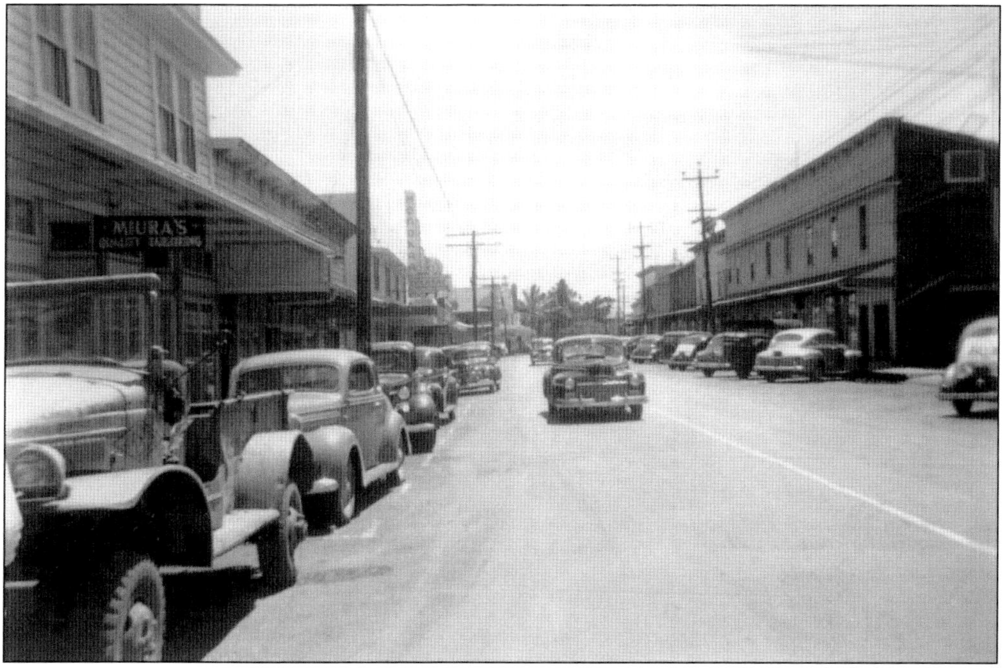

Postwar Mamane Street Scene. Dating photographs is always fun. In this case, the Honokaa Theatre (1939) is identified by its neon sign, the cars are postwar, and Mamane Street's surface has been repaired. Miura's Quality Tailoring, mentioned in the 1945 Honokaa High School annual, is located in the Andrade Building at left. Also pictured are the Kotake, Hirata, Hasegawa, Jesus, Souza and Holmes/Rice Buildings, and the People's Theatre. (Ruis/Botelho Family Collection, NHERC.)

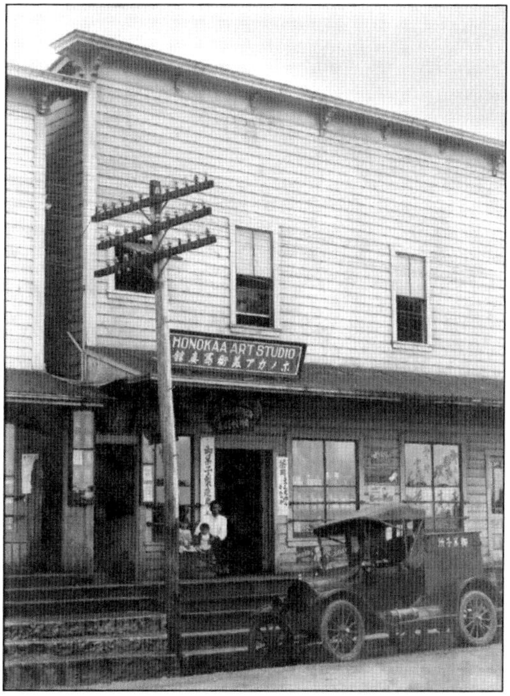

The Hasegawa "Big Store" Exterior. Seishiro Hasegawa and two of his eight children (all born here) sit outside his first candy store. Signs on the Big Store read cookie factory, candy store, catering, *manju*, and *monika*. The Hasegawas lived and worked in the Rice Building for approximately 10 years. Their neighbors reflected the ethnic diversity of the town. Immediately upstairs was photographer Kamenojo Maekawa, who took and developed photos in his Honokaa Art Studio. Next door, to the Hilo side, were the L. Ahfoo Chinese Restaurant (page 73), Castillo Music Store, and Andrade's Honokaa Drug Store (page 73). Note the concrete steps up to the sidewalk, created because the building was constructed before the road was widened and leveled. Multiple concrete steps fronting commercial buildings along Mamane Street continue to be a distinctive feature of Honokaa. (Miyoko Hasegawa Matsuo Collection.) [35]

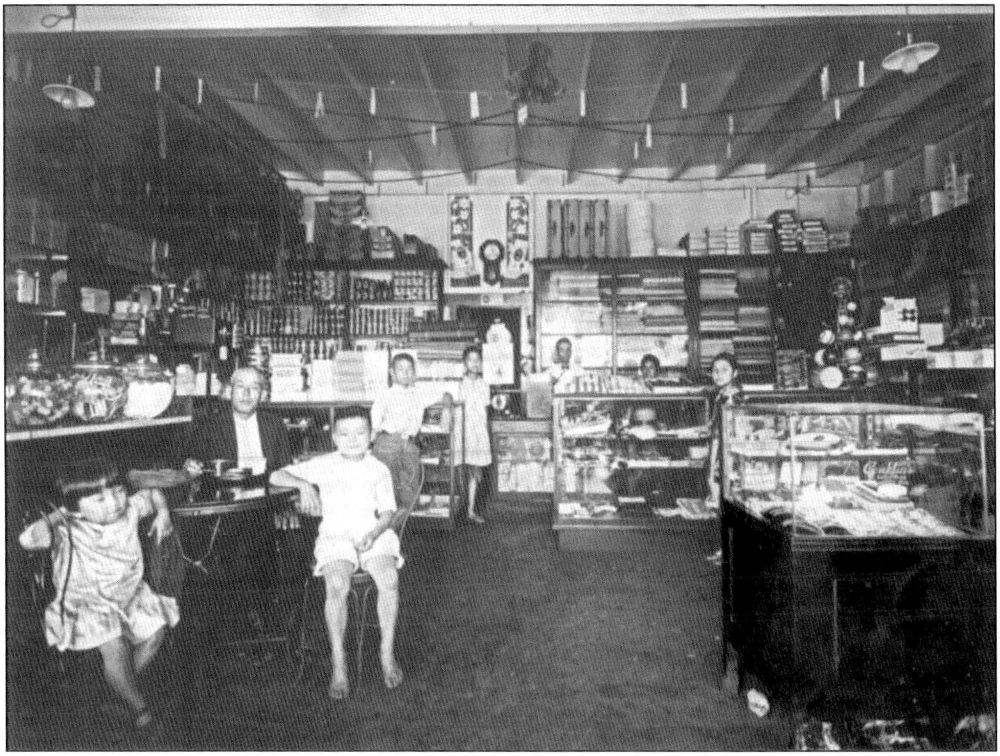

THE HASEGAWA BIG STORE INTERIOR, c. 1929. Besides the treats, the store carried an extensive variety of goods. Note the hatboxes, suitcases, hams, dry goods, jewelry, and a variety of balls. Seishiro Hasegawa declared, "If they did not have it they would get it for the customer." The table was placed for patrons enjoying hand-cranked ice cream such as the dish in front of Hachibe Okubo of Okubo Taxi. From left to right are Misao Hasegawa, Hachibe Okubo, Harold Tatsumi, Kiomi, Irene, Ojichan (grandfather), Obaachan (grandmother), and Fusae Hasegawa. (Miyoko Hasegawa Matsuo Collection.)

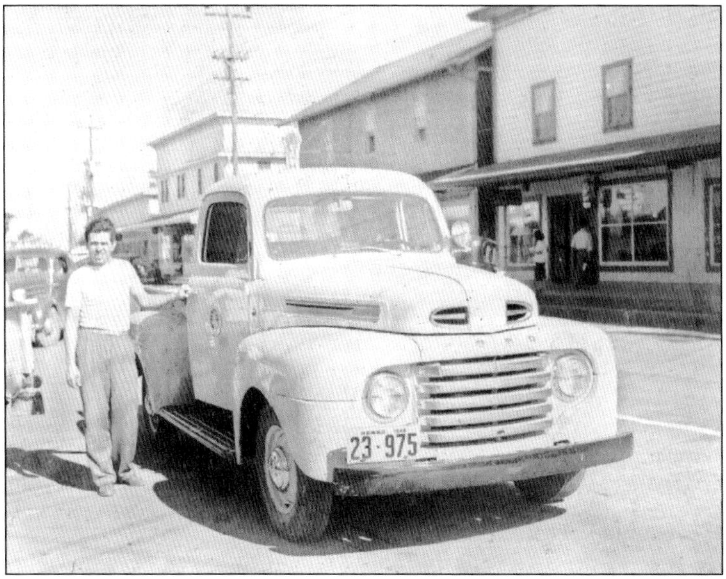

MAN OF MANY TALENTS. David Botelho originally worked as a mechanic at the Botelho Garage before becoming employed by Hawaii Electric Light Company (HELCO). Botelho is standing next to his HELCO truck across Mamane Street from the Rice and Souza Buildings. Note the 1948 five-digit license plate. (Florence Botelho Collection.)

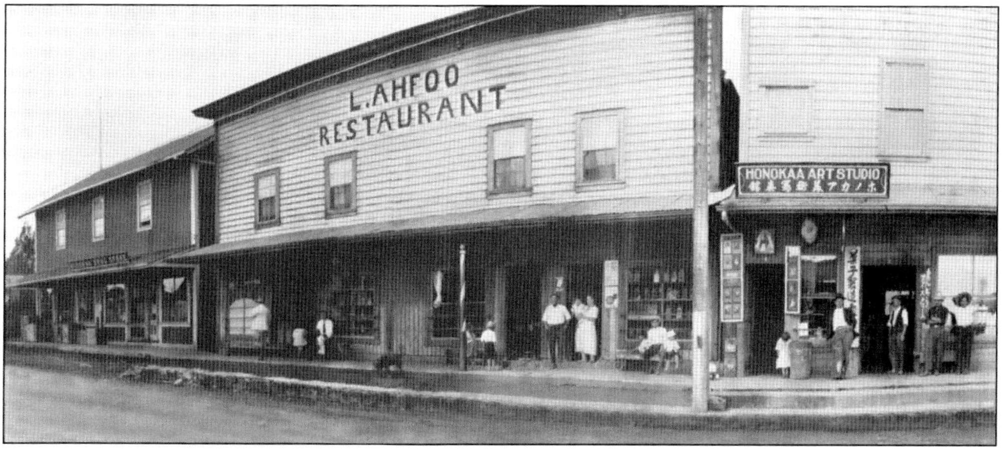

SOUZA BUILDING, C. 1930. Leong Lam Fook acquired this structure in 1912, and it is likely that the L. Ahfoo Restaurant shown here dated from this time. It is popularly known as the Souza Building. John D. Souza acquired it in 1933, and the family retained ownership until 1975. It contained a meat market, barber, and tailor. (Sakata Art Studio.) [36]

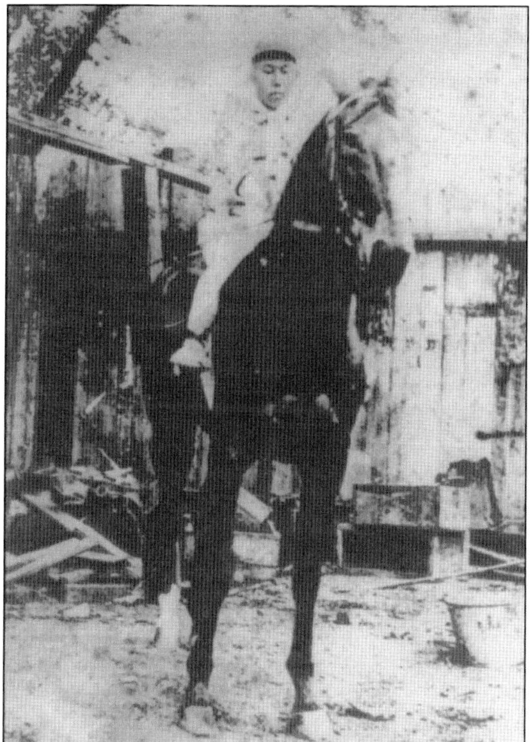

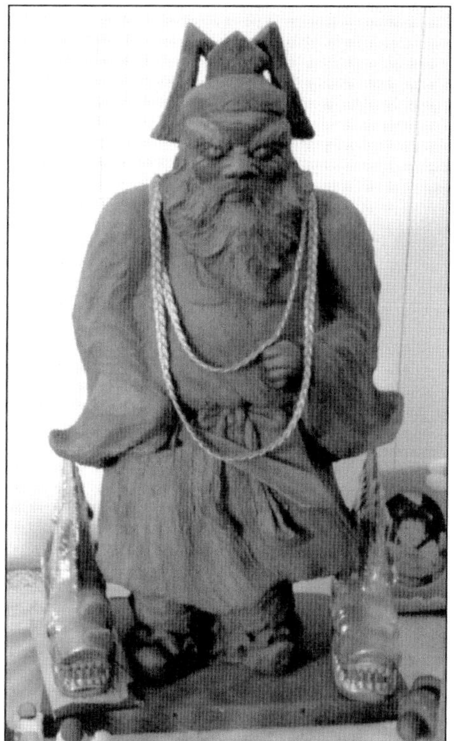

CANDY GIRL AND THE CHINESE GOD SHŌKI. At left, Seishiro Hasegawa sold confections, cookies, and candies on his travels with his horse Candy Girl between Kukuihaele and Laupahoehoe. Once, coming back very late from Laupahoehoe, Candy Girl suddenly stopped and would not budge—the horse had reached its sleep time. So Seishiro slept in the wagon and returned home to Honokaa the next day. On one of his trips to Japan, Seishiro brought back the carved statue of the Chinese god Shōki at right, which was placed prominently on a store shelf. Seishiro selected Shōki to expel demons and help achieve scholastic goals for his many children. (Miyoko Hasegawa Matsuo Collection.)

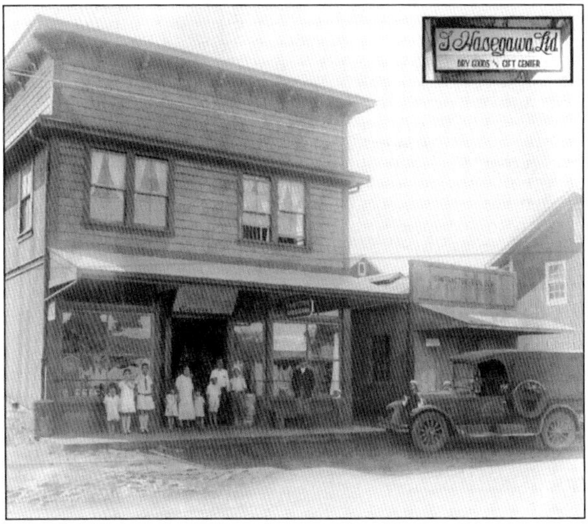

The Hasegawa Building. In 1896, Geraldo Ferreira acquired land from George Hardy on the mauka side of Mamane Street and operated the G.B. Ferreira Blacksmith Shop there. By 1937, Seishiro Hasegawa had acquired the property, built a new two-story building, and relocated the Hasegawa Store there. Hasegawa expanded his new building in 1939 with additions on the Waipio and mauka sides. In common with other two-story retail buildings along Mamane Street, he and his family lived above the shop. (Miyoko Hasegawa Matsuo Collection.) [38]

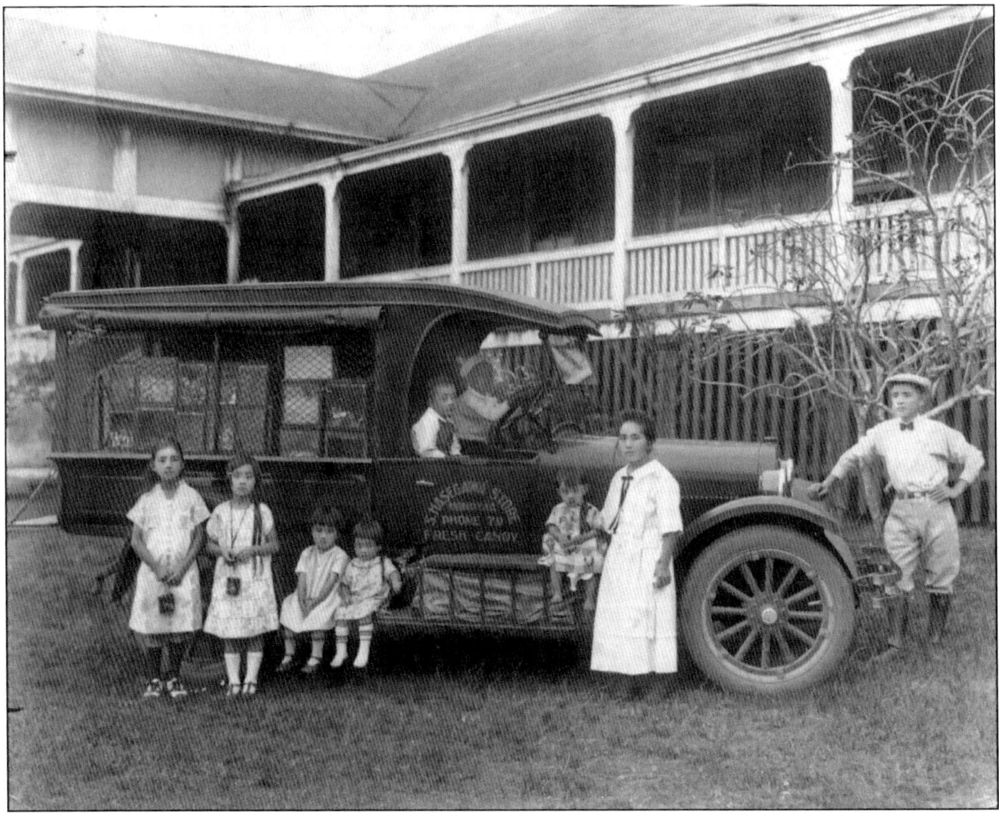

The S. Hasegawa Store Truck. The sign on the truck door has a two-digit phone number—79. Various confections were housed in clear containers so patrons could look in and see the items. Taken at one of the old Japanese school grounds, this family photograph shows, from left to right, Irene, Fusae, Miyoko, Helene, Misao, Obaachan, and Ojichan. The truck driver is Kiyomi, and the passenger is Harold Tatsumi. (Miyoko Hasegawa Matsuo collection.)

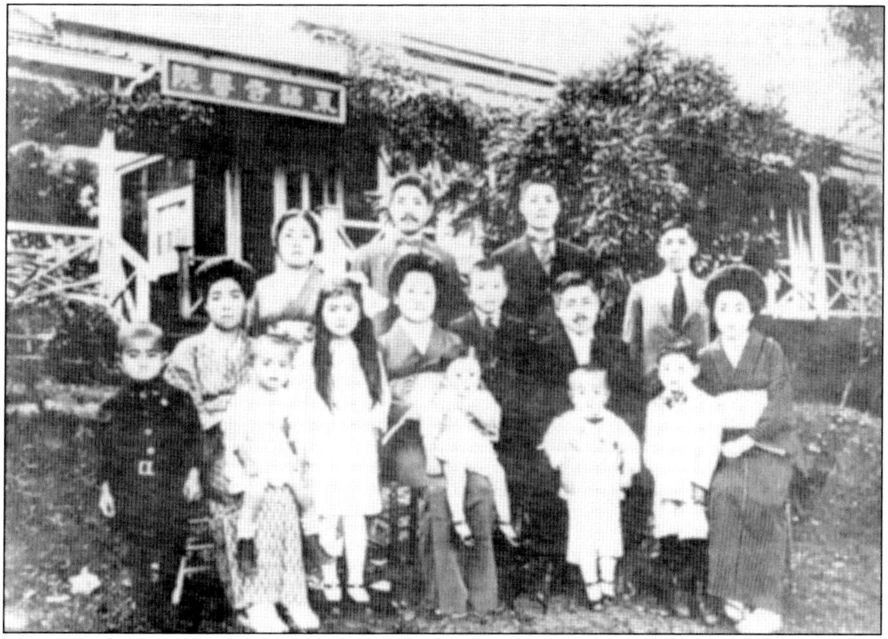

TOFUKUJI JAPANESE HOSPITAL. Dr. Koshiro Tofukuji received his training at Tokyo Saisei Gakusha Medical School and the University of Michigan. He served in the Russo-Japanese War of 1904–1905. In 1906, he established the first Japanese hospital on Hawaii Island in Honokaa on land now owned by the Sakata family. Dr. Tofukuji's hospital operated for 14 years before he moved to Maui in 1921. Dr. Tofukuji was interned and repatriated to Japan in 1943. The Honokaa property was expropriated by the US government. Four buildings remain from the Japanese hospital period, including two now greatly modified structures that are used for housing, a laundry/*furo* building, and a multicar garage. Notice that the photograph below of family and friends also includes the family dog. (Above, *The Private Japanese Hospital*; below, Harunaga Family Collection.) [39]

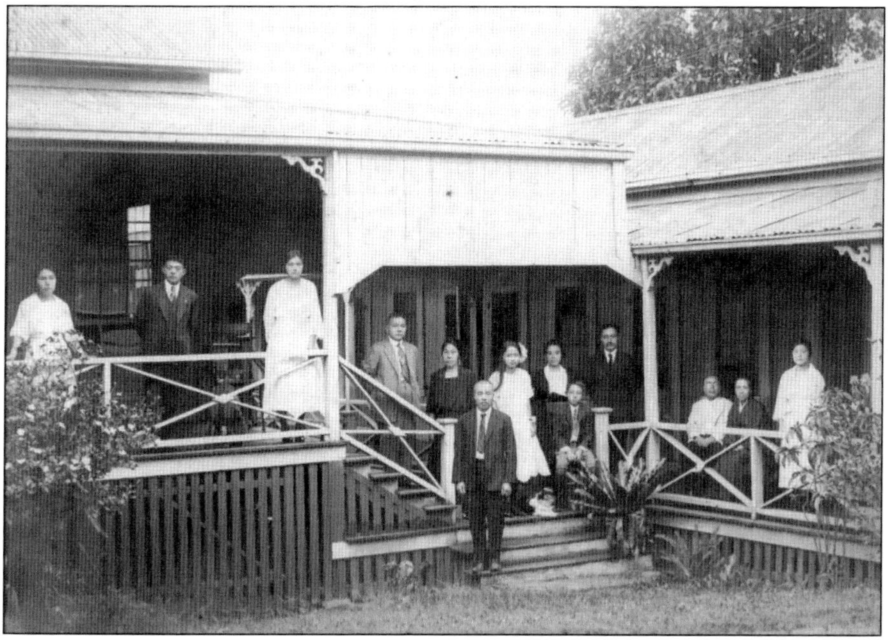

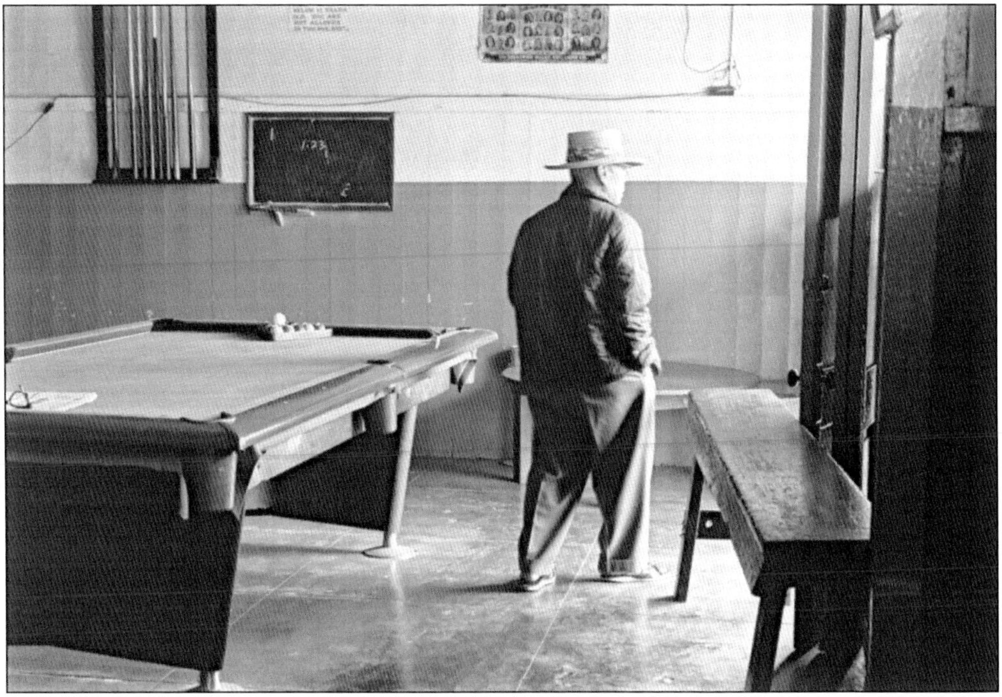

Sakata Building. This is one of the early commercial buildings in Honokaa (note the vertical wood wall construction). Although it does not appear on the 1904 Registered Map 2267, it does appear on the 1914 Sanborn Fire Insurance Map. Early tenants included candy and notions sales, a photography studio, clothes cleaning, dry goods, and sewing machine sales and repair. Recent tenants have included the Galinato and Hernandez Pool Halls (above) and the Filipino Store and Sweet Shoppe (below). (Above, photograph © Franco Salmoiraghi; below, both Yamato Collection, NHERC.)

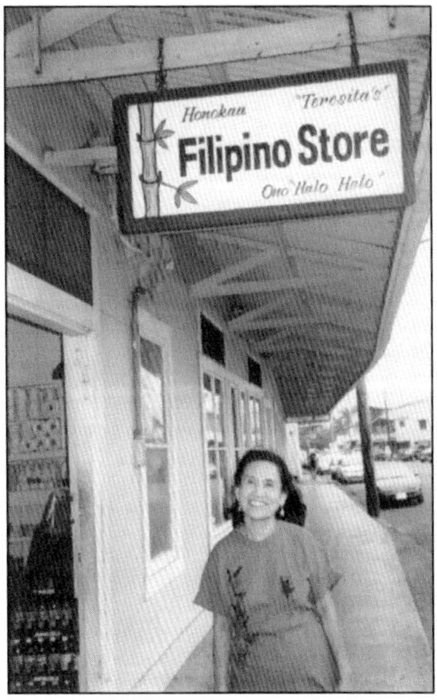

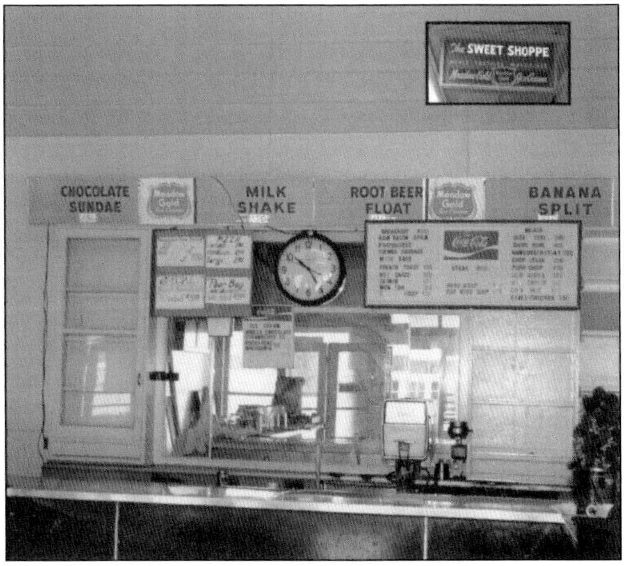

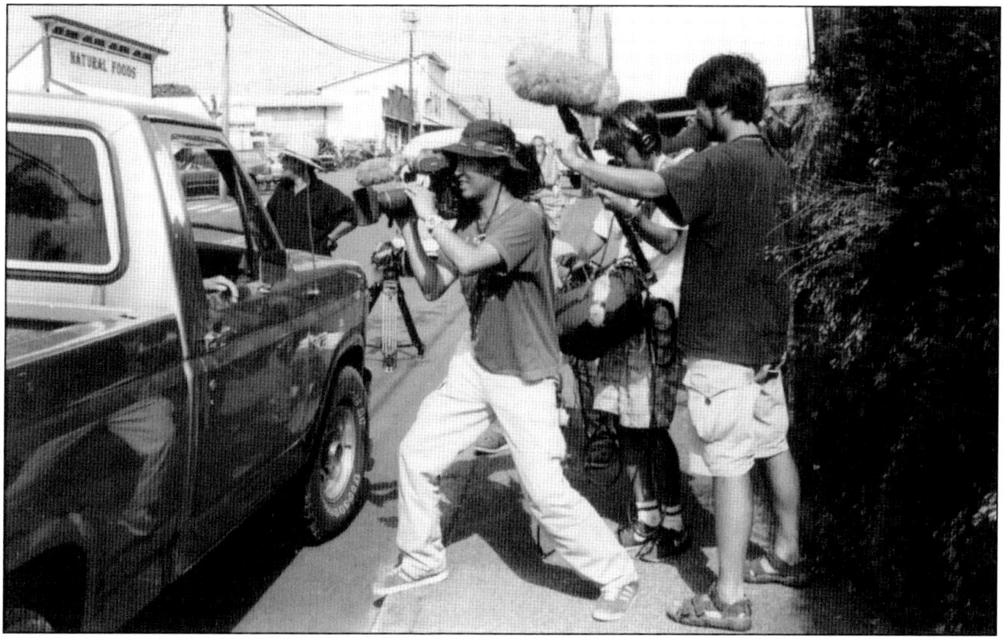

FILMING *HONOKAA BOY*. Based upon the book *Honokaa Boy* by Lee Yoshida and filmed on location in Honokaa in October 2008, this movie revolves around a Japanese college student who finds refuge in Honokaa working as a projectionist at the People's Theatre. He meets an eccentric master chef, an older woman with a zest for life, and is attracted to a young woman. By gaining and losing love, he comes to understand the true meanings of friendship and affection. This popular Japanese movie is regularly shown on flights between Japan and Hawaii. (Yamato Collection, NHERC.)

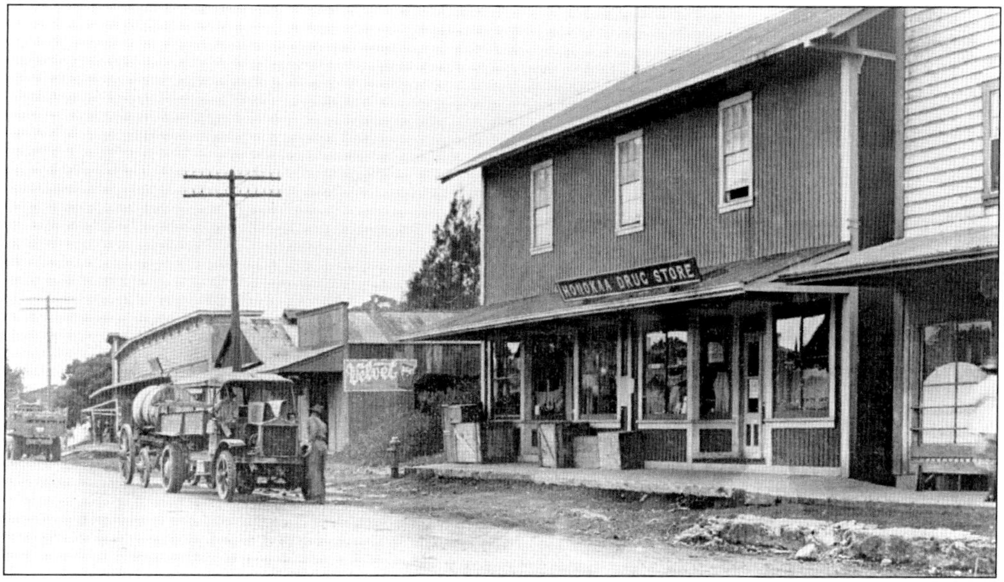

MAUKA SIDE OF MAMANE STREET, BEFORE 1930. All these buildings are recorded on the 1914 Sanborn Fire Insurance Map. From left to right are the two-story parapet of Takata Building, the Sakata Commercial Building's curved roof and parapet, G.B. Ferreira Blacksmith Shop, storage building, Jesus Building, and Souza Building. (Sakata Art Studio.)

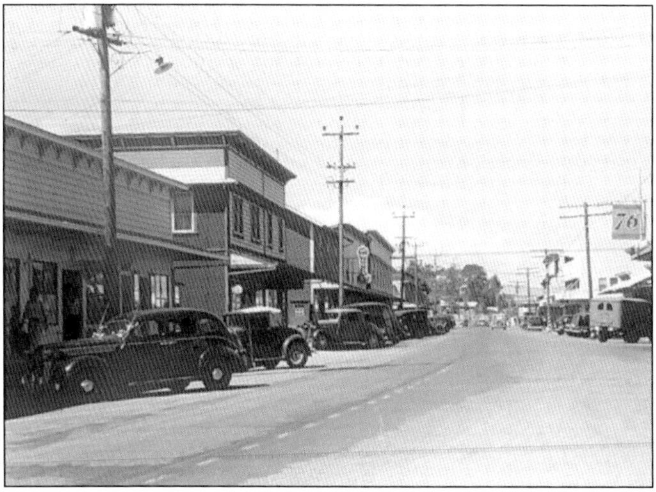

MAMANE STREET, C. 1940S. Evidence of the immediate nature of the war includes the differing types of automobiles and the poor condition of Mamane Street. The Sakata Building is at far left. Most of the landmarks then are still standing now, such as the Hasegawa, Jesus, Souza, and Rice Buildings, but the businesses within (Oshima Hotel, Tanaka Fountain, T. Kaneshiro Market, and Long Soup Corner) have changed. (NHERC.)

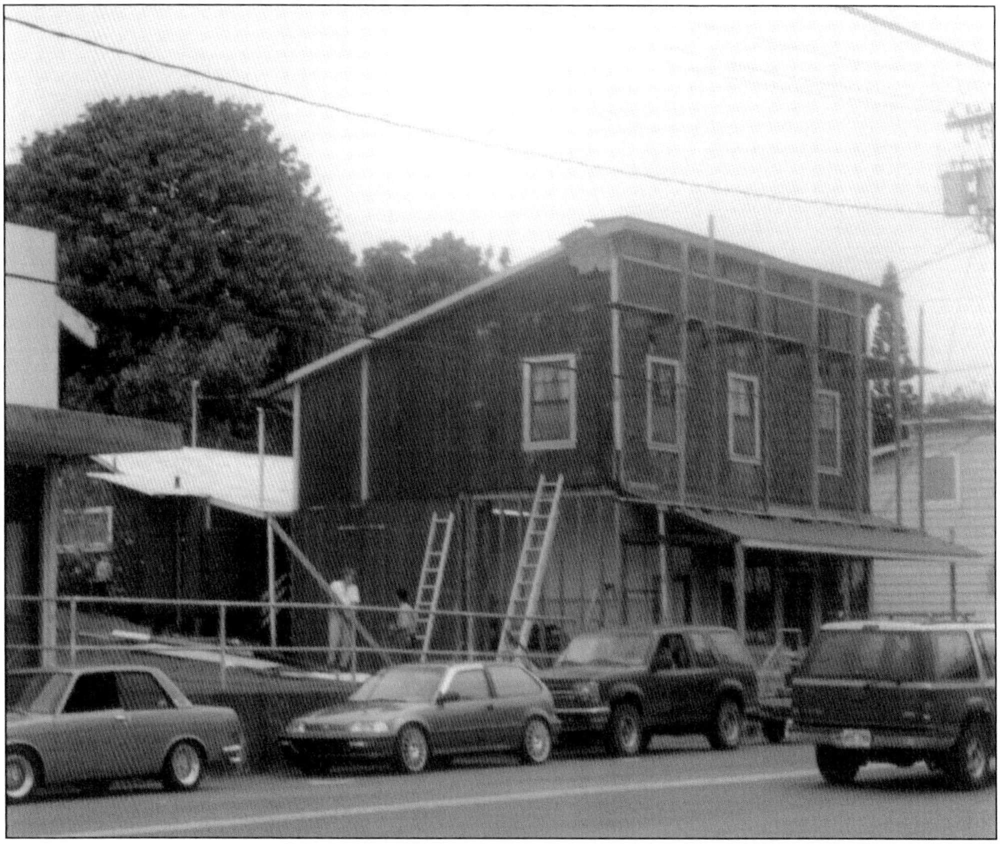

TAKATA BUILDING. Wooden buildings require periodic maintenance to prevent wood rot and termite infestation. Fortunately, wood buildings from the territorial period are usually made up of dense old-growth lumber that was floated in by sea. Both the hardness of the wood and the sea salt discourage termites. The carpenters of the territorial period fit components tightly together. The owners of Honokaa's buildings have been willing to make periodic repairs to protect their investments. In this photograph, the Takata Building is undergoing rehabilitation. (Yamato Collection, NHERC.) [40]

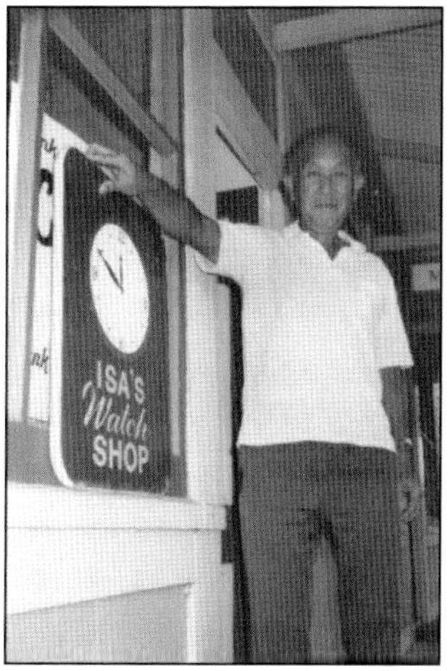

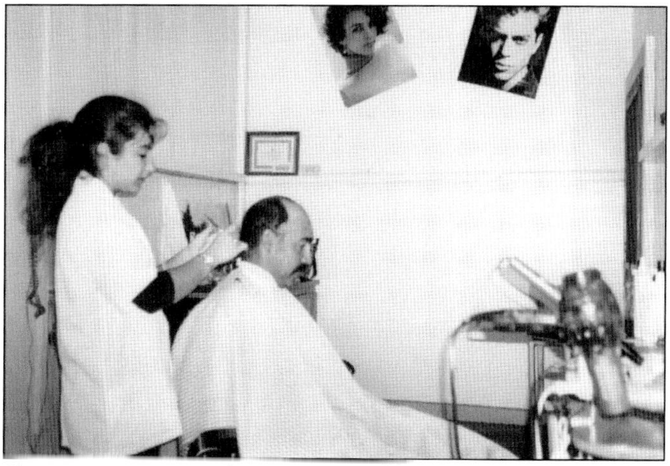

All in One Place. Isa's Watch Shop was a part-time business owned by Isa Kitagawa. The shop was located on the Hilo side of the Takata Building in the same space also once occupied by Zelina's Barber Shop. Zelina's father, Melin Zimbra, owned the building. The Waipio side has been occupied by a pool hall and later a video store. (Yamato Collection, NHERC.)

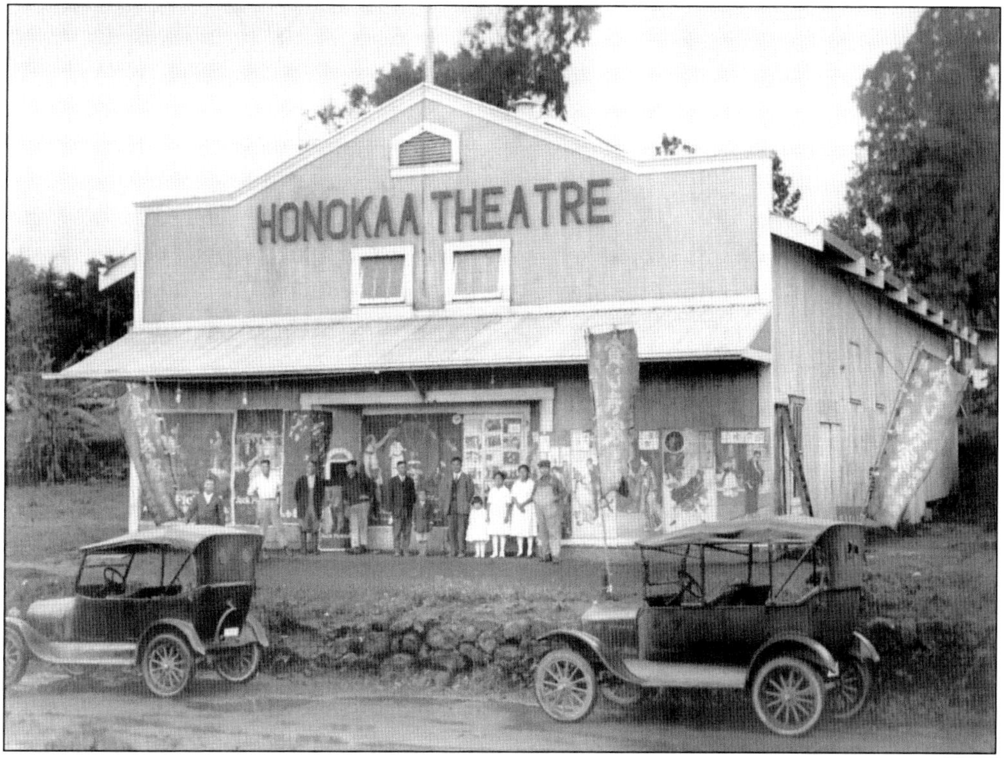

Old Tanimoto Theatre. The Honokaa Theatre, nicknamed the Old Tanimoto Theatre and opened in 1921, was initially operated by Manki Harunaga and J. Fujino. Entertainment was provided by traveling and local troupes in elaborate costumes and makeup who performed acrobatics, *kabuki* (classical Japanese dance-drama), *shibai* (Japanese folk drama), singing, and storytelling. Also presented were silent cowboy films, early talkies, and samurai movies narrated by a *benshi*, who spoke the actors' lines and explained and elaborated the action to the audience. In 1932, Hatsuzo Tanimoto acquired the property and closed the theater. (Harunaga Family Collection.) [41]

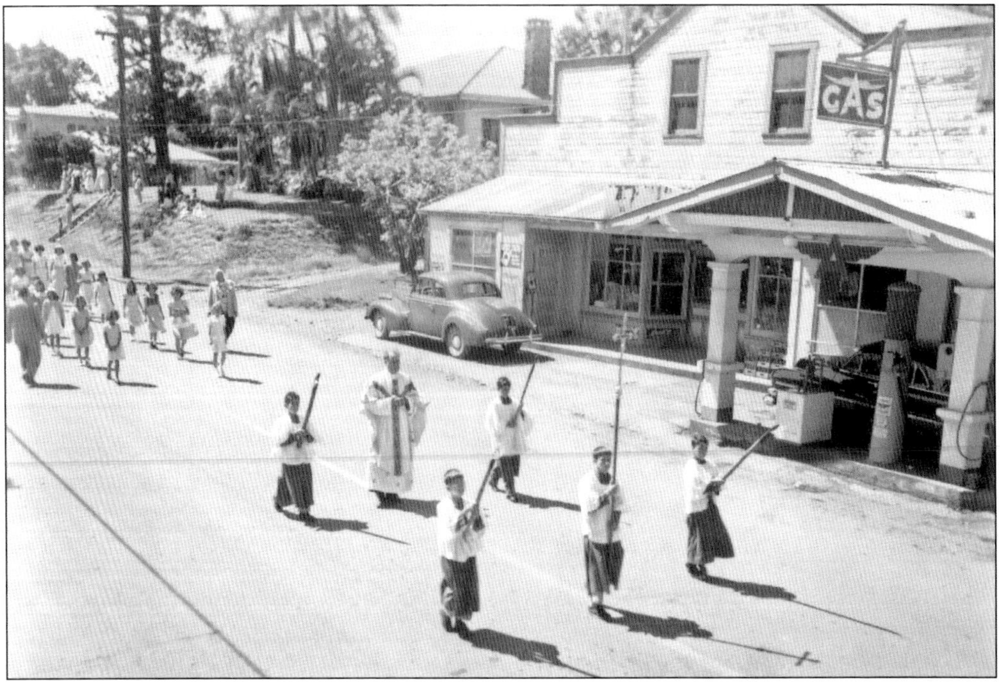

HAMAKUA SHOKWAI INC. This location was the site of the earlier A.B. Lindsay Store. The Hamakua Shokwai, a general-merchandise retailer, was established in 1921 and occupied one of the largest buildings in town. It closed in 1948 when the property was, like the Tofukuji property, seized by the US government after World War II to cover war reparations. This location has held numerous automobile-related businesses, including Higarashi Garage and Coastline Transportation. (Caroline Hart Collection, Peter Tomich.) [42]

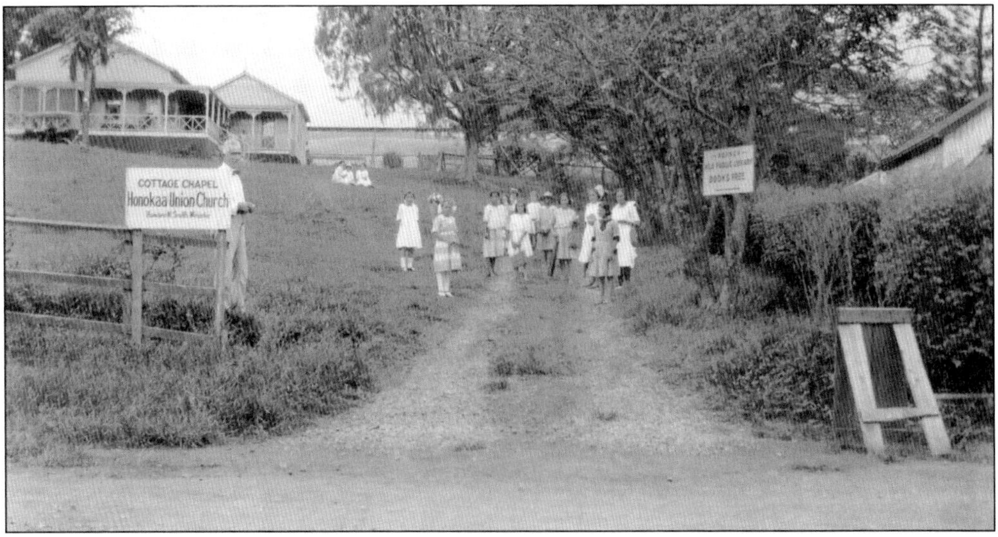

CONGREGATIONAL CHURCH. The Hawaiian Evangelical Association (Congregational church) acquired the old A.B. Lindsay residential property on the mauka side of Mamane Street in 1921, establishing the Honokaa Union Church. As seen in this photograph, the facilities also were once used as one of several informal libraries for local children before the 1937 library was constructed. In 1927, these Victorian-era buildings were replaced by the present structure (page 30). (HSL.) [43]

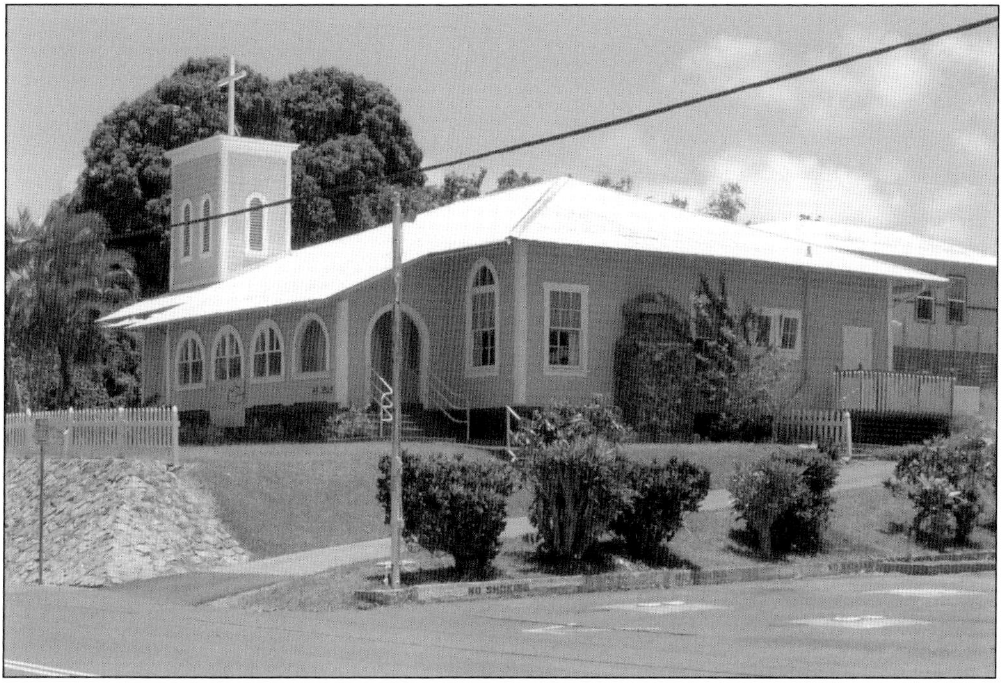

Honokaa United Methodist Church. The catalyst for a Methodist church in Honokaa came in 1910, when the Rev. Cenon Ramos came from the Philippines and, with the help of plantation management, constructed the first Filipino Methodist church building makai of the Catholic church and Hongwanji Temple on Lehua Street. Koreans, who had learned Methodist teachings in the old country, also joined. The United Methodist Church subsequently acquired the more central Mamane Street property and held its first services there in 1950. (CCS.)

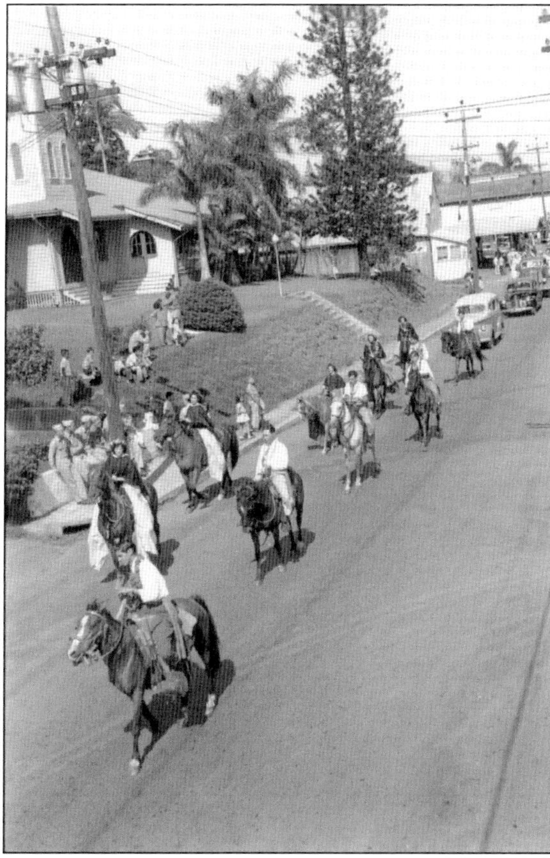

Paniolo Days. Cowboys and *pau* riders (women in long colorful skirts) parade on horseback in front of the Methodist church. Note that Mamane Street has not yet been widened nor the mauka stone wall built, allowing spectators to sit on the grassy slope. Farther toward Waipio, the side of the Hamakua Shokwai can be seen. (NHERC.)

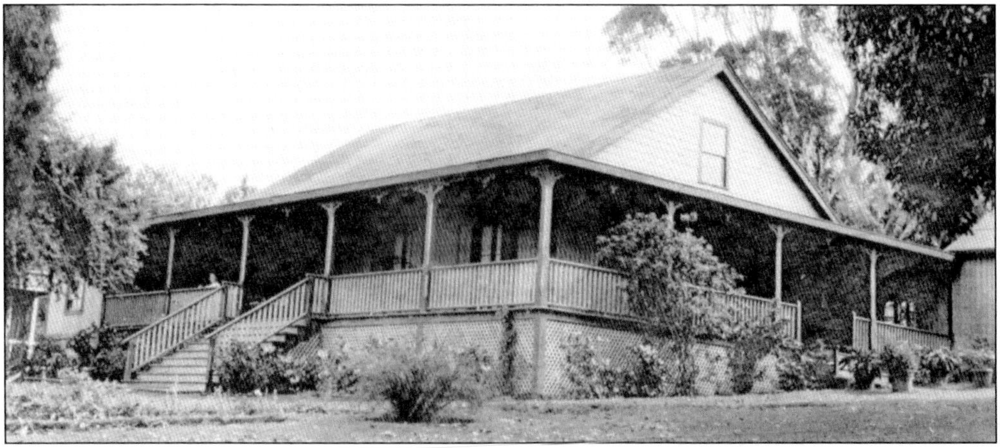

Rickard Hotel. This structure was likely constructed in 1883 by George W. Wilfong, a native of Boston and a sugar planter and postmaster of the town. William H. Rickard, former manager of the Honokaa Sugar Company, moved into the house in 1893. After Rickard's death in 1899, his widow temporarily moved to Canada, during which time Joseph Pritchard started a hotel on the premises. Nora Rickard eventually returned and operated the hotel herself for many years. The Salvation Army acquired the property in 1958. (NHERC.) [48]

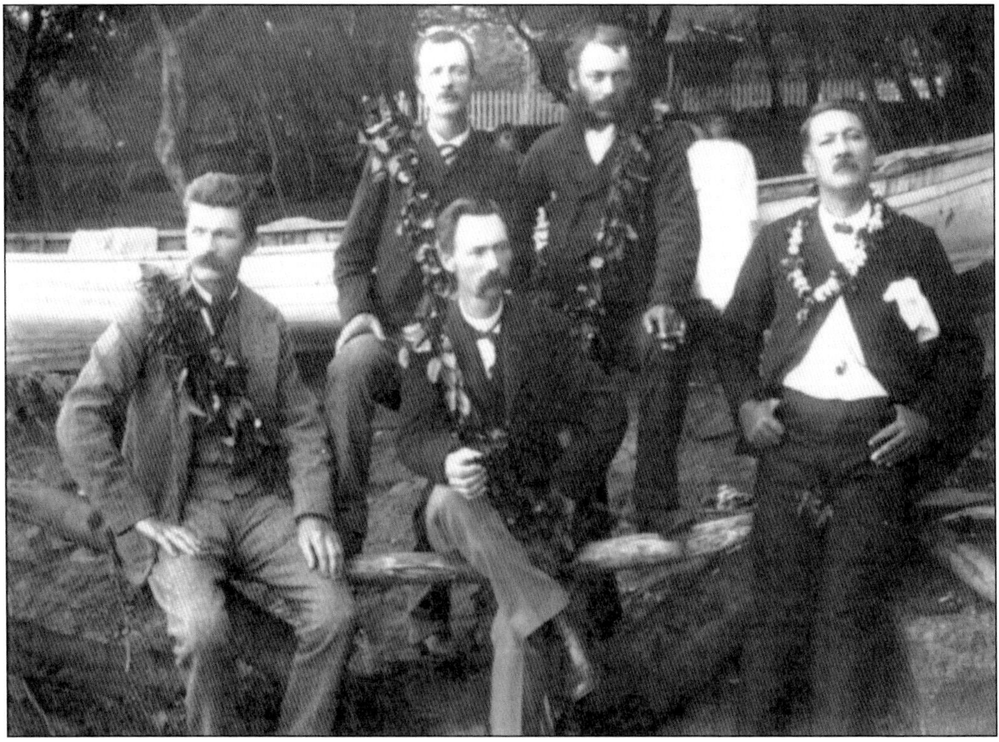

Reception for a Hero. In 1895, an armed counterrevolution was undertaken by Royalists against the Provisional/Republic government. Guns were landed, and battles occurred at Diamond Head, Kaimuki, and Manoa on Oahu, ending in the defeat of the Royalists. Longtime Honokaa resident W.H. Rickard was intimately involved with the restoration attempt and subsequently imprisoned by the Republic. Upon his release, he was honored by the Native Hawaiian community and other Royalists with a huge luau as a "demonstration of affection." (HSA.)

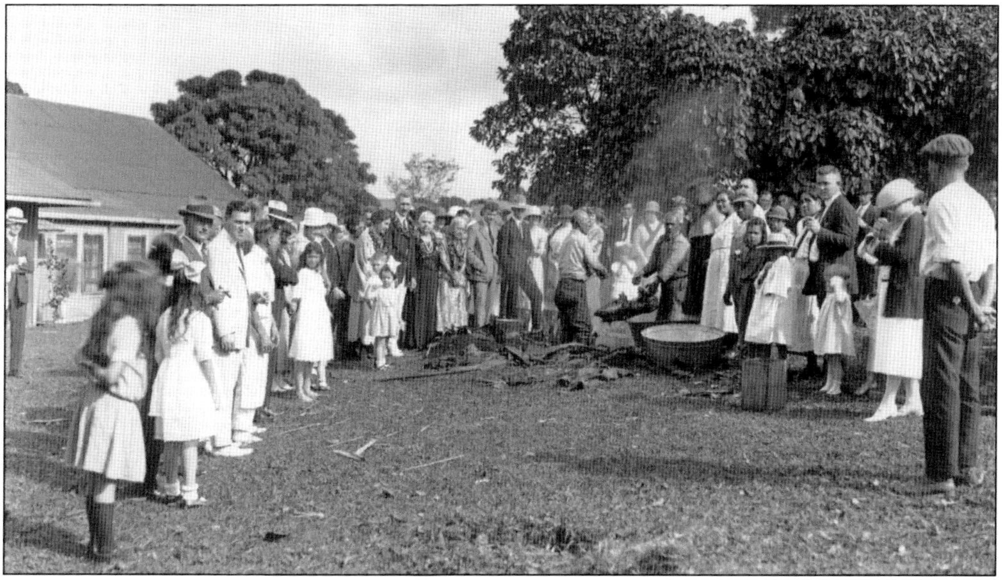

Rickard Descendents at a Luau. Important feasts in pre-contact Hawaii were called *ahaaina* (meal gathering). (The term luau actually refers to young taro tops, especially as baked with coconut cream and chicken or octopus.) Like other longtime residents throughout the islands, the Rickard family periodically returned to their roots on the Big Island. Here, an extended family get-together occurred on the old family site in Honokaa. The pig for the feast has been cooked in an *imu* (underground oven.) (Rickard Collection, NHERC.)

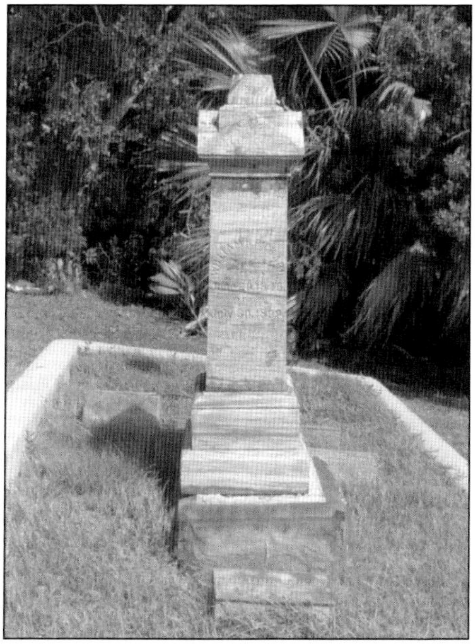

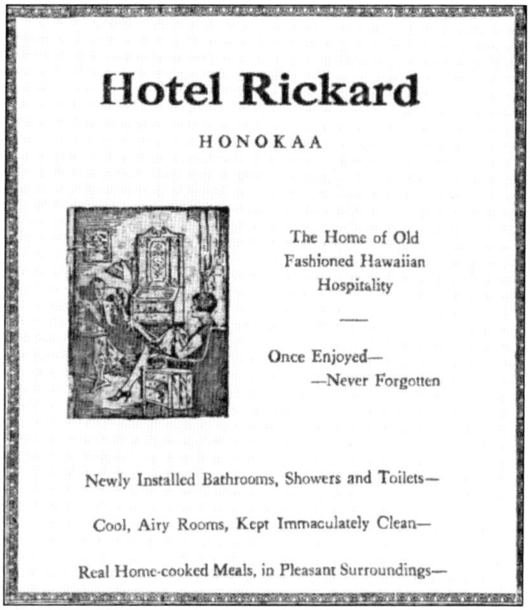

W.H. Rickard Monument and Hotel Advertisement. Rickard died young after catching tuberculosis while imprisoned, and was buried in the Anglican Cemetery off Ohelo Street, which he had helped to establish in 1886. (Note that the column is off-center, due to recent earthquakes.) Rickard's wife, Nora, lived until the age of 96 in 1944. For many years, she was happy to relate stories of her personal relationships with Native Hawaiian royalty to the many guests at the Rickard Hotel. (Left, LR; right, SHPD.) [3]

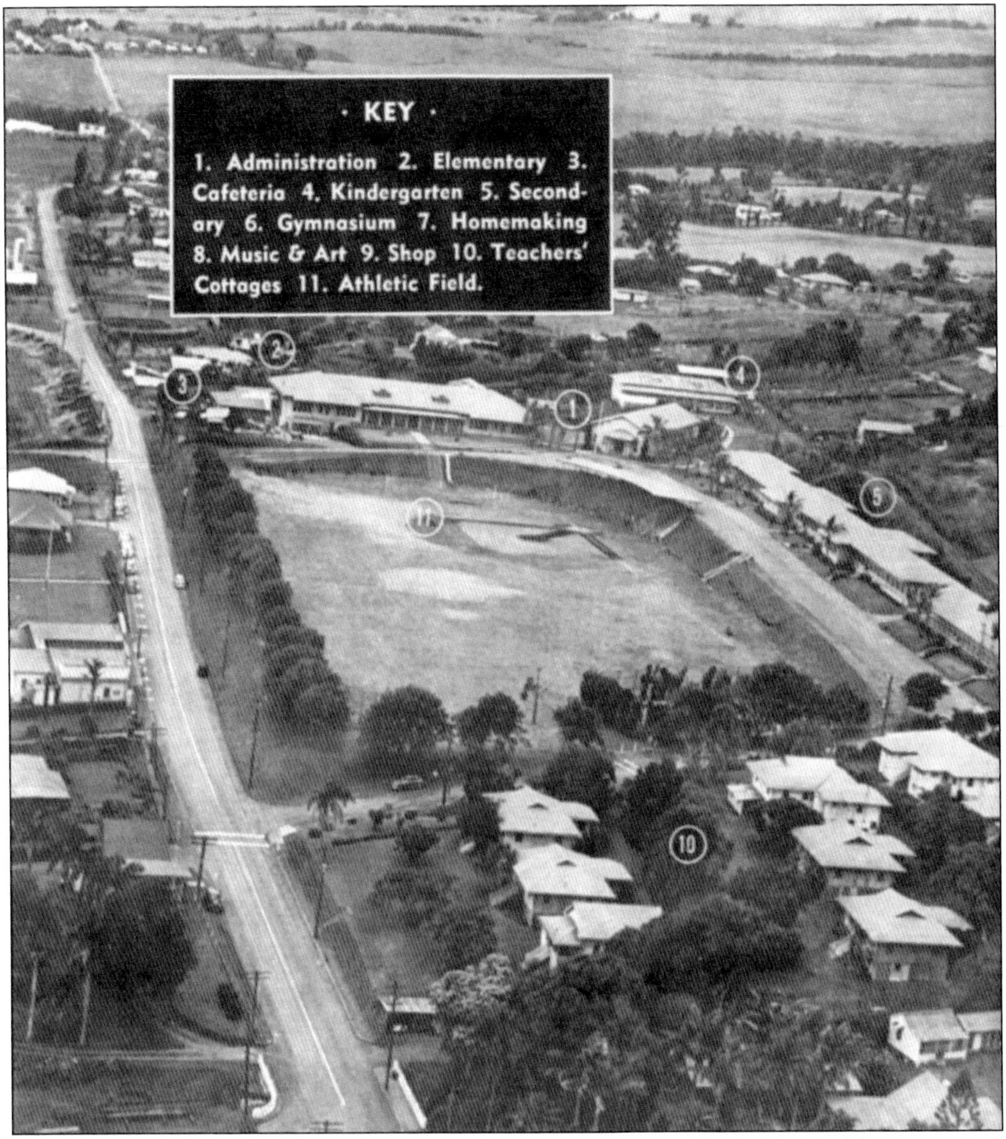

Aerial View of Honokaa School, 1952. Honokaa School has been in several locations, and its function as an educational center for Hamakua is a major reason for Honokaa's existence. It began in 1889 as an elementary school, sited within the present grounds of the cemetery on Ohelo Street makai of Mamane Street (out of picture on the left). There, a three-room schoolhouse was constructed. In 1908, the school needed more space and was moved to the present courthouse grounds along the makai side of Mamane Street (visible at left center). The government subsequently acquired acreage from the Honokaa Sugar Company and Lyceum before moving the school to the present campus in 1924. Junior high classes were added in 1921 and high school classes in 1937. What is remarkable in this 1952 photograph from the *Ka Nani o Honokaa* yearbook is the large number of teachers' cottages on Mamane Street and along Pakalana Street. Note also that both the pool complex and the armory building, now located on the Waipio side of the athletic field, do not yet exist. (HHSY.) [53]

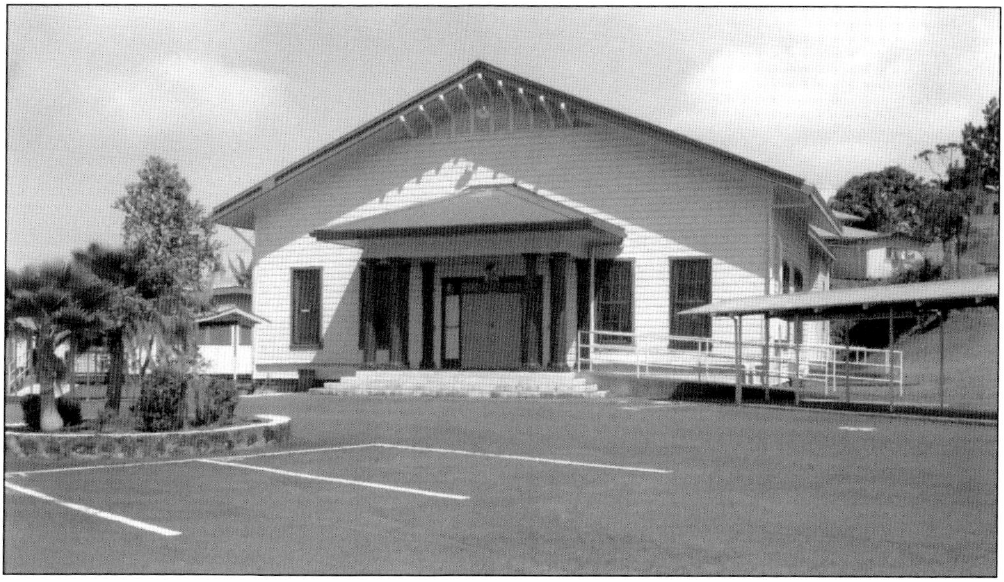

Honokaa High School. W.H. Rickard Auditorium (1925) and Buildings A and E (1927) were designed by Frank Arakawa, Hawaii County's deputy engineer from 1915 to 1942. Arakawa placed columns in many school buildings, including the Hilo High School Auditorium and Hilo Intermediate School Gymnasium; other common design elements included double-hung windows and green totan roofs found throughout the island. Unfortunately, Arakawa was interned during World War II and never returned to Hawaii. (CCS.)

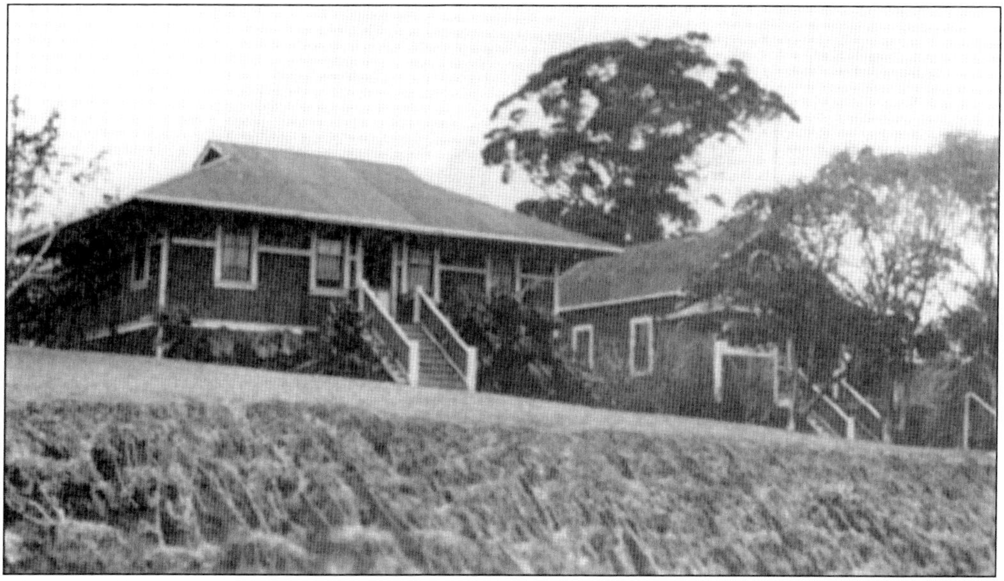

Teachers Cottages, 1939. In the 19th century, the Hawaiian Kingdom became one of the most literate countries on earth. Sending students to Oahu was impractical; successive regimes instead domiciled teachers in government-owned residences on the school lot. Educators were often newly minted, imported from the mainland on contract, adventurous and enthusiastic. The system worked well, with the teachers involved with their students all week long, providing children with improved educations, raising teacher retention rates, and creating lifelong bonds within the community. This photograph is from the 1939 *Ka Nani O Honokaa* yearbook. (HHSY.) [49]

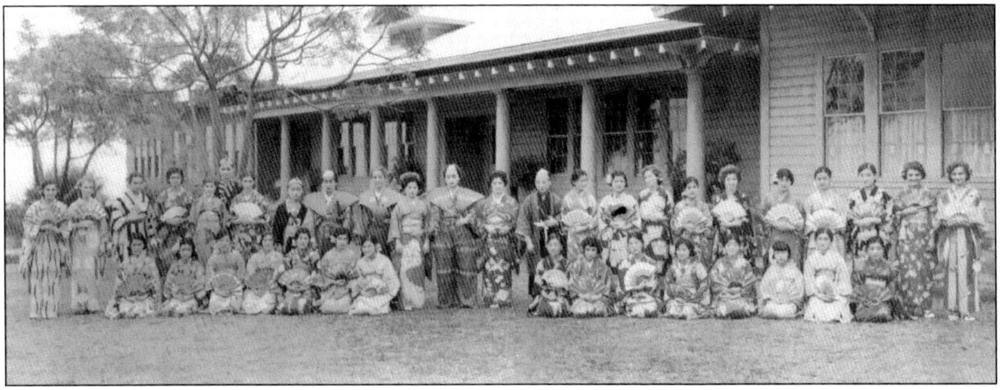

Japanese Drama on School Grounds. After the carnage of the Great War, many citizens with a worldview hoped to prevent the possibility of another such conflict by increasing international understanding. Cross-cultural organizations such as the Hawaii-based Pan-Pacific Union, universities, schools, and labor and business organizations encouraged international exchanges through trade, travel, literature, art, and theater. Pictured here is a multiethnic group at Honokaa School dressed in traditional Japanese attire. (Ujiki Family Collection.)

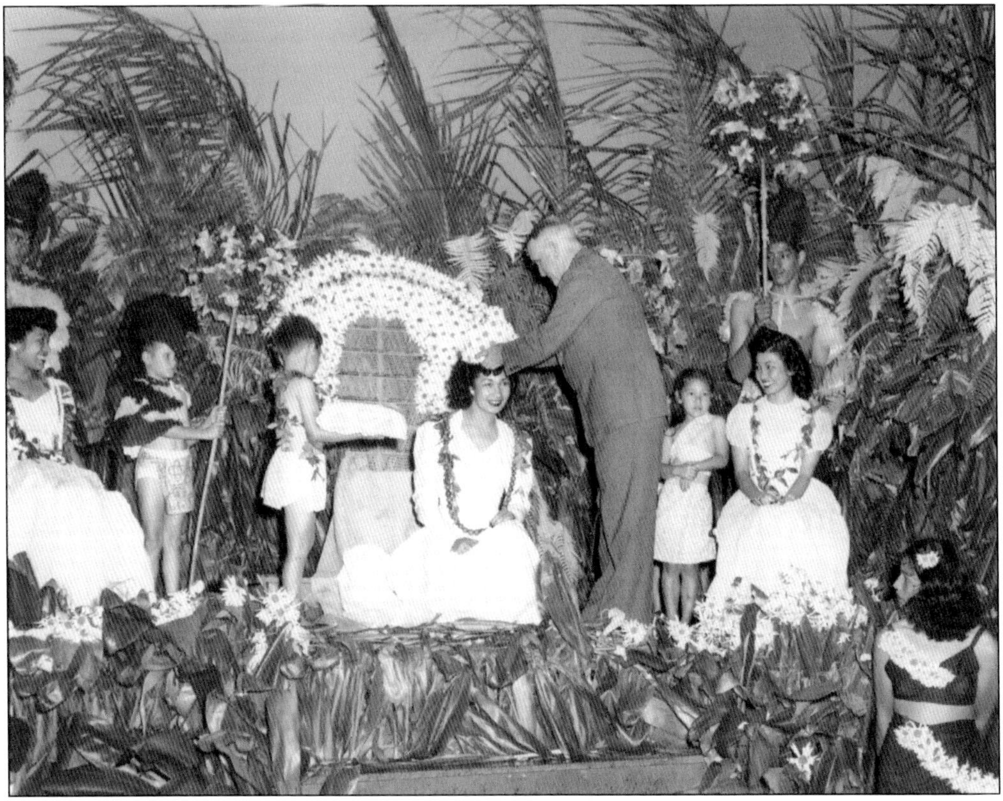

May Day is Lei Day in Hawaii. Writer and Hawaii promoter Don Blanding suggested a celebration centered on the Hawaiian custom of making and wearing *lei*. The first Lei Day was May 1, 1928, with festivities including hula, music, and lei making. Since then, generations of island children have helped produce and enjoy this event, complete with a floral court as seen here, as a highlight of the school year. (Christensen Collection, NHERC.)

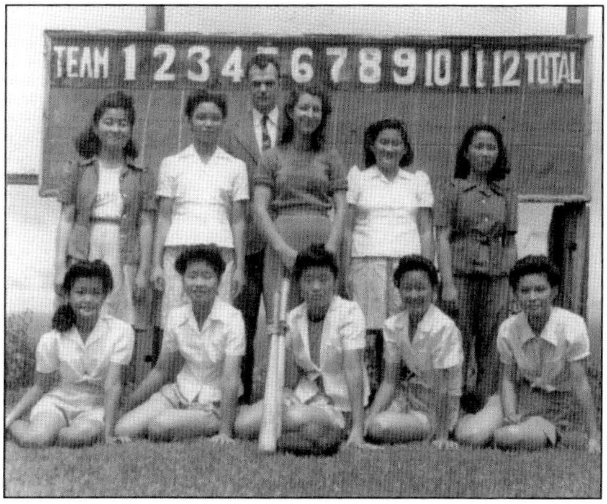

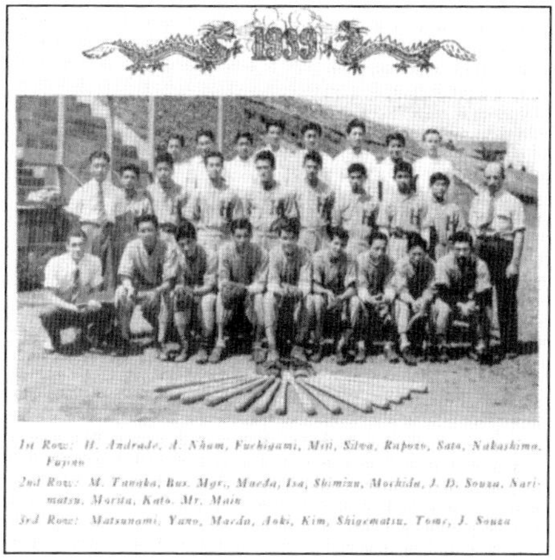

SPORTS IN HAMAKUA. In Hawaii, it is not so much what college one attended as what high school. This identifies people as local and where their roots are. This also includes school sports programs. Competition is often keen, leading to island championships and state championships. Both these groups attended Honokaa High—most of the girls at left, photographed at Kukuihaele, are wearing their school athletic outfits. The boys on the right in this 1939 *Ka Nani O Honokaa* yearbook photograph are on the Honokaa athletic field. (Left, Christensen Collection, NHERC; right, HHSY.)

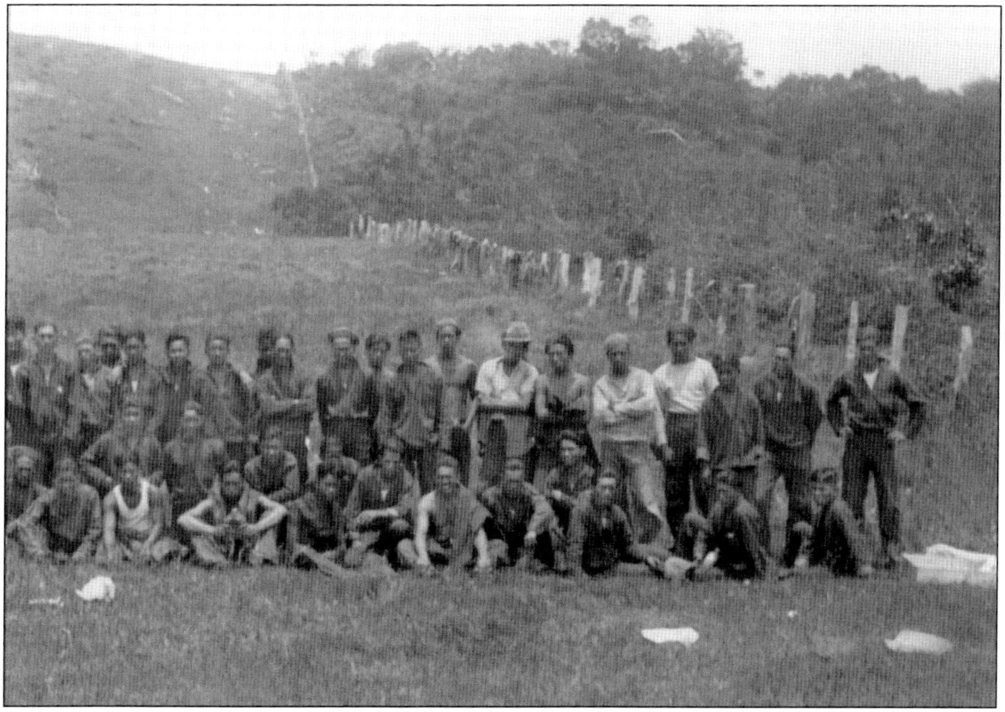

CIVILIAN CONSERVATION CORPS (CCC). The Great Depression of the 1930s slowed the economy. Fear ruled much of daily life, as people worried about possible unemployment and were afraid to spend money, while companies feared further loss of demand for products and so did not hire. This left those without jobs, especially youth, in dire straits. In response, the federal government undertook a public-works program, the CCC, to create temporary jobs (such as building roads and repairing public buildings) for individuals such as the boys pictured here. (Takahashi Watanabe Family Collection.)

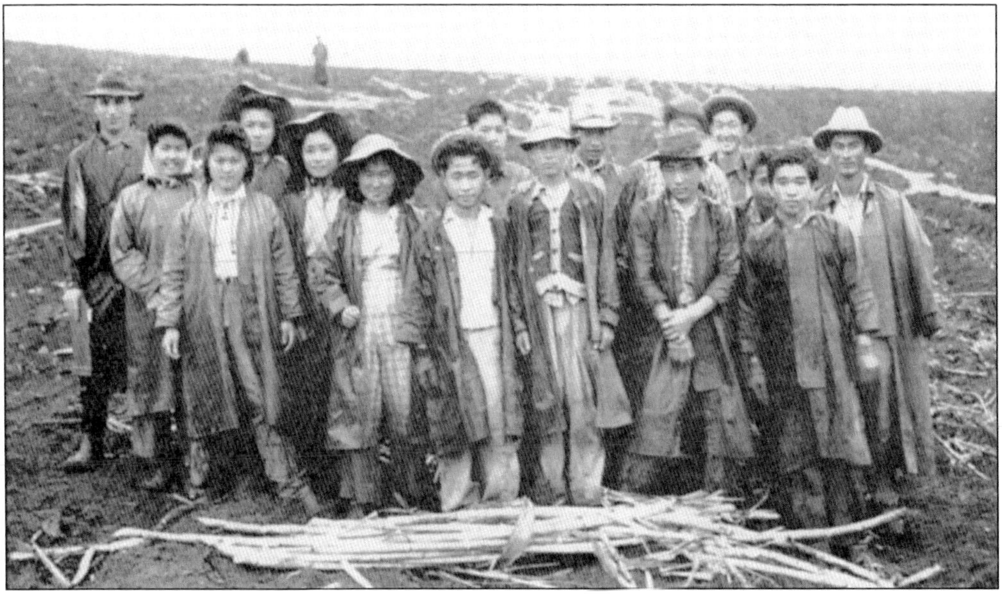

Honokaa Sugar Company Victory Corps. High school students filled in for regular plantation personnel during World War II. The 1945 yearbook noted that they worked Fridays, Saturdays, and over vacations, totaling 4,588 seven-hour days between September 1944 and June 1945. Seventeen students on the poison gang covered 1,052 acres, 16 on the cultivating gang hoed 310 acres, and 28 on the planting gang planted 516 acres. The 1945 *Ka Nani O Honokaa* yearbook staff wrote, "Rain or shine, the Victory Corps students turn out to do their bit." (HHSY.)

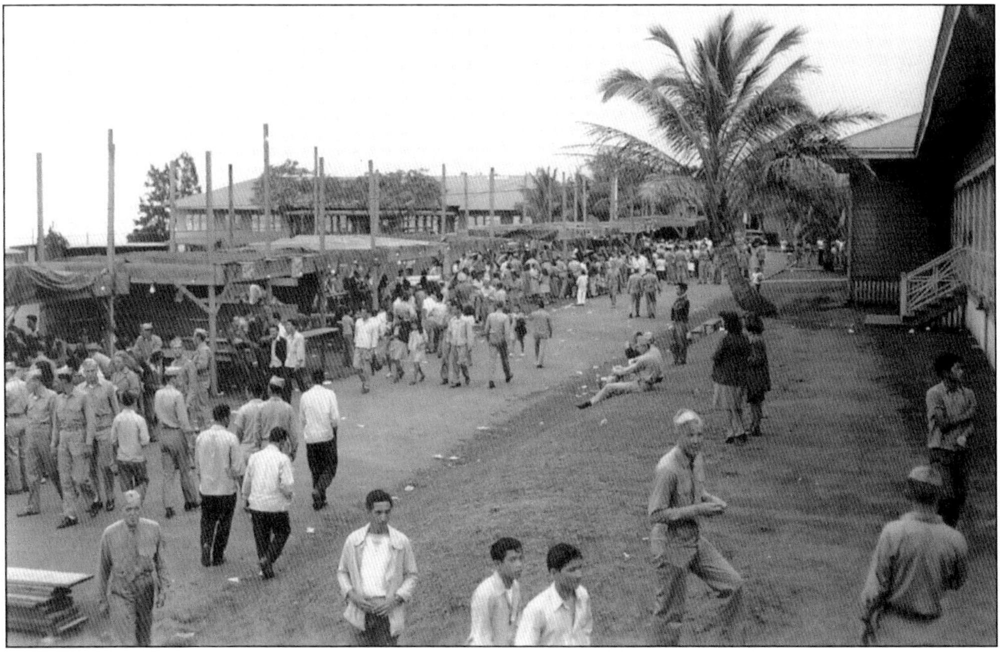

Parades and Carnival for the Troops. With Camp Tarawa close by and a major contributor to the local economy, the Honokaa community went to great lengths to make the soldiers feel appreciated. This is a good old-fashioned American-style midway constructed along the main entrance of the High School. (NHERC.)

WORLD WAR II VICTORY PARADE. Soldiers line Mamane Street to watch this extremely long victory parade. The first float pictured has a flag at half-mast with women in mourning over a coffin, signifying the human cost of war. The second boat-like float reads *Missouri*, representing the ship upon whose deck the peace documents were signed. (NHERC.)

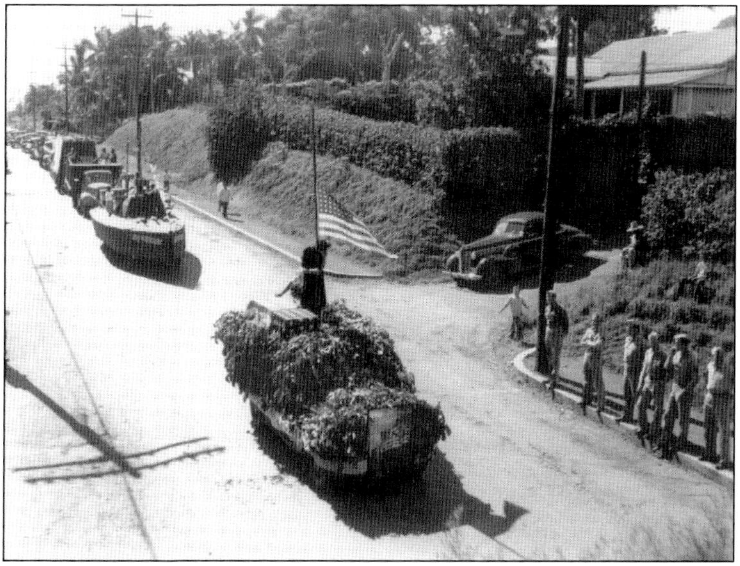

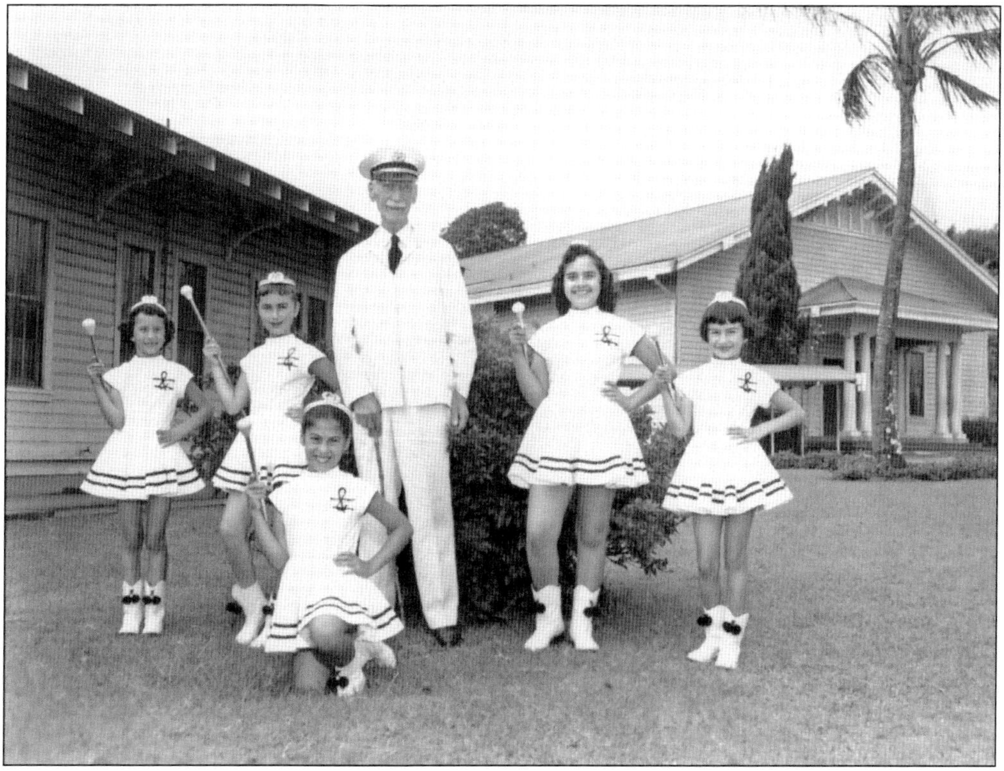

WILLIAM J. RICKARD. Son of W.H. Rickard, he had been employed as a freight clerk, cane weigher, coffee planter, and cattle rancher. He was best known as a longtime deputy sheriff (whose collection of confiscated crime implements is located at NHERC) and for his role in leading parades (see band insignia on cap). Here, the Hamakua County Band majorettes stand with him in front of the Rickard Auditorium at Honokaa School. Pictured are, from left to right, Linda Teves, Beverly Awong, Paula Enanoria, Rickard, Lauri Ann Cypriano, and Alberta Branco. (Awong Family Collection, NHERC.)

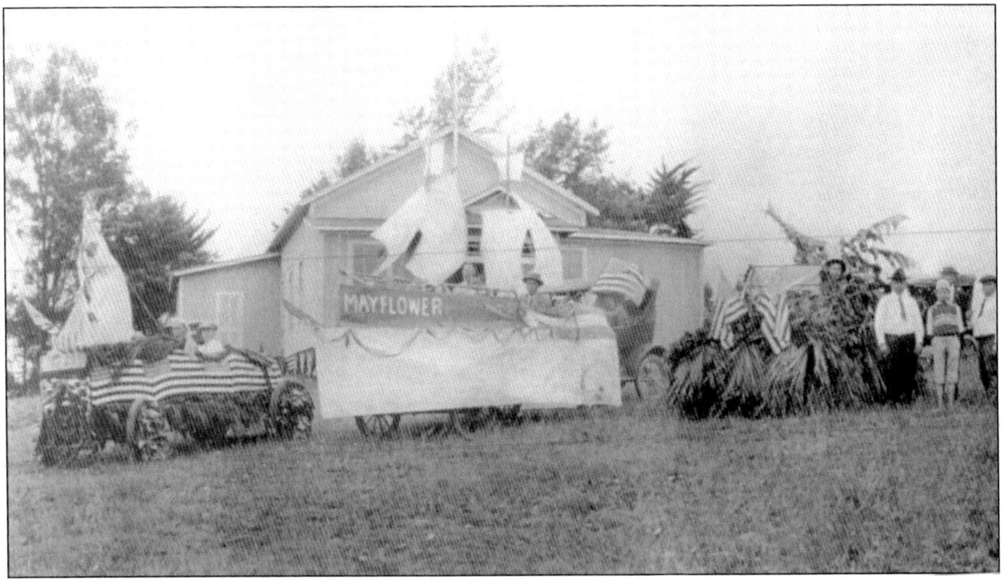

Lyceum. The 19th-century Lyceum Movement established informal associations to improve the social, intellectual, and moral fabric of society. Lectures, dramatic performances, class instructions, and debates were conducted. Here, an Independence Day parade is being organized. Both Honolulu and Honokaa had lyceums; W.H. Rickard helped to organize the one in Honokaa. The Lyceum building was located on the mauka side of Government Road inside the present-day school grounds. (Nancy Awong Teves Collection, NHERC; Peter Tomich.)

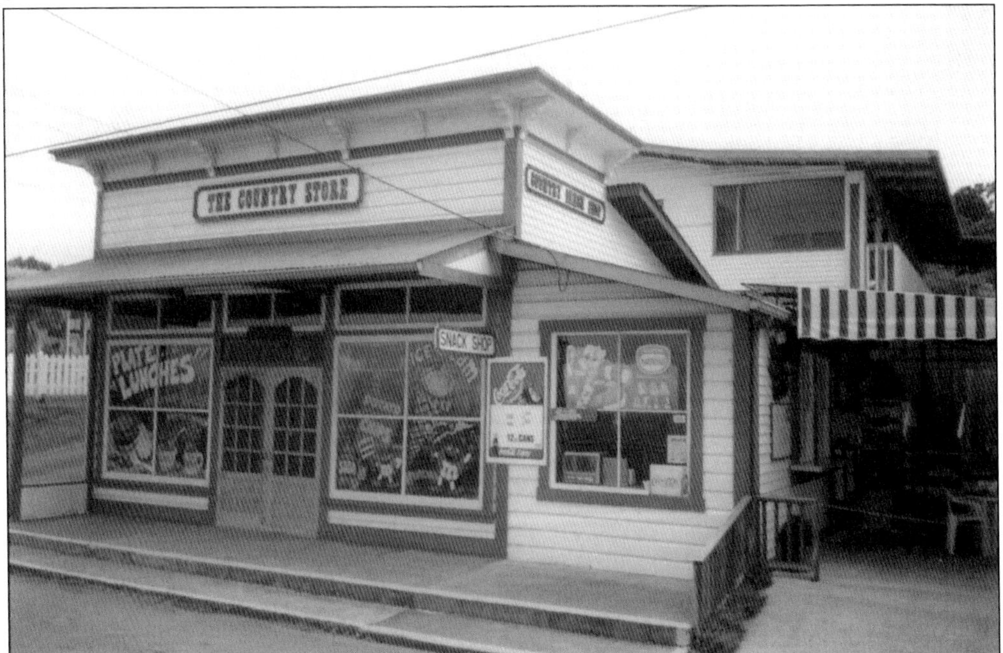

The Country Store. The Paiva family has been involved in numerous Honokaa businesses for generations, with this building, a house on Mamane Street across from the Botelho Building, and the Paiva (Kuramitsu) Garage. This building has contained both the country store pictured and a woodworking shop. (Paiva Family Collection.) [54]

Four

Down Lehua, the Haina Mill, and the Landing

Lehua was the road down to the hub of plantation life.

Makai of the Lehua-Mamane intersection and crossing beneath the road is the Lower Hamakua Ditch. Water had three important uses for Honokaa Plantation: satisfying the needs of a thirsty cane crop (approximately 88 gallons of water are required to produce a five-pound bag of sugar), fluming (placing cane in an artificial channel for downhill transport), and irrigating the macadamia nut orchards. Hamakua had two ditch systems—upper and lower—consisting of tunnels, canals, pipes, and reservoirs, which took water from Waipio Valley as far as Paauilo. One engineer on the ditch system was Michael M. O'Shaughnessy, who later developed the municipal water system for San Francisco, including the Hetch-Hetchy Reservoir.

In 1924, the Honokaa Sugar Company became one of the world's first commercial macadamia nut producers. The former Honokaa Plantation Store, later converted to the Hawaiian Holiday Macadamia Nut Factory, lies on the Hilo side of the road.

Portions of Haina Camp, a typical collection of worker housing that includes single wall, post-on-pier, double-hung window bungalows, is situated mauka of Haina Mill; the separate former manager's housing area lies farther east.

The mill was the center of the Honokaa Sugar Plantation. Begun in 1876 by Siemsen and Marsden, it was reorganized in 1878 by F.A. Schaefer, who remained president for 40 years. Operations were initially very primitive, with the first mill employing a two-roll cane crusher. By 1899, a new six-roll mill had been installed. The mill once featured twin overhead cable systems to carry sugar and supplies from Honokaa Town, to the mill, and to Honokaa Landing below. A narrow-gauge private plantation-owned railroad followed the coast to the Pacific Sugar Mill to the west. The sugar warehouse remains.

Farther makai is Honokaa Landing, one of the few places on this coast that ships could load and offload cargo. Before road improvements and the Hawaii Consolidated Railway, access to Hamakua was through a series of coast derrick landings, operated only in good weather. Andrew Smith Hallidie, who helped develop the materials for improved cable landings, is best known for building the San Francisco cable-car motive system.

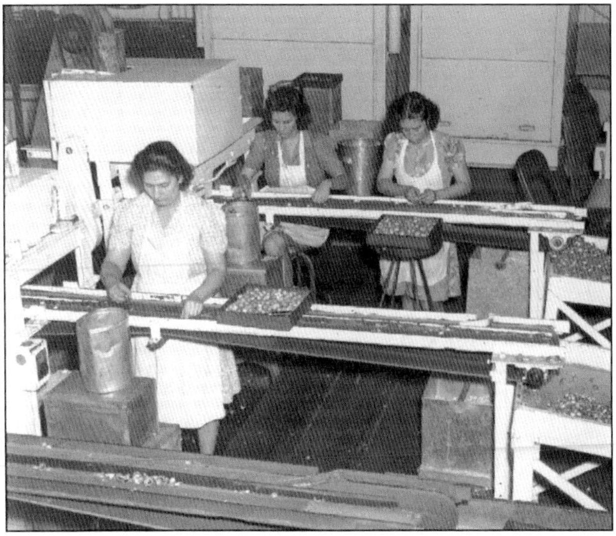

Macadamia Nut Factory. Macadamia nuts were introduced to Hawaii from Australia in 1881 by William H. Purvis, a manager at Pacific Sugar Mill. These were planted at Kapulena, between Honokaa and Waipio. Walter Naquin began commercial production of macadamias in 1924, and the factory on Lehua Street was opened in 1940. Here, nuts are sorted for packaging in the Lehua Street Hawaiian Holiday facility. Unfortunately, the company overextended its acreage and declared bankruptcy in 1990. (Christensen Collection, NHERC.) [56]

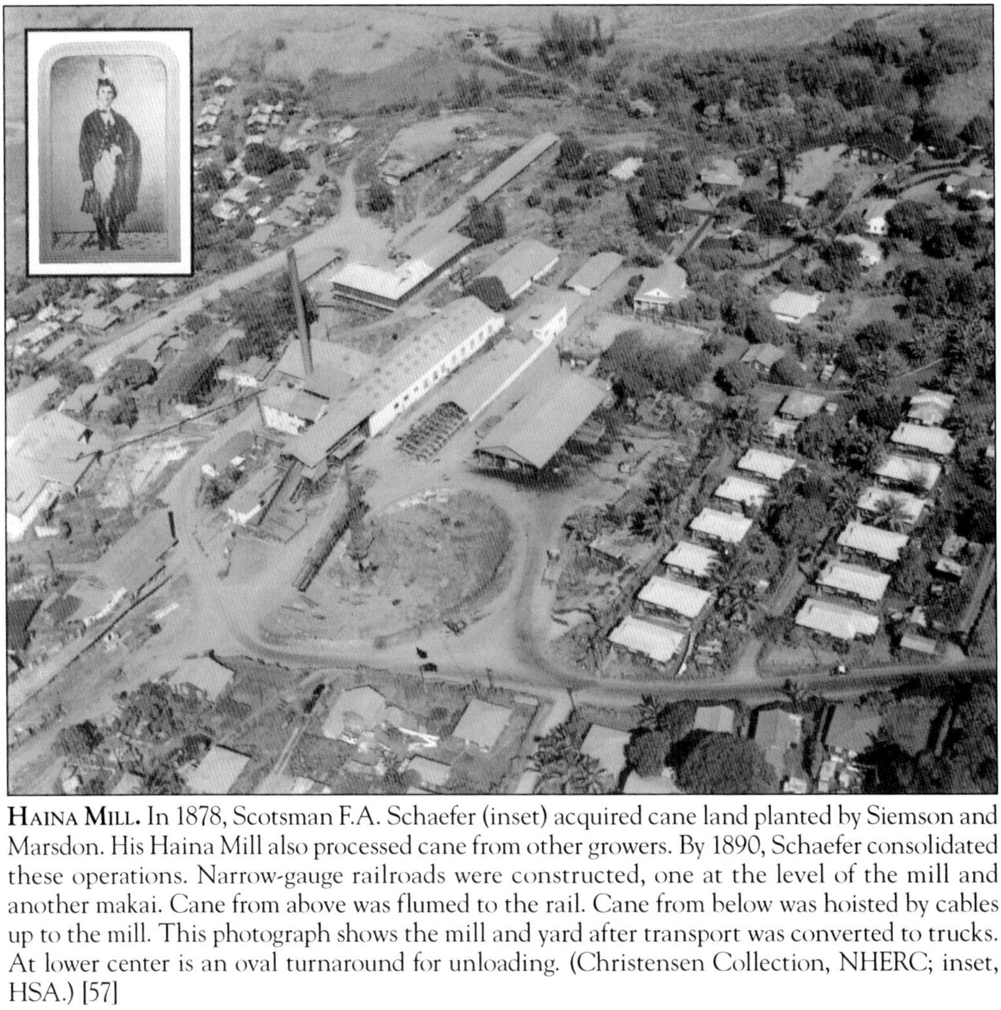

Haina Mill. In 1878, Scotsman F.A. Schaefer (inset) acquired cane land planted by Siemson and Marsdon. His Haina Mill also processed cane from other growers. By 1890, Schaefer consolidated these operations. Narrow-gauge railroads were constructed, one at the level of the mill and another makai. Cane from above was flumed to the rail. Cane from below was hoisted by cables up to the mill. This photograph shows the mill and yard after transport was converted to trucks. At lower center is an oval turnaround for unloading. (Christensen Collection, NHERC; inset, HSA.) [57]

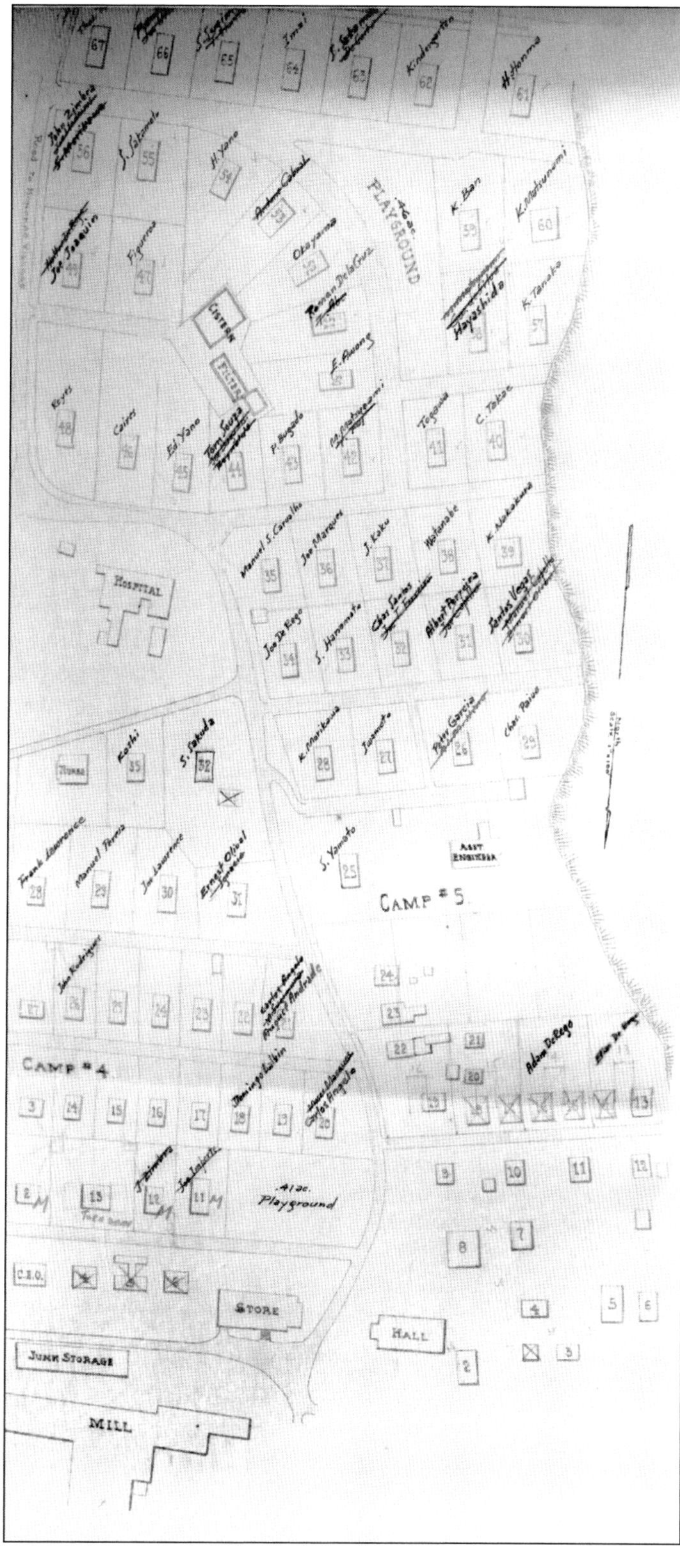

HAINA CAMP NO. 5. Camps were initially segregated to provide continuity in the lives of first generation immigrants and facilitate the management tactic of playing different groups against each other. Poor working conditions created labor shortages, forcing management to improve conditions and promote non-white groups into more responsible positions. The physical consolidation of camps for efficiency and the union's need to universalize the labor struggle helped integrate the camps, especially postwar. This map illustrates that ethnic groups lived side by side after the war and their children attended school and played together. Names on the map include: Chinese: E. Awong; Portuguese: J. Zimbra, T. Souza, J. Joaquin, M. Carvalho, J. Marques, J. Rego, C. Santos, A. Perreira, P. Garcia, C. Paiva, M. Peresa, E. Olival, J. Rodrigues, A. Andrade, A. DeRego, E. De Rego, J. Importe, C. Angelo, and Caires; Japanese: Imai, S. Sato, H. Honma, S. Sakamoto, H. Yano, Okayama, M. Matsunami, E. Yano, K. Matsunami, K. Tanaka, Hayashida, Togawa, C. Takae, J. Kaku, Watanabe, K. Nakamura, S. Hanamoto, K. Morikawa, Iwamoto, S. Yamato, Koshi, S. Sakuda, R. Hino, S. Sugimoto, and K. Ban; Filipino: R. DelaCruz, P. Bugado, Reyes, Figueroa, S. Vegar, and D. Lalbin; other: F. Lawrence and J. Lawrence. (UHHL.)

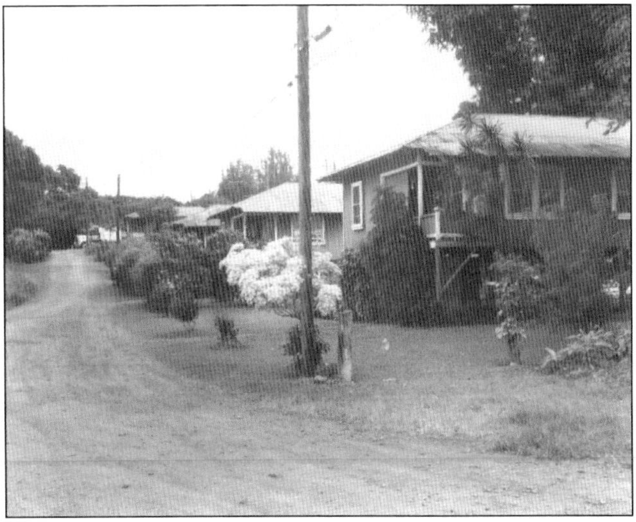

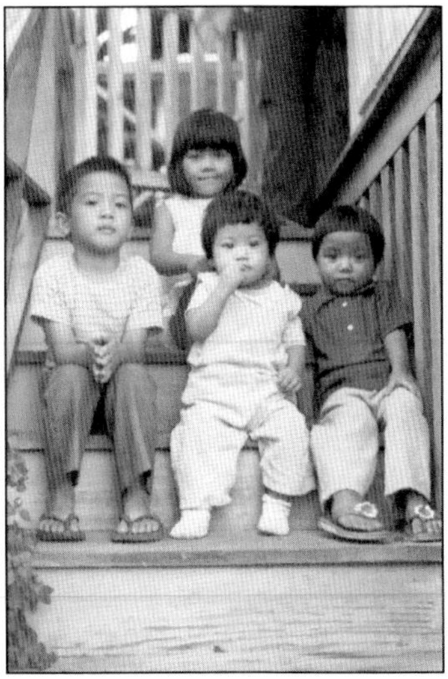

Haina Camp. The plantation mill camp was located within walking distance of work. Such camps were the catalyst for plantation-style architecture, based upon designs by local architect Theodore Vierra for the Hawaii Sugar Planters Association. Buildings featured post-and-pier foundations, single vertical wood walls, double-hung windows, and totan roofs. Yards provided the opportunity for gardening. There were no carports, as most workers could not afford automobiles. Two playgrounds, a hospital, and a hall were provided. (Above left, SHPD; above right, NHERC; below, UHHL.)

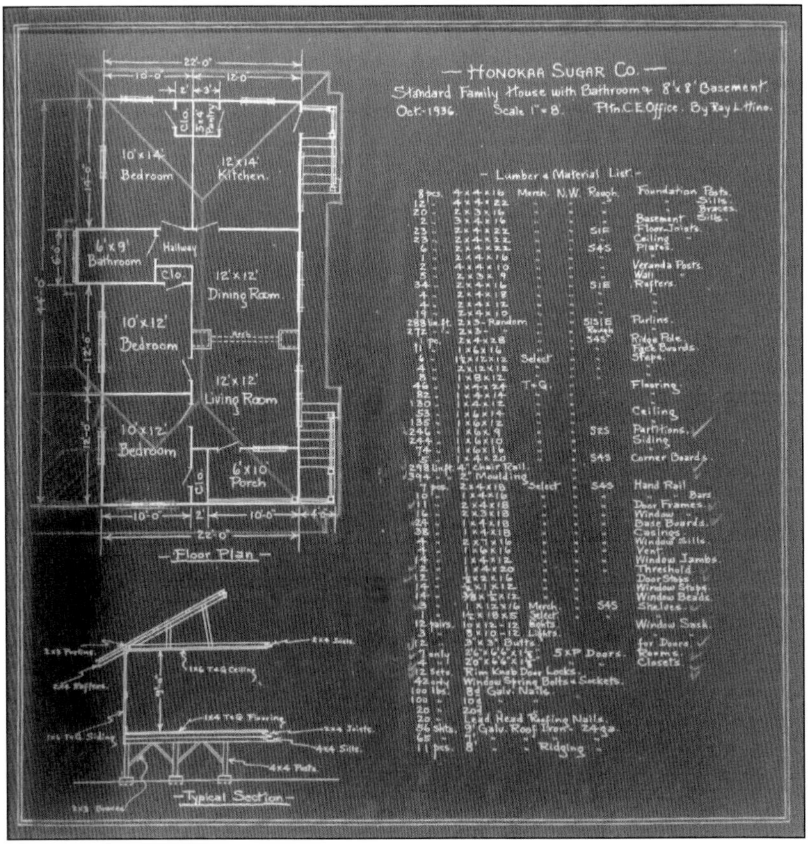

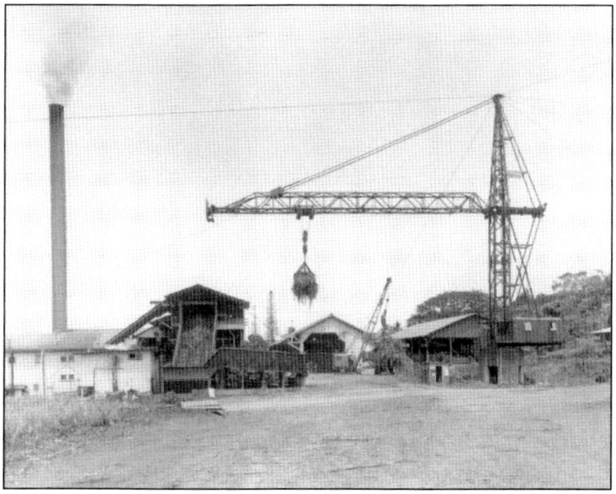

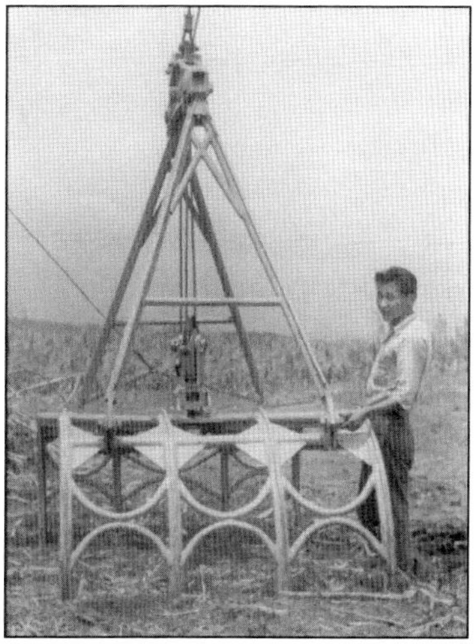

HAINA MILL YARD. Taken in 1951, this photograph centers on the tower crane employed to lift a load of sugarcane from one of the cane haul trucks. The cane will be placed in a hopper and travel via conveyor into the mill. This structure, so critical to operations at the rural mill, is the same basic design employed to construct high-rise buildings in urban areas. At right is a giant crane claw in Paauhau with Tsuneichi Takahashi standing in for scale. (Left, BM; right, Takahashi Watanabe Family Collection.)

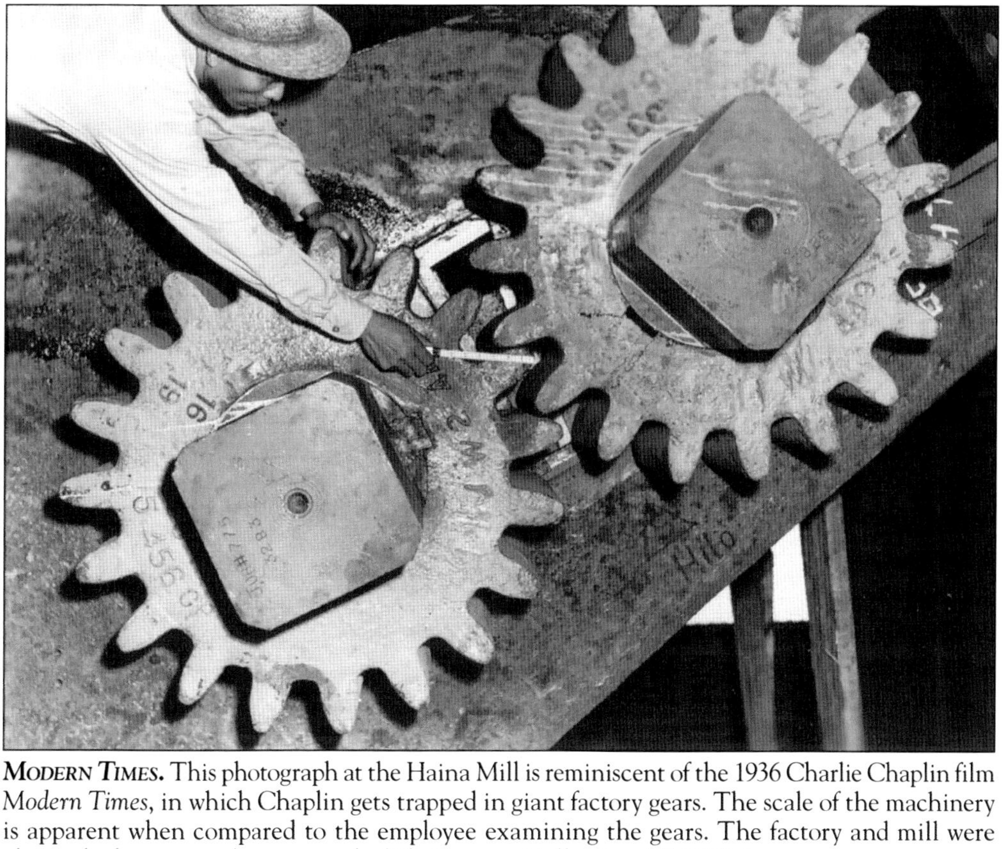

MODERN TIMES. This photograph at the Haina Mill is reminiscent of the 1936 Charlie Chaplin film *Modern Times*, in which Chaplin gets trapped in giant factory gears. The scale of the machinery is apparent when compared to the employee examining the gears. The factory and mill were obviously dangerous places to work. (Christensen Collection, NHERC.)

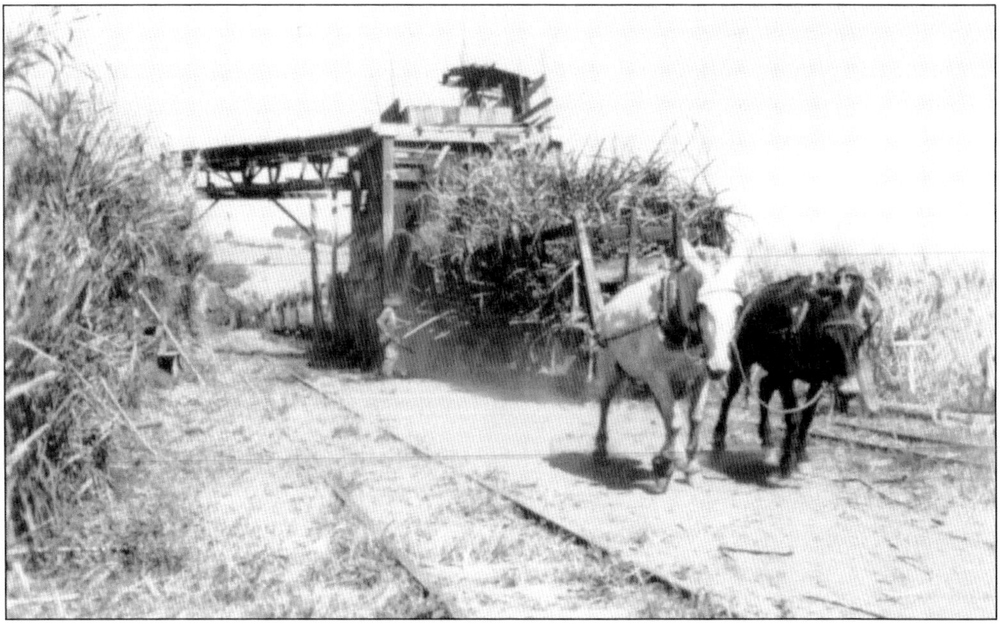

Cane Hauling. While gravity lines, rails, and flumes were useful in moving harvested cane downslope, moving cane across flatter land was more problematic. The initial solution was mule power, which unfortunately was hindered by the rough roads upon which the hauling wagons moved. Great hauling efficiency was provided by the installation of portable rails, which created a uniform surface able to sustain the weight of the train and its load. (Christensen Collection, NHERC.)

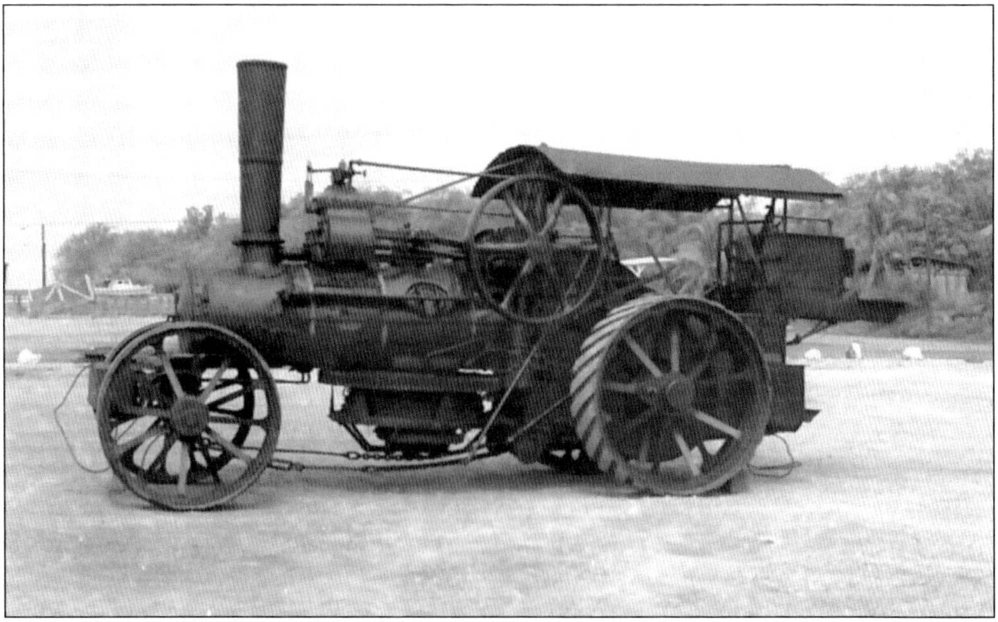

Fowler Engine. John Fowler, working in Leeds, England, has been credited with the invention of steam-driven plowing engines that revolutionized (mechanized) large-scale commercial agriculture. Such devices were placed on either end of a field and a plow pulled by cable across the field between them. These machines were highly prized worldwide because of their portability and flexibility. This example dates from approximately 1916. (Christensen Collection, NHERC.)

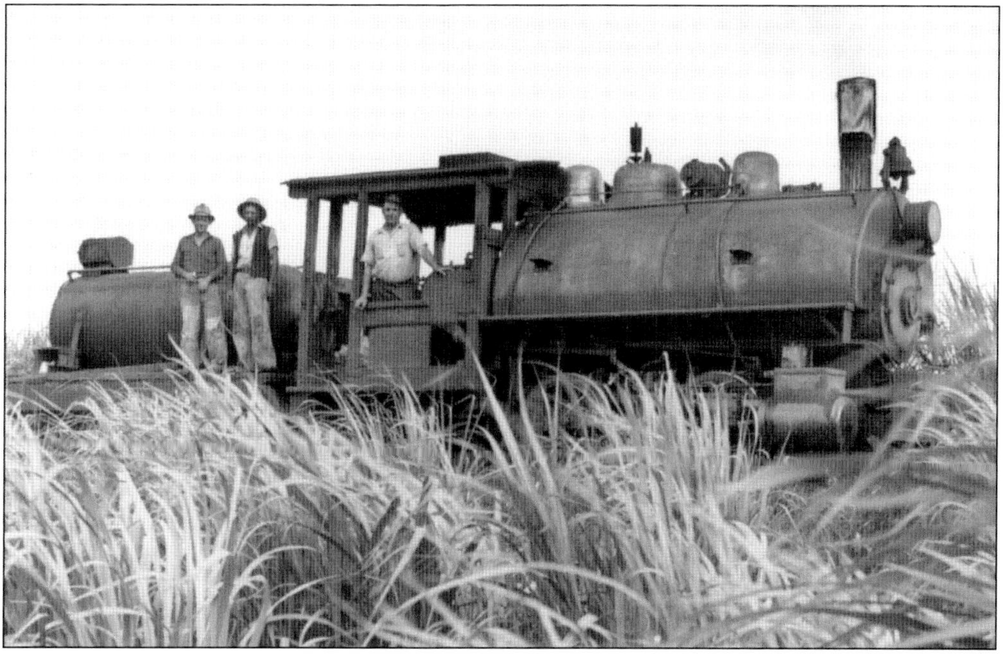

Plantation Private Railroads. The introduction of steam engines to the plantations' systems of permanent and portable track further increased efficiencies. Steam engines could carry larger and heavier loads than the mules could haul. While this meant replanning planting schedules, the increased hauling capabilities, combined with agri-science, facilitated improved yields and potentially greater profits. Eventually, however, trucks proved even more flexible and replaced the private railroads. Below, junked engines rust away. (Both, BM.)

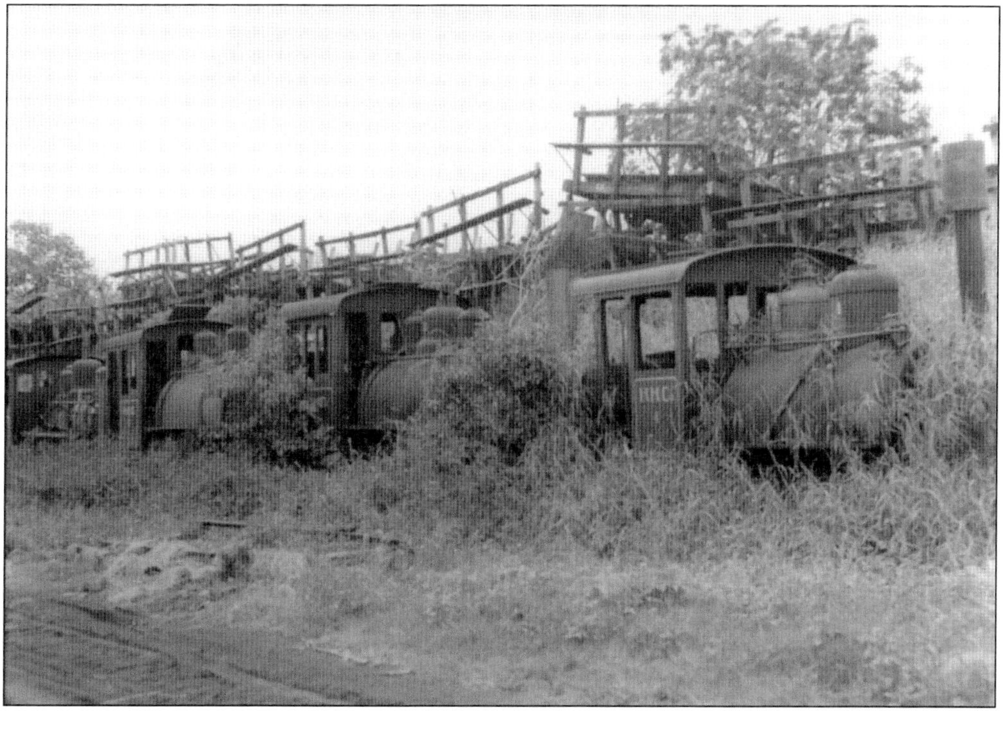

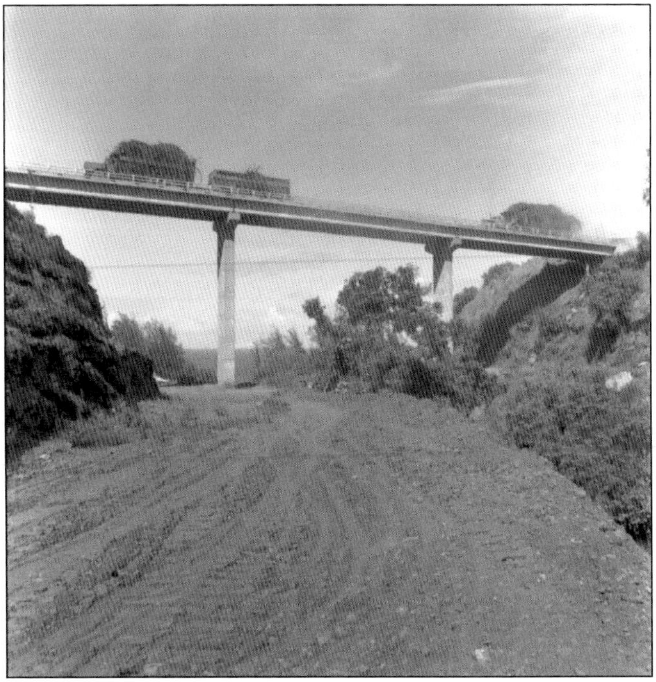

Cane Haul Trucks. Plantation consolidation continued throughout both the plantation railroad and truck-hauling periods, increasing the number of miles traveled carrying cane to the mill. The weight, speed, and size of trucks required development of cane haul roads separate from the highway system. Where loaded trucks did use state and county roads, crews were required to periodically clean up debris. During harvesting season, residents close to the highways would recognize the periodic shifting of gears and sounds of the large truck engines. (Christensen Collection, NHERC.)

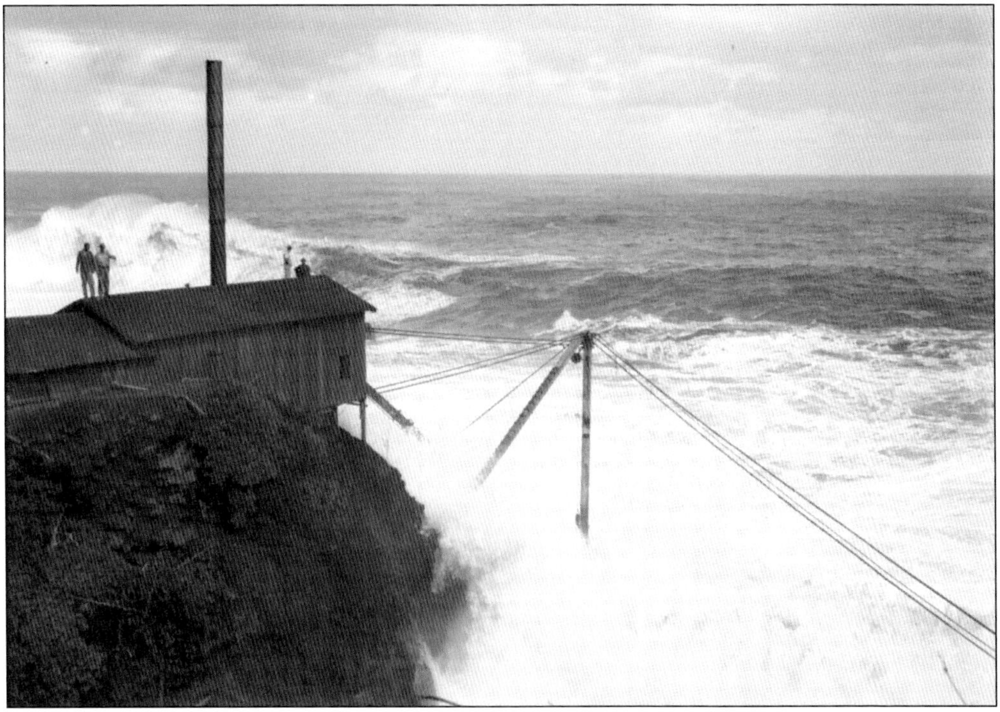

Fierce Waves at the Landing. Hamakua has no natural harbors. Without any natural barrier reef, and subject to wind-driven storms from the northern Pacific Ocean, the landing facilities that developed along the Hamakua Coast were subject to debilitating wave action. In this photograph, two men stand atop the Honokaa Landing watching the power of winter surf. Note the derrick being swamped by white water. (Christensen Collection, NHERC.)

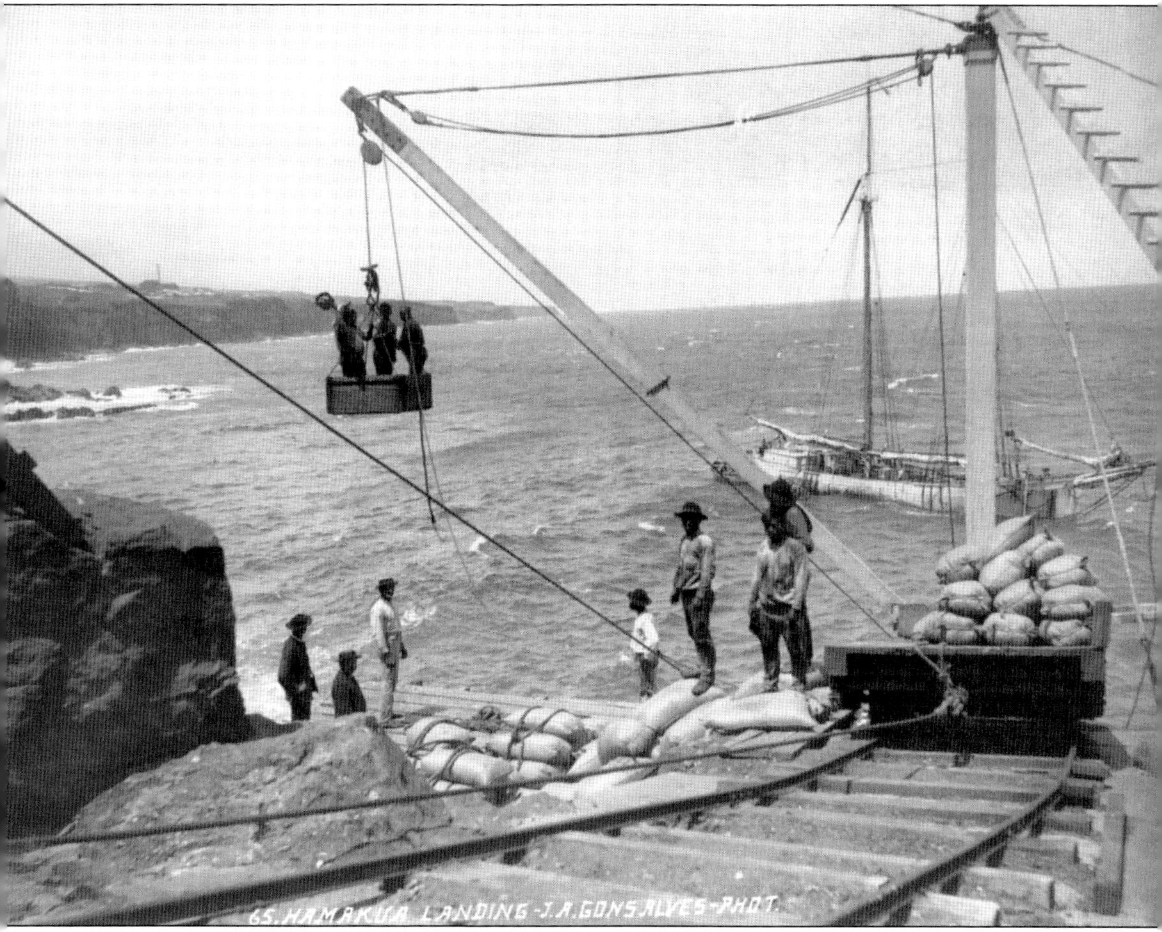

Hamakua Landing, c. 1900. The Hamakua Coast extends approximately 50 miles, with cliffs anywhere from 100 to 400 feet in height. There are no natural harbors; worse, the Hamakua Coast is on the windward side of the island, with winds and waves pushing vessels towards shore while squalls limit visibility. This coast has been deeply cut by streams in numerous places over eons; the overland transportation system into this previously minimally populated area was poor. The small plantation operations begun in the late 19th and early 20th centuries near Honokaa Town (Pacific Sugar Mill, Honokaa Sugar, Paauhau Sugar, Hamakua Mill, Kukaiau Mill, Kaiwiki Sugar, and Laupahoehoe Sugar Companies) were forced to build landings at Ookala, Paauhau, Honokaa (Haina) and Kukuihaele to import supplies and export sugar. Although weather could always close down a landing, even on days with relatively benign ocean conditions, getting to or from shore using derricks was not for the faint of heart. This photograph illustrates that people journeying to and from the ships were treated much like cattle or other cargo: placed in a wooden box and lifted over the ocean and rocky shore by an overhead derrick, subject to sun, wind, or rain. Near to shore, an agile schooner has sailed close to the rocky landing, dropped its sails, and moored to allow small boats to transport other adventurous people. The bagged sugar at the landing also awaits transport to the schooner by derrick; it could easily be lost if transported by small boat. In the distance is Kukuihaele Mill above the pali. (Photograph by J.A. Gonsalves, BM.)

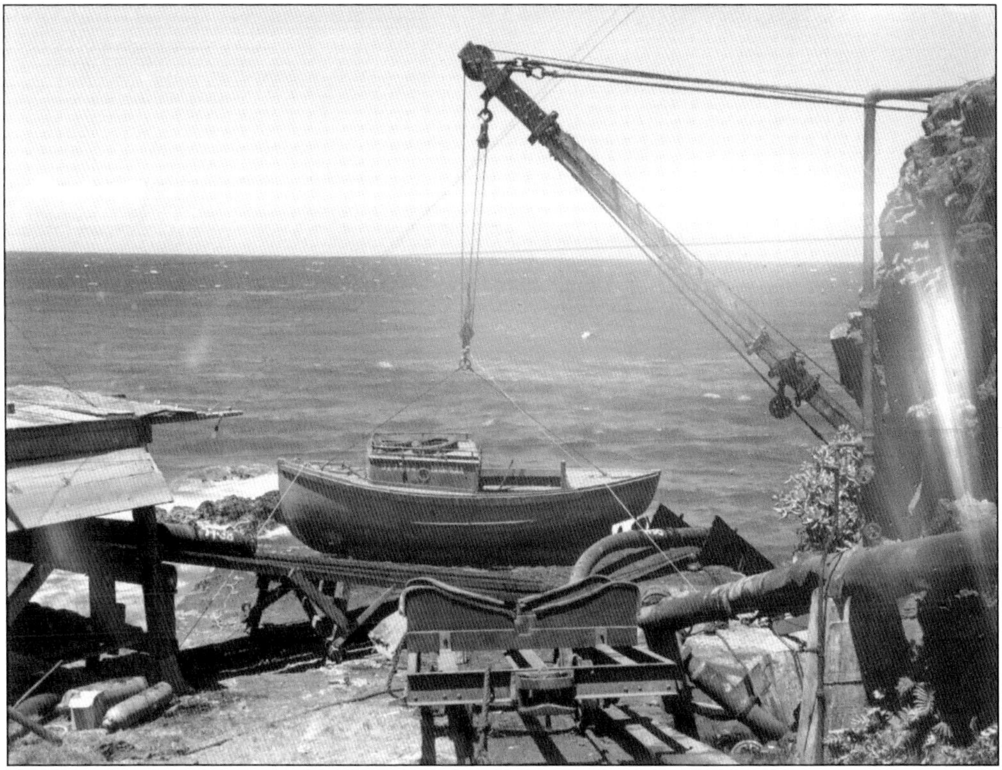

Necessary Equipment at the Dock. Derricks could be used to lift small vessels (such as the appropriately named *Honokaa*, pictured here) into and out of the ocean; the *Honokaa* could facilitate the stringing of heavy cables to and from larger oceangoing ships at the tie-up area. Derricks could also be used to lift cargo from the railhead (foreground) off and onto ship decks. The flexible pipes were used to pump molasses from storage tanks higher ashore directly into ships offshore. (Christensen Collection, NHERC.)

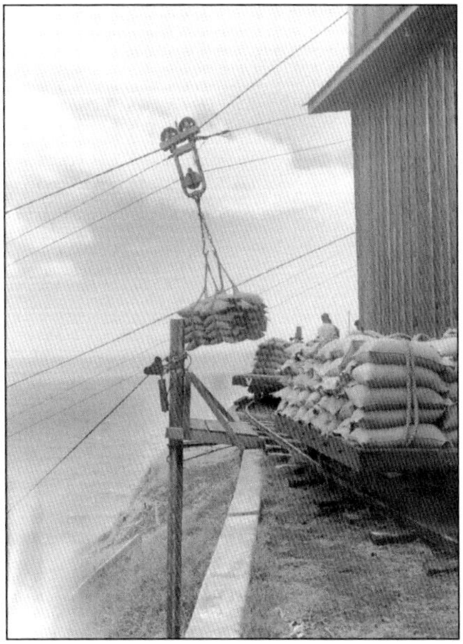

Sugar to the Ship. The major problem with operating the landings along the Hamakua Coast was, when using shore derricks, ships and personnel had to come close to the actual coast. During inclement weather, this was very dangerous. Initial efforts to facilitate cargo movement focused on maximizing handling during calm intervals. The introduction of ship-to-shore wire cable landings allowed operations to occur in most weather. Ships would enter a designated mooring area and tie up using a series of permanent buoys and anchor positions. Steel wires extended to a buoy seaward of the ship, across the hatches of the vessel, and to the winch house above the shoreline. This system allowed ships to rig up quickly and disengage rapidly if sea conditions deteriorated. A series of pulleys was employed to move goods across the overhead wires between the two line ends. Here, sugar bags are just leaving the railhead on their way offshore. (Christensen Collection, NHERC.)

Five

Going Waipio

Interestingly, in the early 20th century, the Government Road on the Waipio side of Lehua Street was a major commercial area. But at that time, most Honokaa Town business activities moved toward the Hilo side of town in anticipation of the arrival of the railroad's terminus.

This early settlement pattern of the town is confirmed by period maps. In 1881, the area contained a school and housing. By 1904, Japanese stores existed at the main intersection. In 1914, numerous Japanese businesses operated along Waipio Road, including a candy store, bathhouse, hotel, and garage.

Most of these are gone. The makai side of the highway was subdivided in the 1930s, sold off to, again, mostly Japanese. Remaining structures include a former Flying A gas station and an even older homegrown petrol station whose owner is considering restoring the pumps [62].

Also makai of the highway is the International Longshore and Warehouse Union (ILWU) hall. The ILWU organized harbors and plantations, ending decades of paternalism. The Quonset hut, likely World War II surplus, reflects civilian reuse as an organizing and recreational center.

Farther toward Waipio is evidence of the Chinese, some of the earliest post-contact immigrants, who once dominated rice growing in Waipio Valley. Two Chinese cemeteries, one on each side of the highway, contain numerous mostly unmarked remains. Also on the mauka side of the highway is the site of the Chee Ying Society clubhouse. The two-story wooden structure served two functions: as a cultural center for immigrants from Kwantung, Fukien, and Shantung Provinces, and as a place to practice traditional Chinese (mostly Taoist) religious beliefs.

The Japanese are also represented in a large cemetery on the mauka side of the highway, Waipio of the Chinese sites. A large communal monument dedicated to the immigrants greets visitors who make an uphill trek to a tree-shaded plateau above.

Camp Eight, on the mauka side of the highway, contains relocated housing from the Overend Camp that once stood on the Hilo side of Honokaa. The original plantation-era buildings, constructed mostly on wooden piers with single wood wall construction and totan roofs, were designed to be portable (many plantation houses were moved at least once). Portability was beneficial as economics and sociability increasingly made larger camps more desirable than isolated housing.

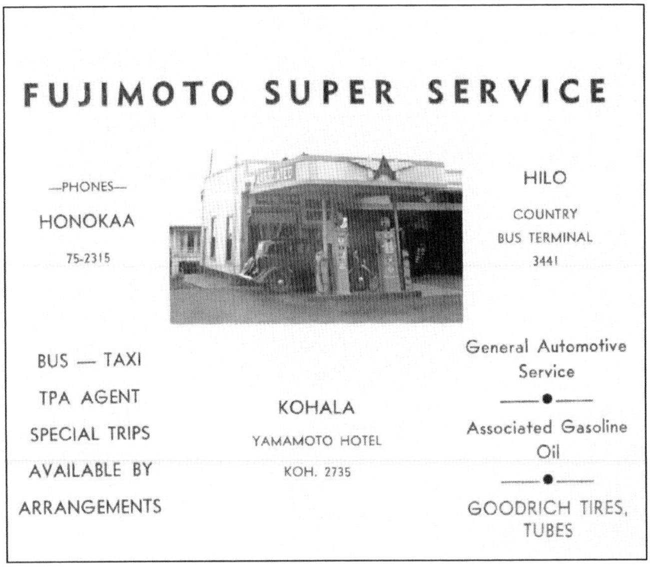

Fujimoto Super Service, 1955. Once associated with Flying A (Associated Oil Company) and later Phillips 66, in the 1960s, the Fujimoto family operated a school bus service into Honokaa from the Hilo side. Vicente Bargado operated school buses into Honokaa from the Waimea side. The Fujimoto buses were yellow, the Bargado baby blue. Bargado was most unhappy when the state required that all school buses be painted yellow. The state compromised and let him retain a blue stripe. This advertisement appeared in the 1955 *Ka Nani O Honokaa* yearbook. (HHSY.) [58]

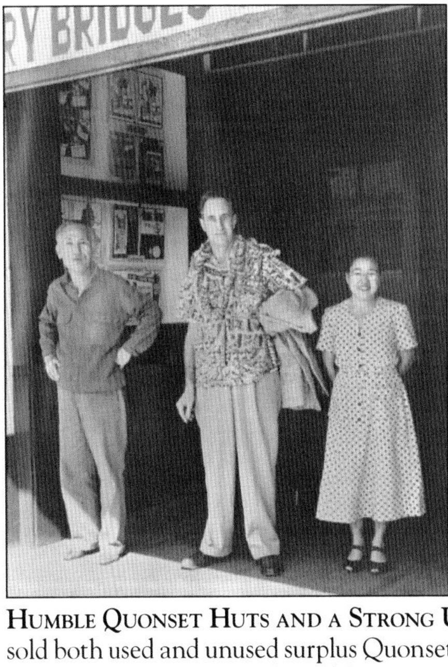

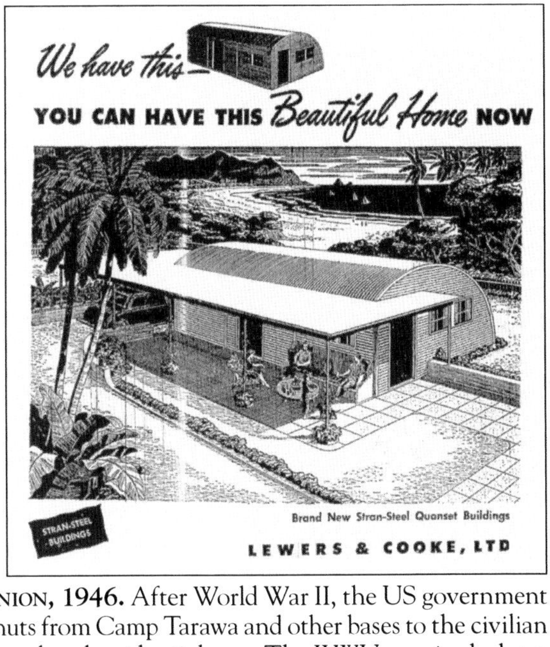

Humble Quonset Huts and a Strong Union, 1946. After World War II, the US government sold both used and unused surplus Quonset huts from Camp Tarawa and other bases to the civilian population. Units were adapted for institutional and residential uses. The ILWU acquired a large surplus Quonset hut for its Hamakua headquarters. ILWU president Harry Bridges (seen at left with Christian and Peggy Tanimoto at the People's Theatre) was an experienced West Coast labor organizer who had strengthened the coast union by organizing beyond the docks into industries that fed shipping. ILWU Hawaii's vice president Jack Hall did the same here with the sugar, pineapple, and hotel industries. (Left, HPT; right, *Honolulu Star-Advertiser*.) [62]

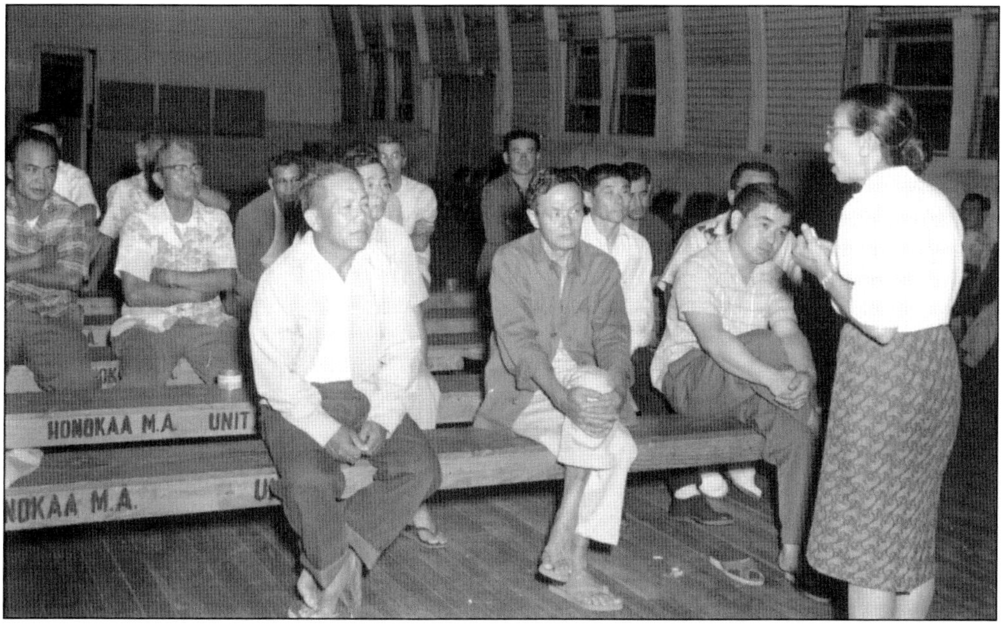

INTERNATIONAL LONGSHORE AND WAREHOUSE UNION. The ILWU was responsible for major post–World War II political and economic changes in Hawaii. Through a series of dock and plantation strikes in 1935, 1938, 1946, 1947, 1948, 1949, 1951, and 1954, the union prevailed against an entrenched political and economic oligarchy. Sugar workers gained such benefits as an industry-wide medical program, sick leave, paid vacations, holidays, and a pension plan. Above, ILWU union activist, labor leader, and social worker Ah Quon McElrath gives a presentation on dental benefits to ILWU Local 142 members at the union hall in 1963. The Jack Wayne Hall building has served three purposes: its primary role as the scene of labor organizing and strike support, a place for general community organizing, and, below, a social center. (Above, ILWU Local 142 Archives; below, Miyoko Hasegawa Matsuo Collection.)

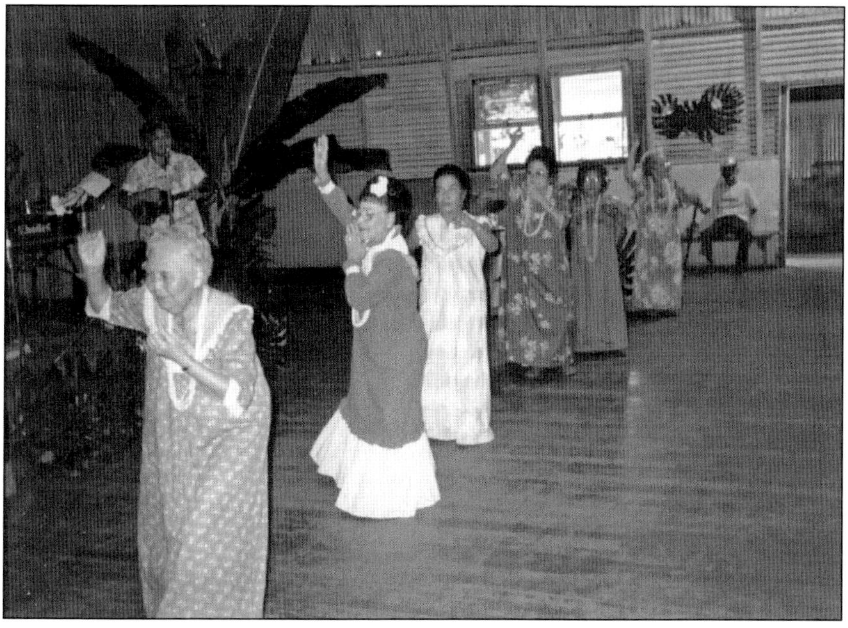

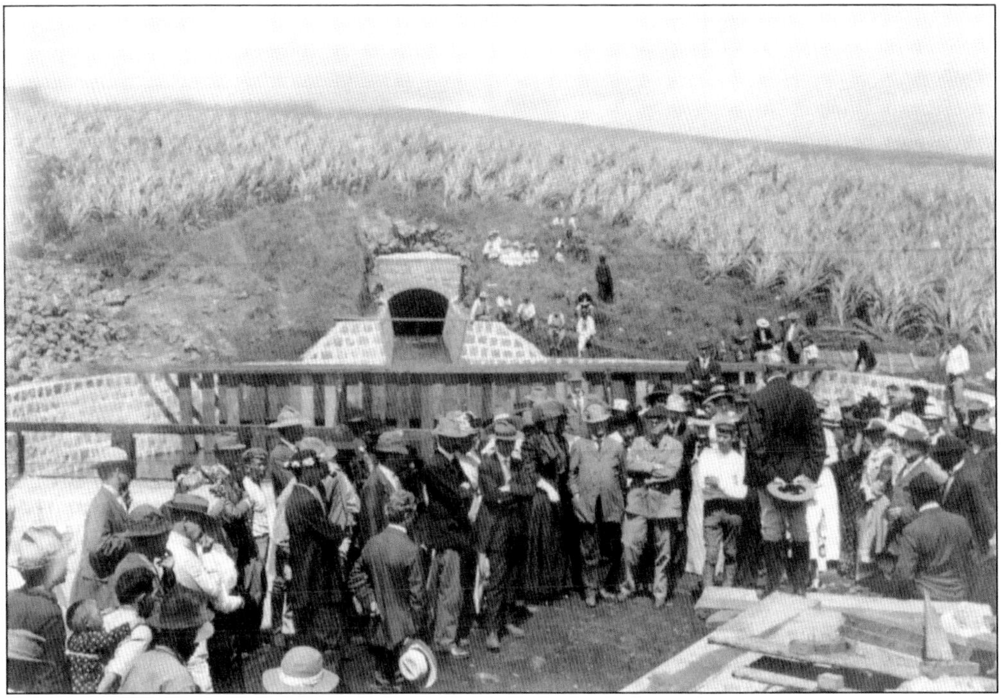

THE UPPER AND LOWER HAMAKUA DITCHES. Water coming from the Waipio and Waimanu Valleys into the Hamakua irrigation ditches began at the highest possible elevation; the route then followed contours and specific gradients to facilitate flow over long distances. This also maximized field areas between ditches and coast, which could be irrigated by secondary canals. The Upper Ditch (1907) was a failure, the Lower Ditch (1910) a success. Here, the community celebrates the opening of the Lower Hamakua Ditch. (Peter Tomich.) [55]

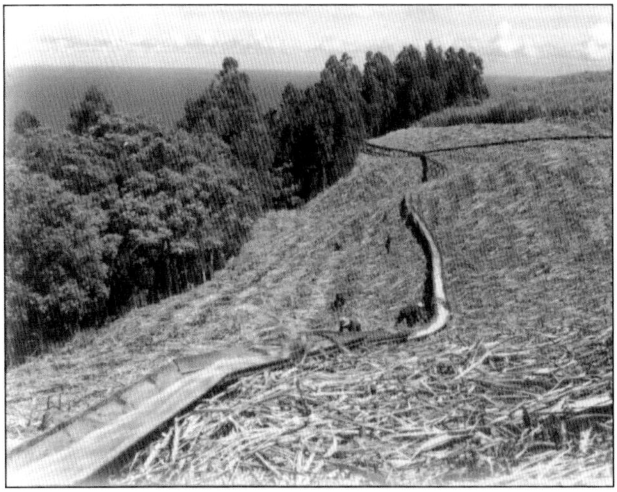

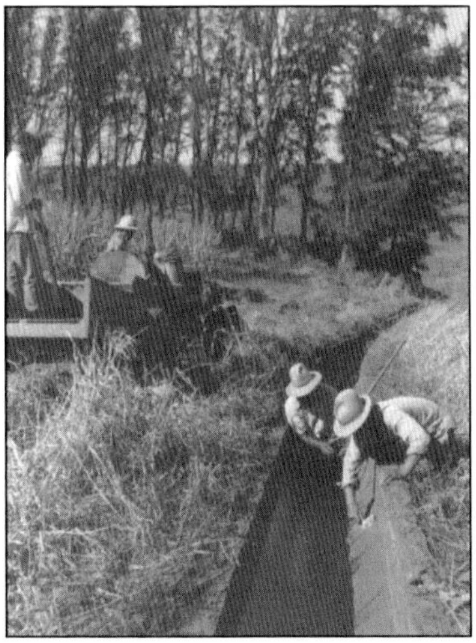

FLUMES. To maximize cane growth, fields were mapped, numbered, and plowed; soil quality gauged; a reliable source of irrigation developed; ditches and tunnels kept clear of debris; concrete linings installed to prevent ditch and tunnel seepage; insect and disease-resistant cane planted; growth monitored; fertilizer added; pesticide and herbicides applied; and finally, waste material burned. Then the issue became transport of the cane to the mill. Flexible portable flumes were employed to float cane downhill toward the mill. (Christensen Collection, NHERC.)

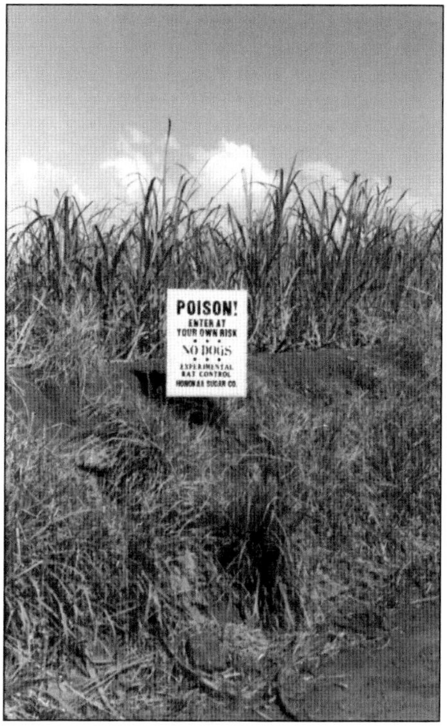

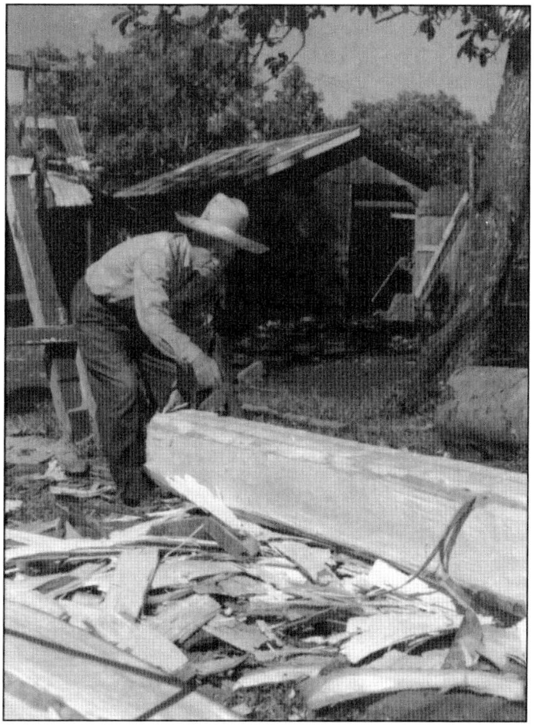

ON THE PLANTATION. Scenes familiar to those living on the plantation included application of fertilizers, herbicides, and insecticides; burning cane fields; and rat-control programs (see sign at top left). Workers regularly displayed ingenuity and multiple skillsets. To the right, a carpenter is preparing an unusually heavy beam, possibly as a flume or tunnel ceiling support. (Both, Christensen Collection, NHERC.)

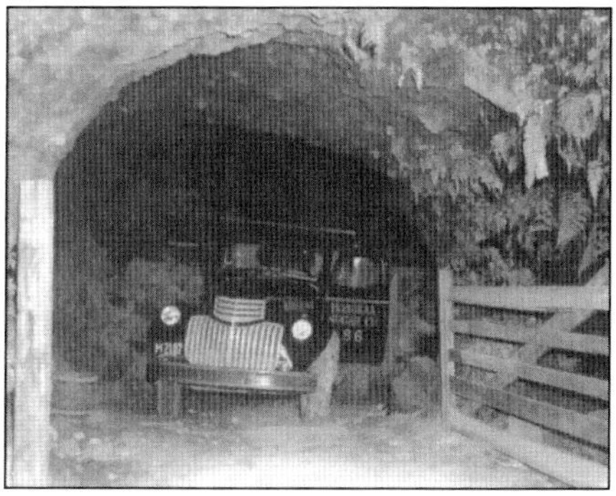

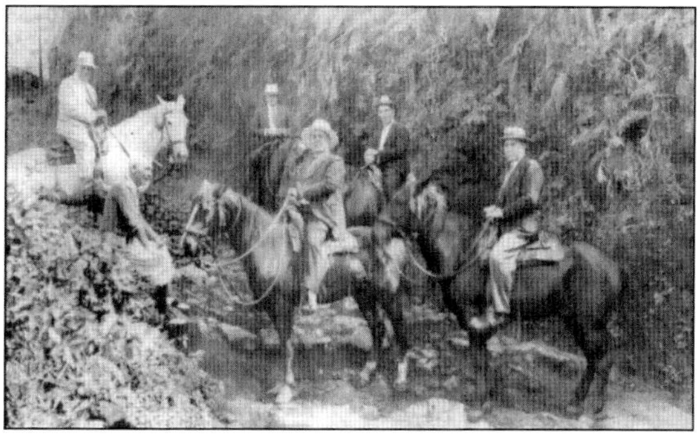

MORE INFRASTRUCTURE IMPROVEMENTS. On the left, the DeLuz family mines the core of a cinder cone in Ahualoa Mauka. Honokaa Plantation purchased such material for its own roads, here using its own truck for transport. On the right, community leaders ride surefooted horses down a rough and steep road to Waipio Valley even into the first decades of the 20th century. From left to right are county supervisor A.M. Cabrinha, unidentified, bandmaster and store owner Alfred Awong, county board chairman (mayor) Samuel "Mahuka" Spencer (for whom Spencer Park at Kawaihae is named), road overseer Antone Luce Ferreira, and Kalopa homesteader Joe Pestana. (Left, Christensen Collection, NHERC; right, Ferreira Family Collection).

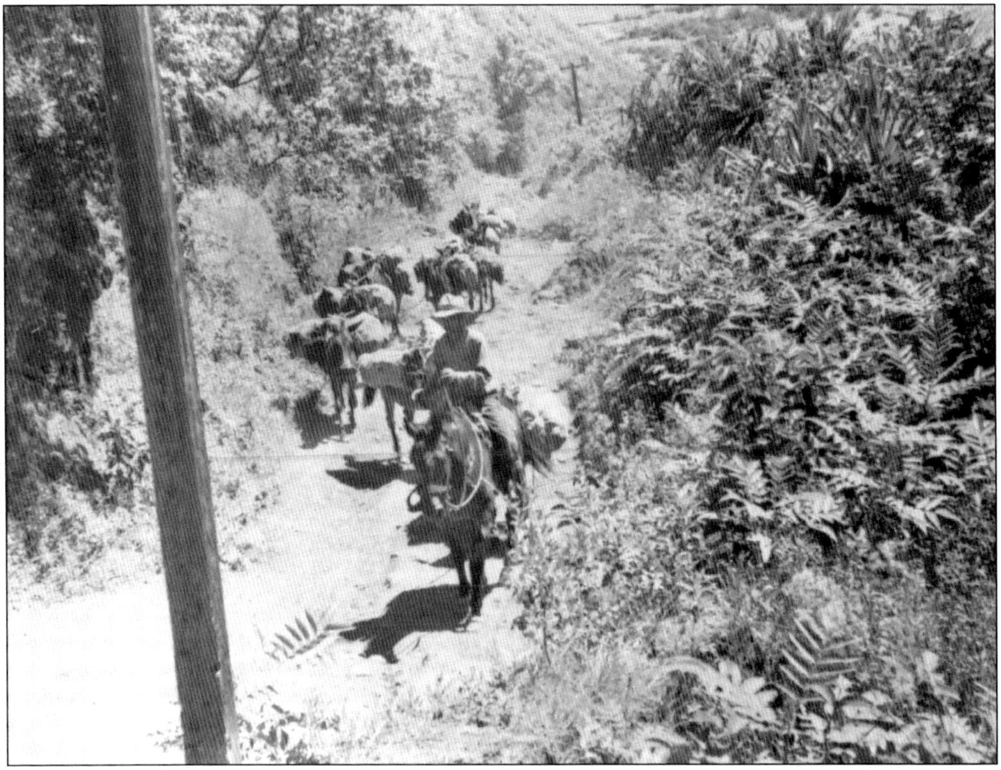

UP FROM WAIPIO VALLEY. As late as the mid-20th century, donkeys were used to bring taro and rice up out of the steep Waipio Valley adjacent to Kukuihaele. The trek would then continue on to Waimea via Mud Lane or to Honokaa by the coastal road. The route remains a narrow, four-wheel-drive road in 2015. (Okada Collection, NHERC.)

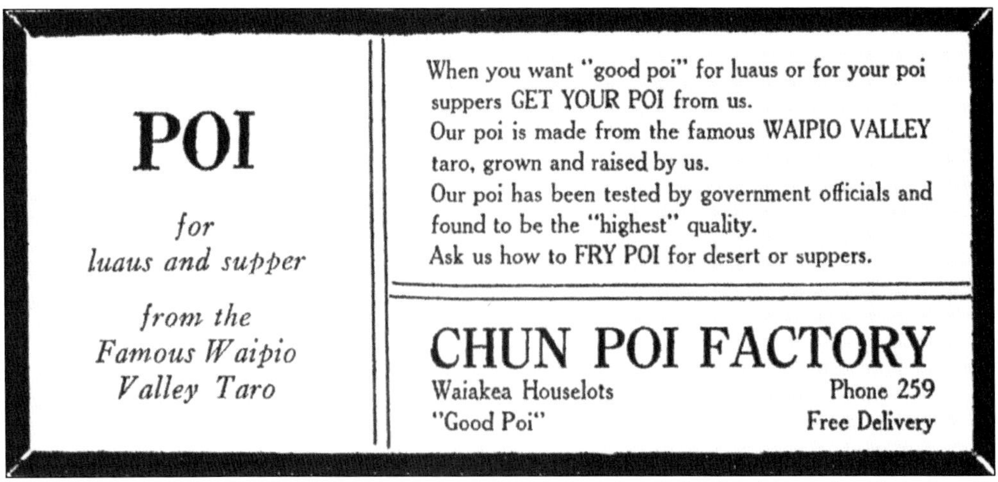

POI

for luaus and supper

from the Famous Waipio Valley Taro

When you want "good poi" for luaus or for your poi suppers GET YOUR POI from us.
Our poi is made from the famous WAIPIO VALLEY taro, grown and raised by us.
Our poi has been tested by government officials and found to be the "highest" quality.
Ask us how to FRY POI for desert or suppers.

CHUN POI FACTORY

Waiakea Houselots — Phone 259

"Good Poi" — Free Delivery

POI. Although commercial rice production supplanted taro in most lowland agricultural areas such as Waipio by the turn of the 20th century, the cultivating of taro in Waipio and the production of poi from taro remained an important cultural food for Native Hawaiians and a supplement to the diets of many other ethnic groups. This advertisement is from 1927. (HTH.)

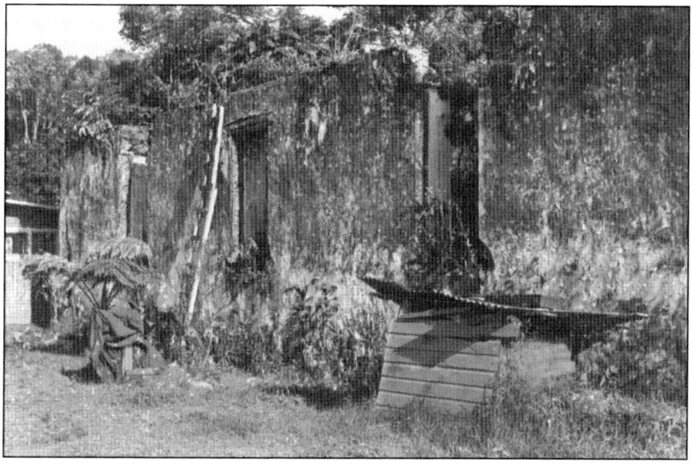

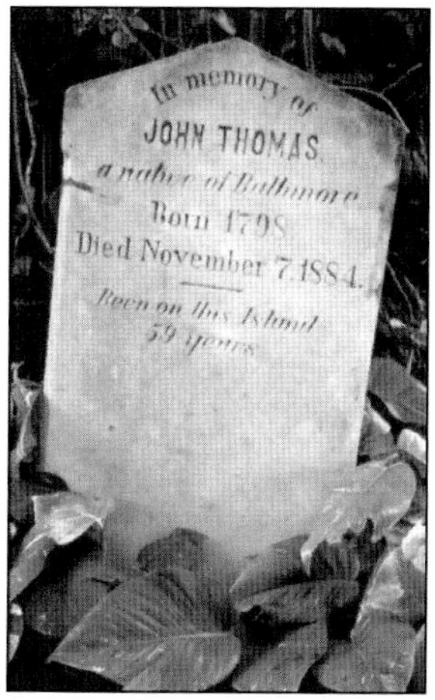

KUKUIHAELE CHURCH. The Rev. Lorenzo Lyons, one of the Congregational ministers sent to Hawaii by the American Board of Commissioners for Foreign Missions, first arrived in Waimea on July 16, 1832. He spent 54 years constructing 14 churches throughout North and South Kohala, Waimea, and Hamakua. The first Hamakua Native Hawaiian church in Kanahonua ahupuaa, called Ele-io ("to go after speedily"), was established by Lyons in 1835. A permanent stone edifice (later named Kukuihaele Church) was erected in 1859; its ruins and graveyard are still visible today. The Reverend Lyons is also remembered as the author of "I Left it All with Jesus," also called "Hawaii Aloha." (Left, SHPD; right, LR.)

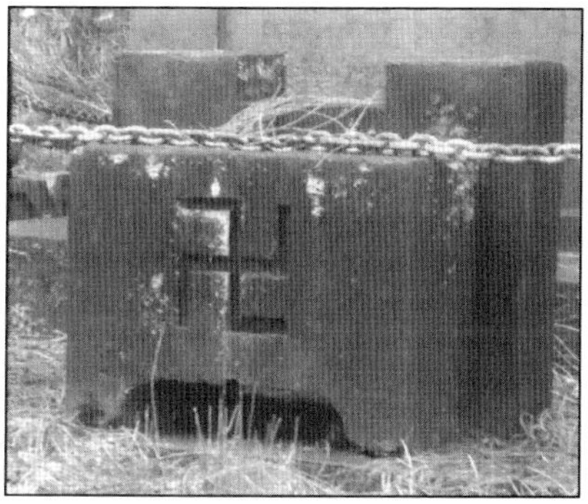

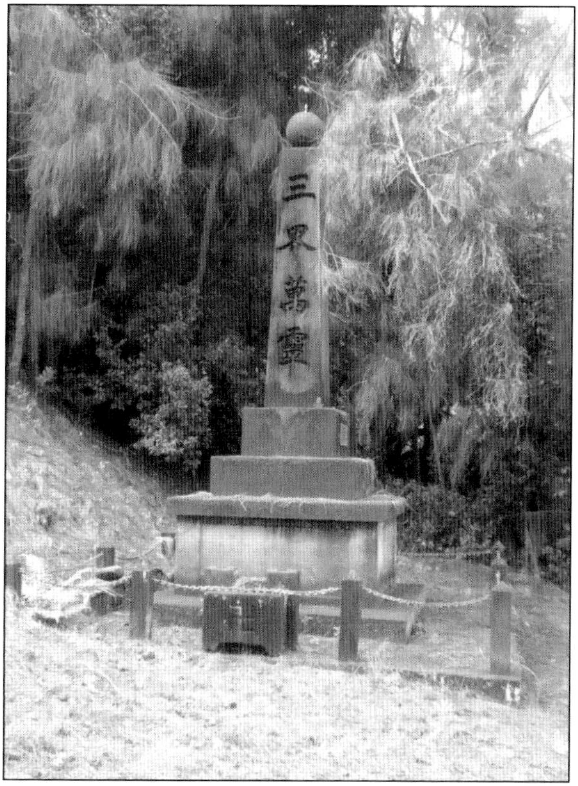

JAPANESE CEMETERY MONUMENT. The monument at right reads *sangai banrei*, "All the Reincarnating Souls." The *svasstika* (swastika) above symbolizes good fortune or wellbeing. The monument also has inscribed in English, "In Memory of Unknown Pioneers—erected by Ukichi Kuramitsu, July 28, 1941." Kuramitsu was the proprietor of the Honokaa Garage (1920s–1950s). Ironically, this was erected a few months prior to the Japanese attack on Pearl Harbor. (Both, LR.)

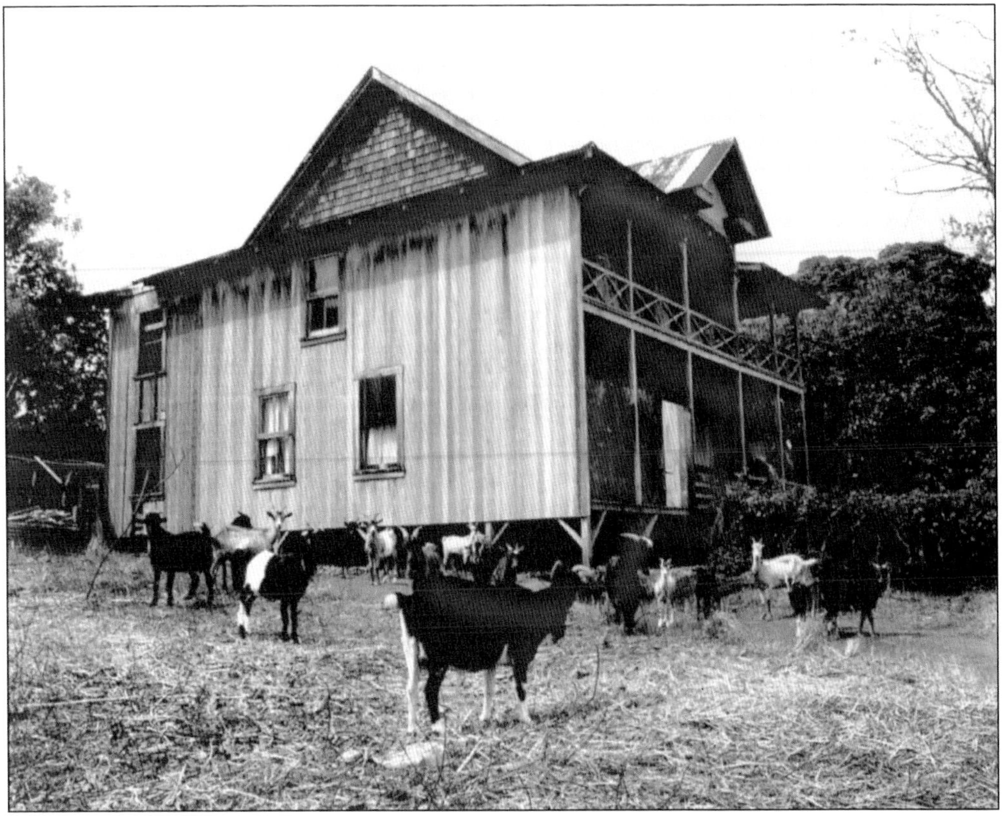

Chee Ying Society Hall. Founded mostly by Chinese immigrants from Kwangtung, Fukien, and Shantung Provinces, the society sought to maintain ties with China and provide mutual protection and welfare. These included celebrations of festivals, care for the elderly, and burial for the dead. The hall's first floor held a community room, and the second floor a Taoist temple room. Two cemeteries, a cookhouse, a pork cooker, and a cistern also occupied the property. (All, SHPD.)

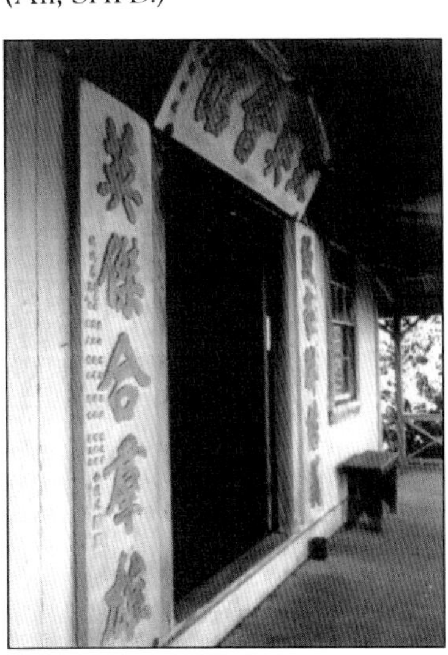

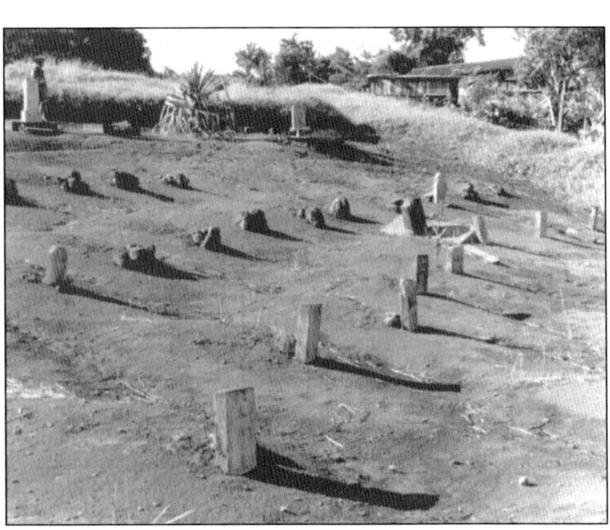

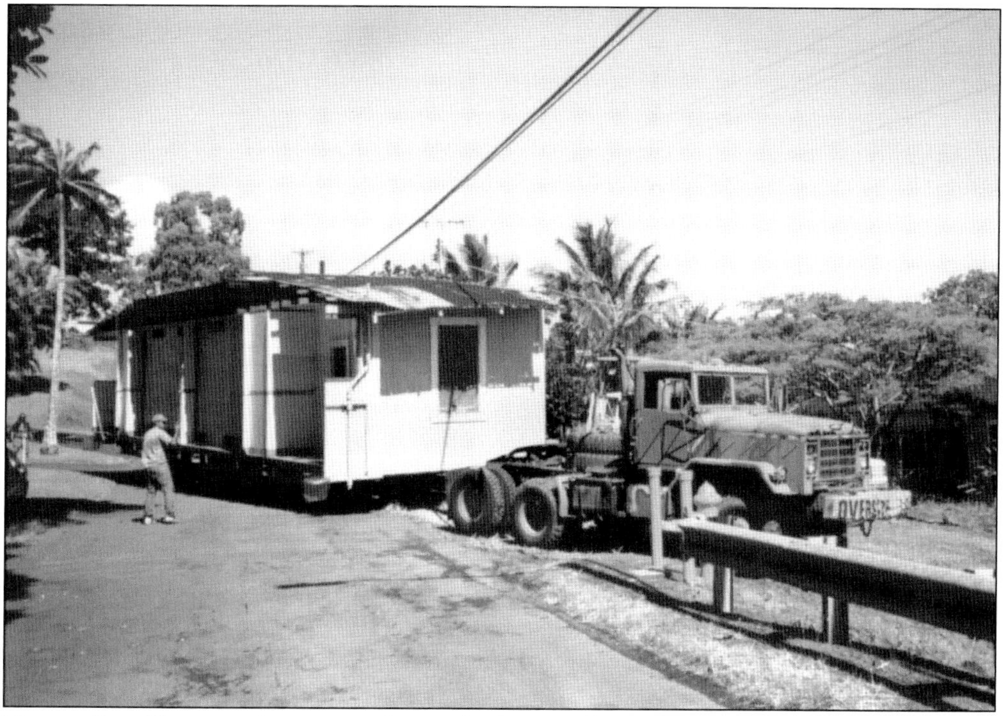

Moving Day. Plantation homes were designed to be portable, constructed on posts and piers, which allowed the buildings to be lifted onto trailers for moves. And move they did. The introduction of trucks allowed workers to live far from worksites. Plantation management subsequently consolidated camp housing, creating residences in one central place to warrant construction of amenities such as sewers, electricity, and running water to improve plantation living conditions and retain employees. In Honokaa, the best-known relocation of houses was from the old Overend Camp to Camp Eight. Such moving of residences had an unanticipated side effect on many plantations, because for inventory purposes, plantation-owned houses retained their unique numbers. So, for example, instead of housing addresses in the reconstituted camps reading 103, 105, 107, and so forth down the street, addresses could read 103, 109, 151, 227, with no other numbers in between. (Christensen Collection, NHERC.)

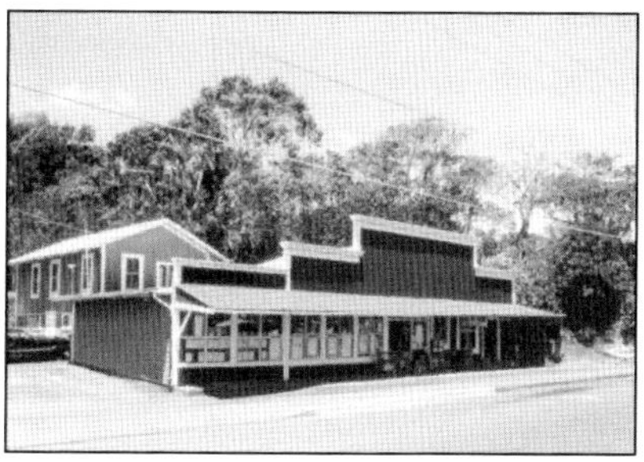

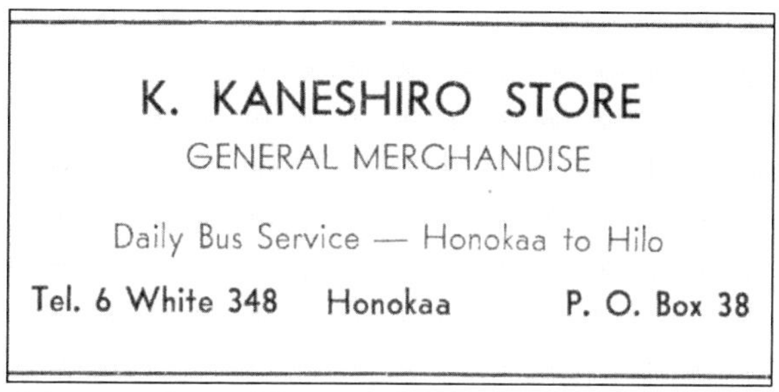

Cash and Carry. As mentioned earlier, Mamane Street Waipio side of Lehua once was much more commercial. The 1914 Sanborn Fire Insurance Company map lists a tailor shop, cakes and candy, general merchandise, a harness shop, a blacksmith, a photographer, a barber, and soda bottling there. Poi manufacturer Mock Chew of Kukuihaele acquired this particular property in 1925. Naozo Kaneshiro purchased it in 1931, and the K. Kaneshiros operated a general cash-and-carry store into 2008. The advertisement on the right is from the 1939 *Ka Nani O Honokaa* yearbook. (Left, SHPD; right, HHSY.) [63]

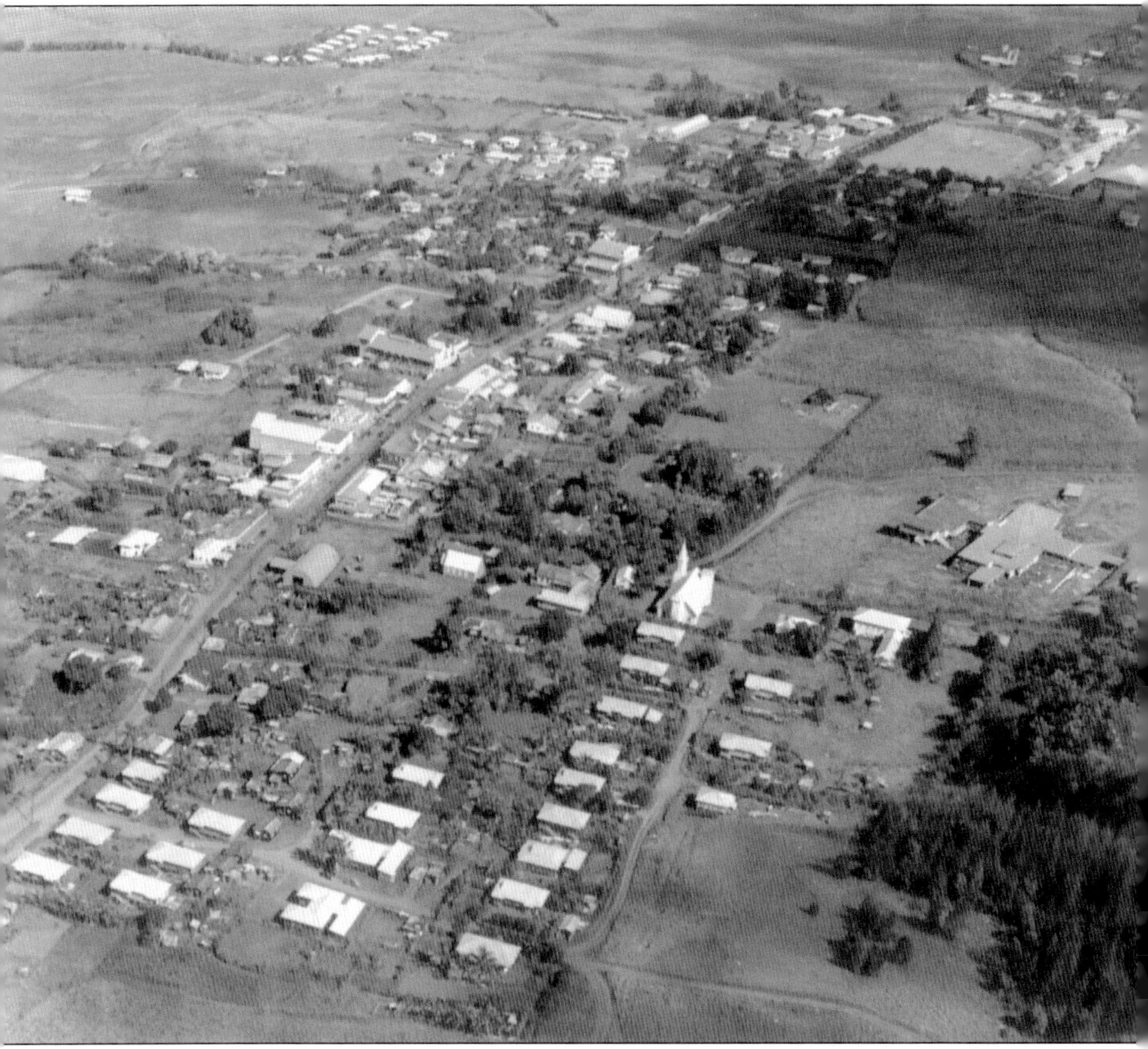

Aerial Photograph of Honokaa, 1953. The first systematic aerial photography of the Hawaiian Islands was undertaken by the military for defense purposes in the 1930s. Introduction of crop dusting of fertilizer and other substances by the Honokaa Sugar Company allowed employee Paul Christensen to document sugar cane fields, mills, camps, and towns within Hamakua in the 1950s. In the foreground are the orderly rows of Camp Eight housing. Looking toward Hilo, the Haina (Lehua) Road splits the photograph in half. Out of view to the left is the Honokaa Sugar Company Mill. To the right of the Government Road intersection and up the hill are the old Methodist church, the Hongwanji Buddhist Temple, Our Lady of Lourdes Catholic Church, and the newly opened Honokaa Hospital. At center along Government Road are three prominent landmarks: the "Doc" Hill Theatre, the Honokaa People's Theatre, and the Botelho Building and Garage. On the far Hilo side, in the makai direction at upper left, is the separate Overend Camp before it was dismantled. On the mauka side (to the extreme right) are the fields and buildings of Honokaa School. (Christensen Collection, NHERC.)

Six

Up Lehua to Waimea

Religious organizations settled on the Waipio side of Honokaa. There is a reason for this.

The Roman Catholics came first. Catholic priests arrived on Hawaii Island at Kailua-Kona in 1839 before establishing a center at Waimea. Church officials followed the population, with Father (later Bishop) Gulstan based in Waipio Valley but responsible for adherents throughout Hamakua. As the sugar plantations began organizing, Father Paul Raulin established two temporary churches "up top" at Honokaa. Land was then purchased from Catholic George Hardy in 1879 and 1886. The parish has changed its name over time from St. Georges, to Church of the Immaculate Conception, to Our Lady of Lourdes, and moved twice, remaining near Lehua.

The Anglican (now Episcopal) church established a cemetery in Honokaa in 1886. In 1904, the Hamakua (now Honokaa) Hongwanji Mission established a temple. The 1914 Sanborn Fire Insurance Company map lists a Japanese Christian church and a Korean school not far from the Lehua-Plumeria intersection. The Honokaa Kinpukuji Shingon Mission, organized in 1916, was there also.

The reason for this religious amalgamation near Lehua is because of the policies of the Honokaa Sugar Company. As happened at many other plantations, management came to view religious instruction as a community-stabilizing influence, which was in their own best interest. The plantations began to treat these institutions equally and provided land for temples and churches. "Church Rows" proliferated in Honokaa, Waimea, and Paauilo.

Other institutions nearby are the state's Honokaa Hospital, which opened in 1952 and replaced most of the private hospitals (ethnic and plantation), and, on the same campus, the North Hawaii Education and Research Center (NHERC), which contains the local Heritage Center and Gallery.

Farther mauka are ranch activities (including a rodeo arena) and beyond, in Waimea, the site of Camp Tarawa. Camp Tarawa was the location where US soldiers from the 2nd Marine Division recovered after invading the island of Tarawa in World War II. The camp was also the training ground for the 5th Marine Division before the invasion of Iwo Jima. Camp Tarawa is indelibly linked to Honokaa because the soldiers came to Honokaa for liberty.

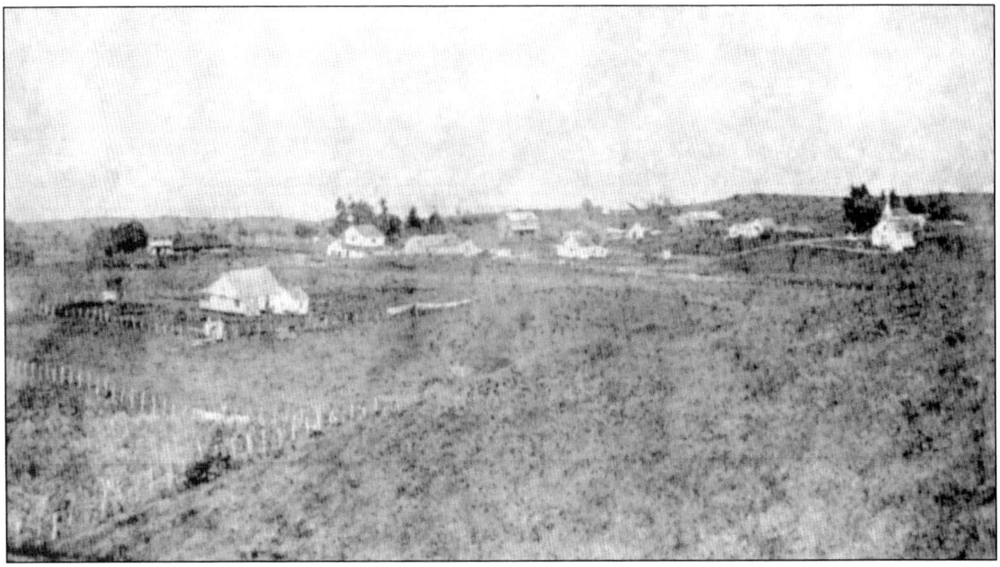

Early Honokaa Town. This is the earliest known photograph of Honokaa Town, credited to Marcus D. Monsarrat. Monsarrat worked as a government surveyor from 1873 to 1877 and in private practice until at least 1917. The quality of the photograph and its contents suggest that it predates the turn of the 20th century. Lehua cuts across the landscape from left to right, with Mamane farther right crossing Lehua. Visible in the foreground are St. Georges Catholic Church and the Lumaheihei homestead. (Photograph by M.D. Monsarrat, HSA.)

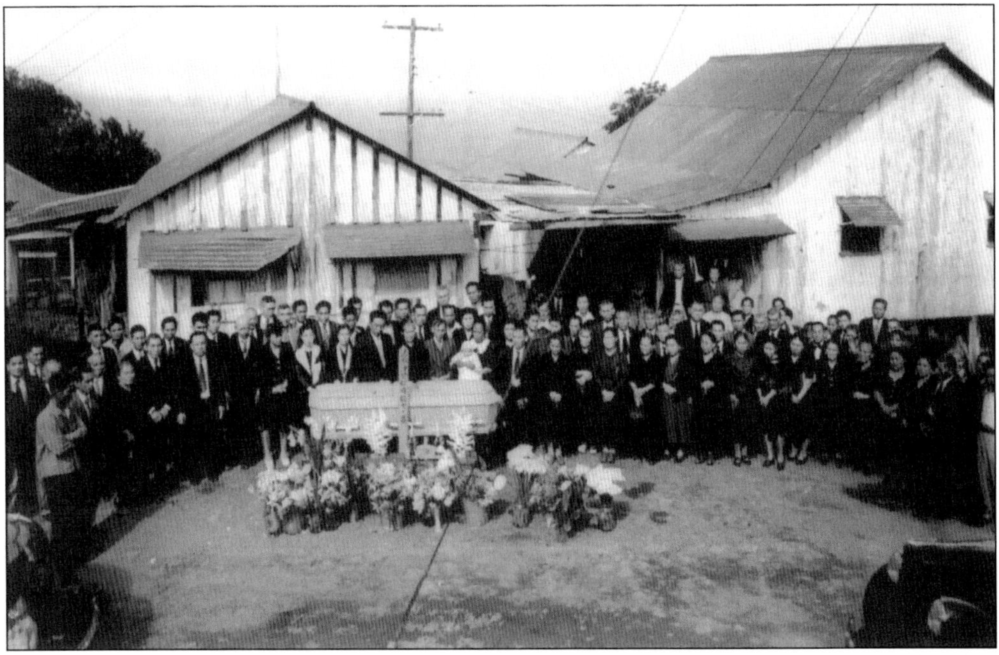

Kinpukuji, the Shingon Buddhist Mission Funeral. Built in 1907, the temple building has vertical board walls, homemade windows and window awnings, and no vent or gable ornamentation. This pre-war photograph depicts a Buddhist funeral service for a woman. The *kaimyo* (posthumous name) is written on the *stupa* (wooden post) in front of the casket. This event predates the Seniors' Club in 1949 (page 113). (Larry Ignacio Collection.) [13]

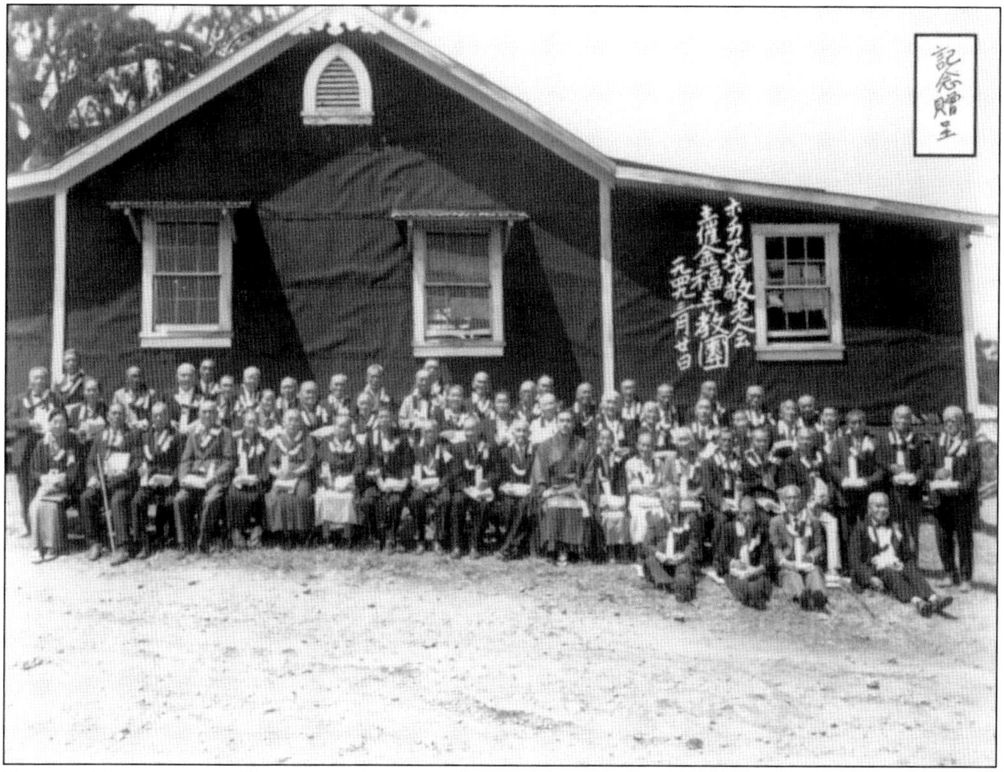

SENIORS' CLUB AT THE KINPUKUJI SHINGON TEMPLE. Members of Honokaa District Seniors' Club pose in front of the Kinpukuji building for this Gift of Commemoration photograph on March 20, 1949. It would appear that the temple was undergoing renovations, as it was covered with tarpaper. In recent times, the Shingon Mission (clad in vertical boards) was moved in one piece through the Hongwanji grounds to its present location just off Maile Street. (NHERC.)

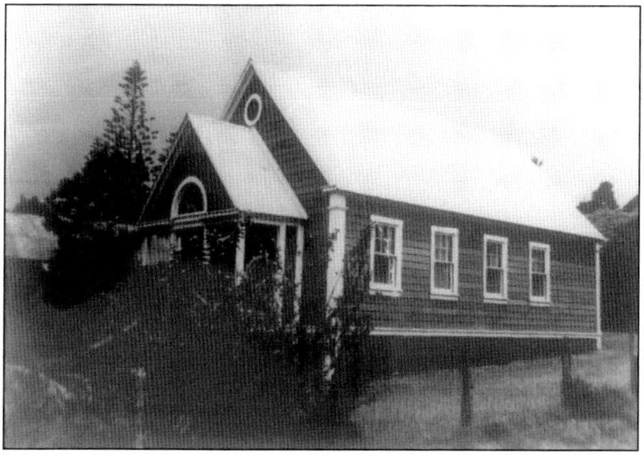

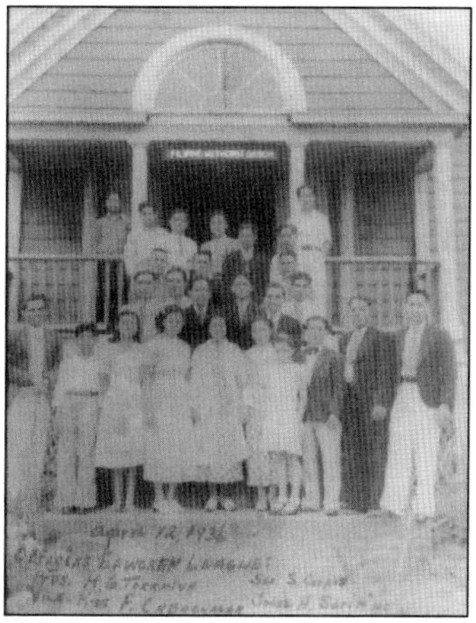

METHODIST CHURCH. In 1906, Koreans and Filipinos began arriving as plantation labor. Both groups had been introduced to Methodism in their home countries. In 1910, the Rev. Cenon Ramos raised $1,746 for a church, which was constructed by Honokaa Plantation carpenters on land provided by that company. In 1937, the Rev. S.G. Afalla was appointed. The membership moved to the present site on Mamane Street in 1950. Today, all ethnic groups are represented. (Methodist Archives.) [65]

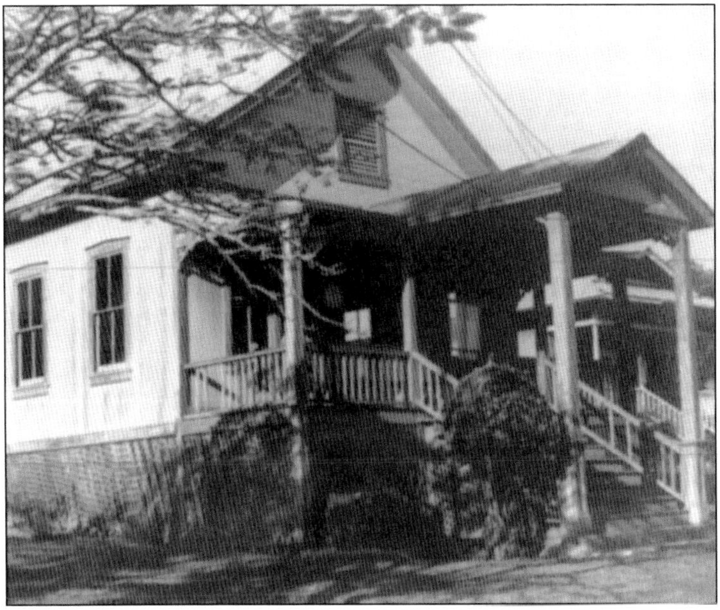

Hamakua Hongwanji Mission. The first Buddhist Hongwanji services at Honokaa were conducted in 1904 by the Rev. Joei Abe at the site later occupied by the Old "Doc" Hill Theatre on Mamane Street. In 1905, under the leadership of the Rev. Keigetsu Shibata, first resident minister at Honokaa, a permanent temple was constructed at the present site on Lehua Street. (LM.) [67]

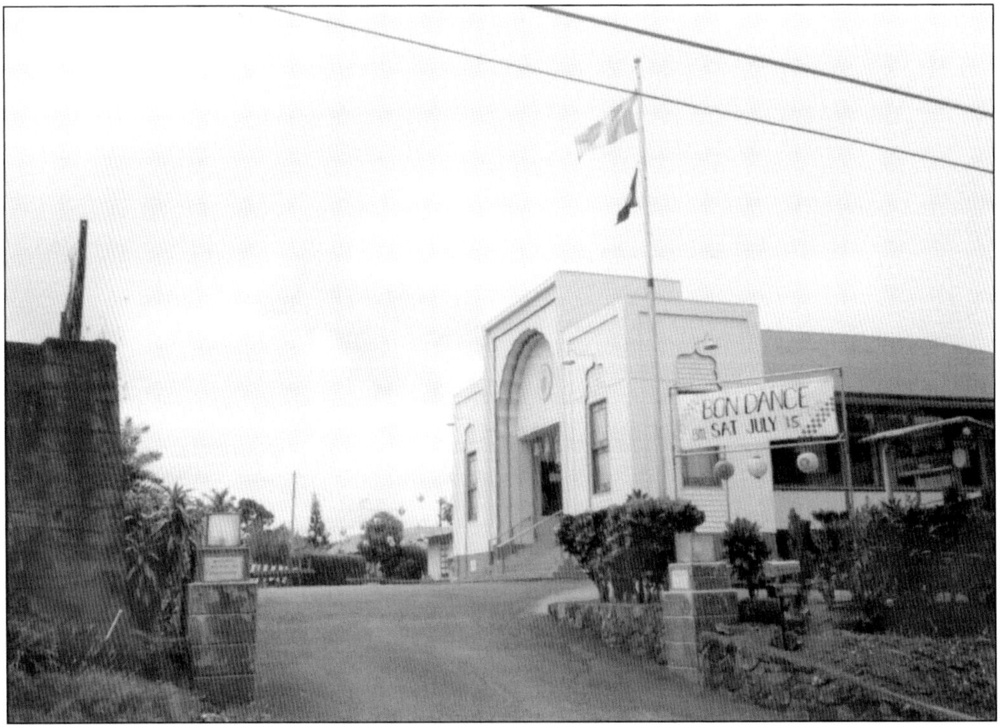

Honokaa Hongwanji Temple. This building dates from 1951, but the architecture of the façade was influenced by Bishop Yemyo Imamura's ideas for the Honpa Hongwanji Hawaii Betsuin in Honolulu. The building entrance has Indian and other cultural design elements to reflect the universality and internationalism of Buddhism. The grounds include a minister's residence, assembly hall, and columbarium. (Yamato Collection, NHERC.)

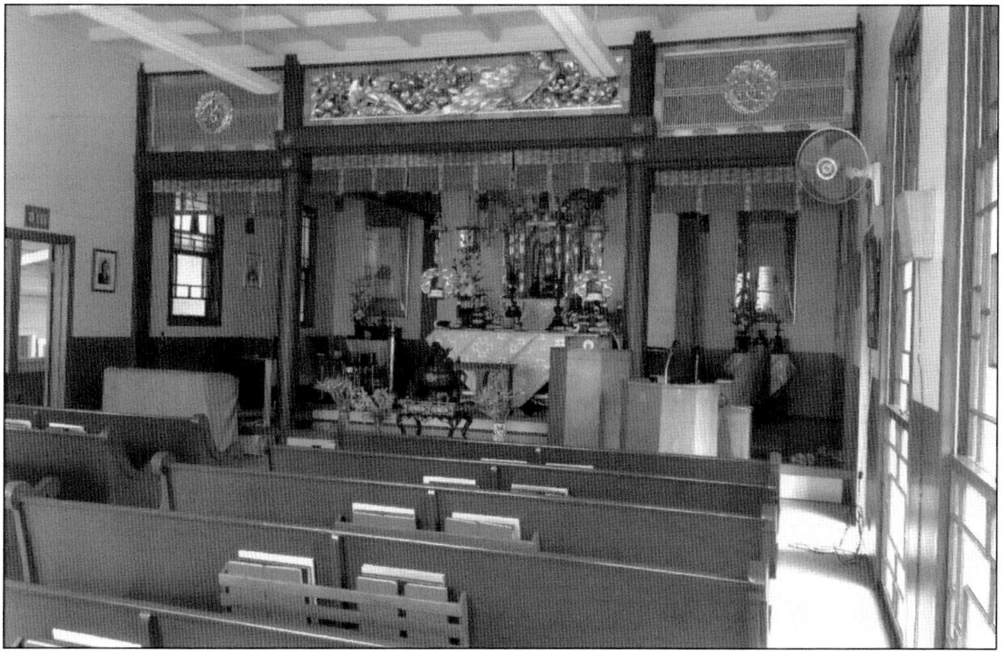

The Hongwanji Sanctuary. Not only did Bishop Imamura employ international elements in the external architecture of Hongwanji temples, he also Americanized Buddhist service practices. Pews, piano and organ, and hymns were American Christian adaptations. An interesting feature of this and other Hongwanji buildings are the big double-hung windows opening to side galleries to accommodate an overflow worship service. (LR.)

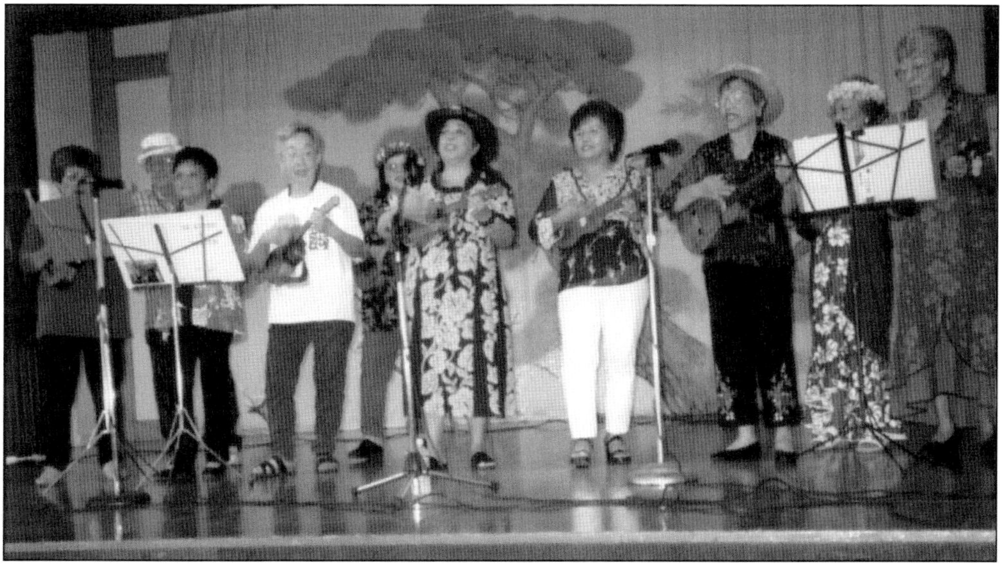

Music at the Hongwanji Meeting Hall. Note the stylized Japanese pine tree on the stage curtain. In traditional Japanese culture, the pine, an evergreen, represents longevity, strength, and good fortune. The tree is represented in Hawaii at New Year's celebration with a *kadomatsu* (arrangement of pine and bamboo) often placed at the entrance to a home. In the foreground is a Honokaa music group playing ukulele—an instrument introduced to Hawaii by Portuguese immigrants. (Maria Yano Collection.)

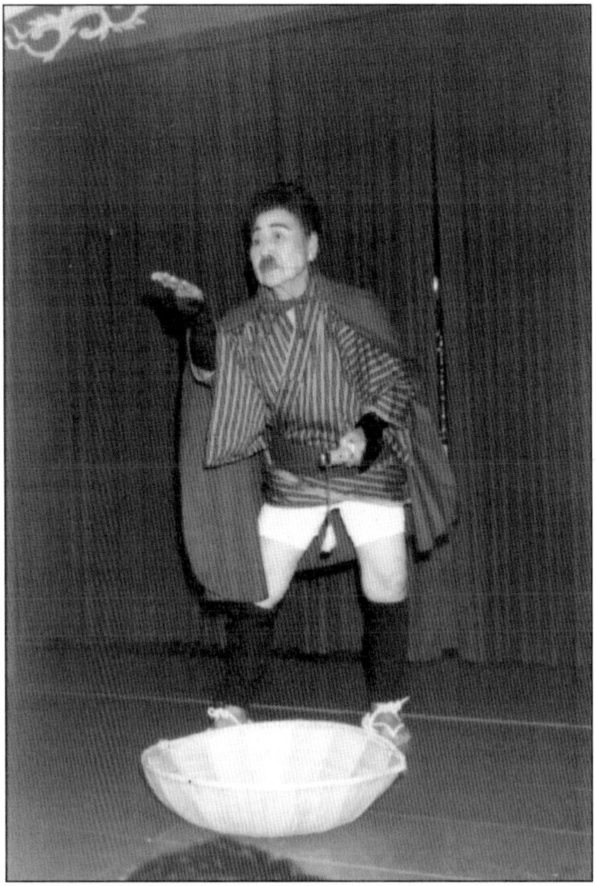

In Costume. Peggy Tanimoto (co-owner of the Honokaa People's Theatre) gestures during a theatrical performance at the assembly hall. She is dressed in the traditional attire of a Japanese man, complete with moustache. (Miyoko Hasegawa Matsuo Collection.)

Obon Festival. This annual Japanese Buddhist season honors the spirits of ancestors. People return to ancestral family sites and clean ancestors' graves; departed spirits visit household altars. A dance, known as *bon-odori*, is conducted in a circle around a *yagura* (tower with raised platform). The dance is often performed with singers, musicians, and *taiko* drummers. The colorful hanging *chochin* (lanterns) add to the festivities. (NHERC.)

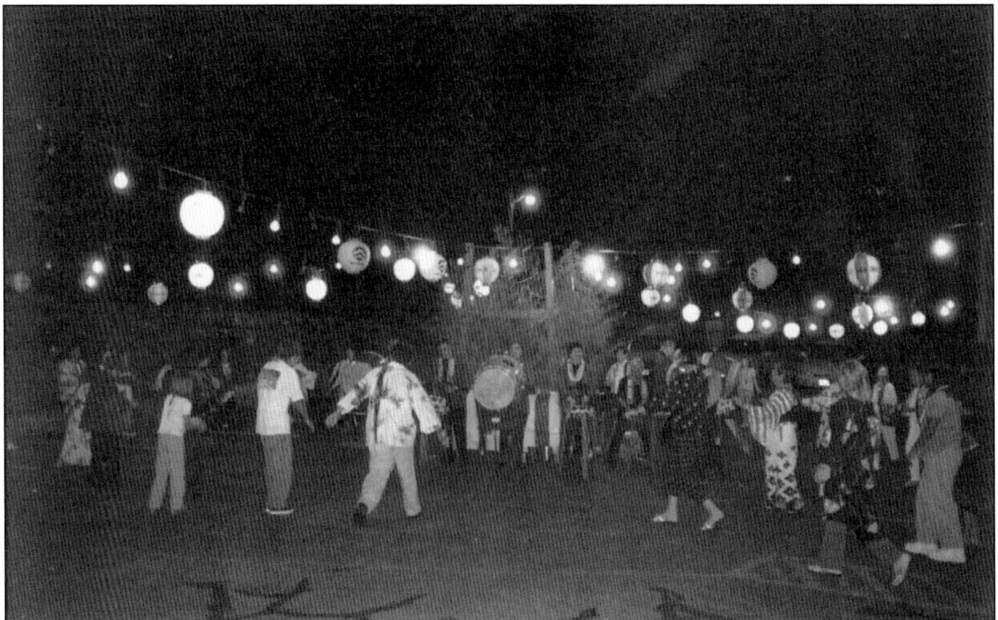

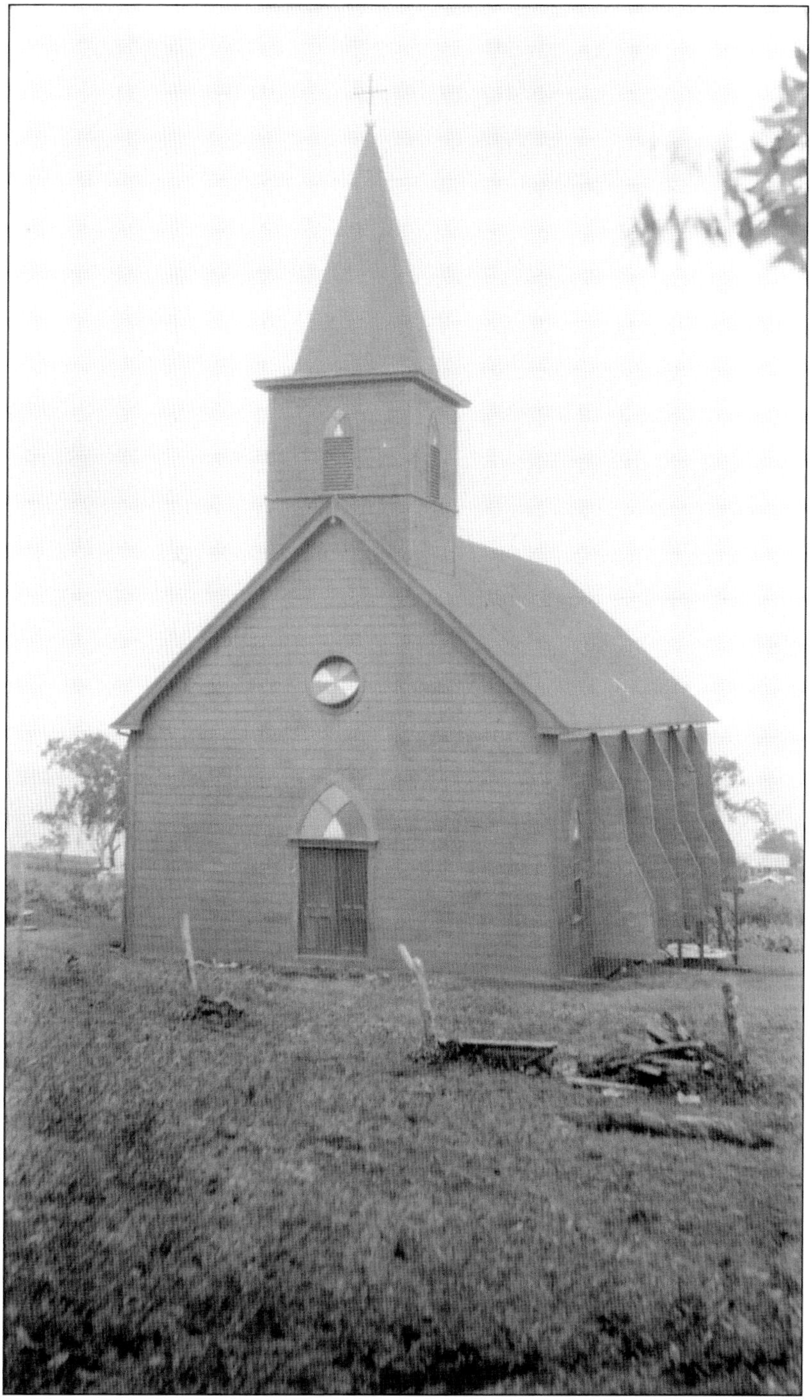

Church of the Immaculate Conception. The first permanent Catholic church in Honokaa was St. Georges, just Hilo side of Lehua Road. A second and later church, on the makai side of the main Catholic cemetery, was named the Church of the Immaculate Conception. This wooden church, seen here, had wooden buttresses reminiscent of European medieval religious structures. The present Our Lady of Lourdes was constructed farther makai in 1927. (CA.) [69]

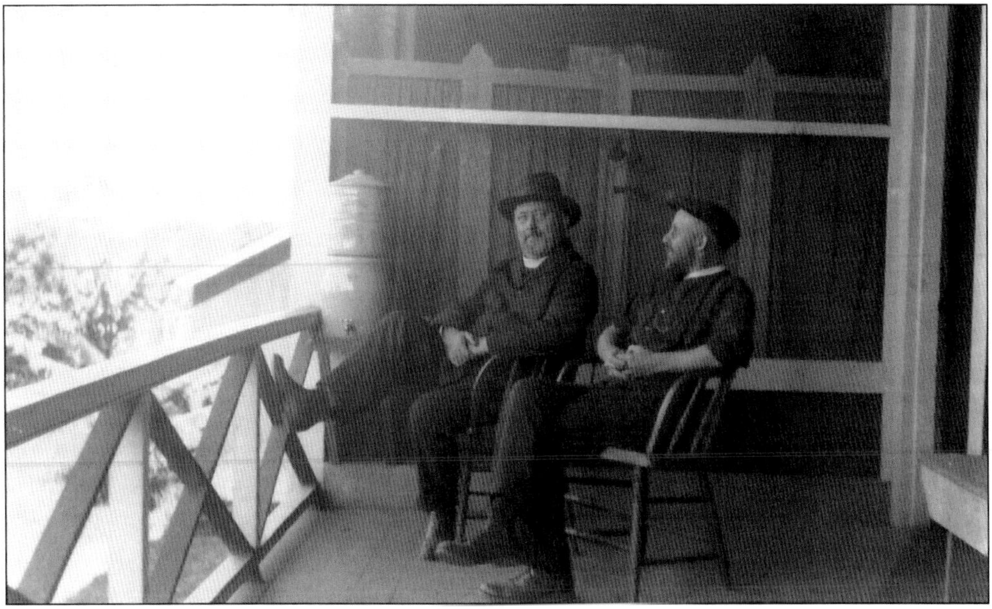

CATHOLIC FATHER OTTO AND BROTHER WENCESLAS. These two men are "talking story" while sitting on the lanai of the priest's Honokaa residence. While earlier priests such as Father Gulstan Ropert lived in Waipio, the growth of sugar-plantation employment led later priests such as Father Paul Raulin to live in Honokaa. Father Raulin arrived in 1882 and served until 1918. The present Our Lady of Lourdes was constructed by Father Athanasius Bons. (CA.)

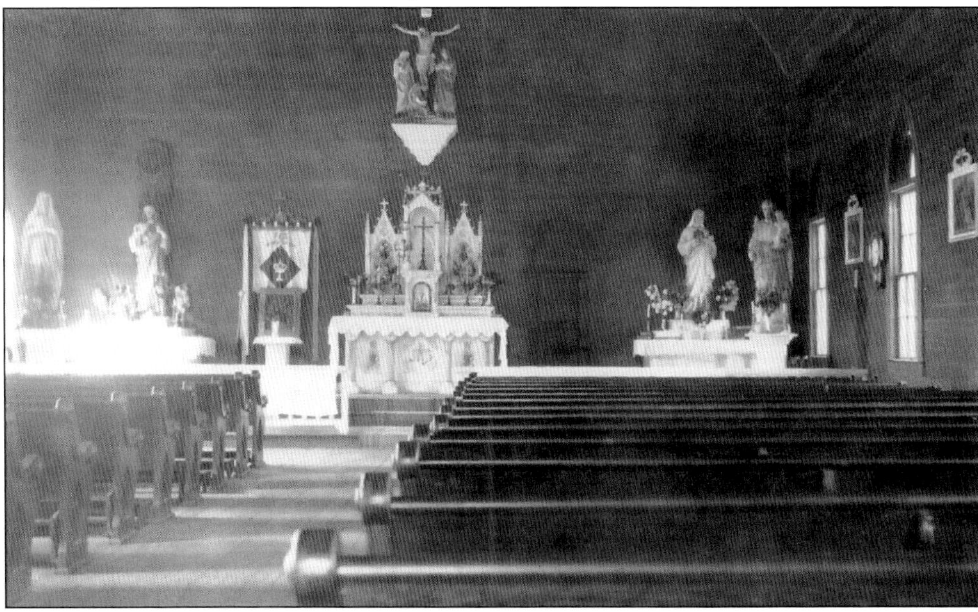

INTERIOR OF THE CHURCH OF THE IMMACULATE CONCEPTION. This photograph shows that the building was entirely made of wood, including a plank floor (following the common period practice). Interesting architectural features included unusual horizontal board construction (suggesting double walls), either dark paint or stain wall surfaces, use of white or light-colored paint to draw attention to the chancel area, larger than usual double-hung windows to bring in light, and lancet arches over the windows. (CA.)

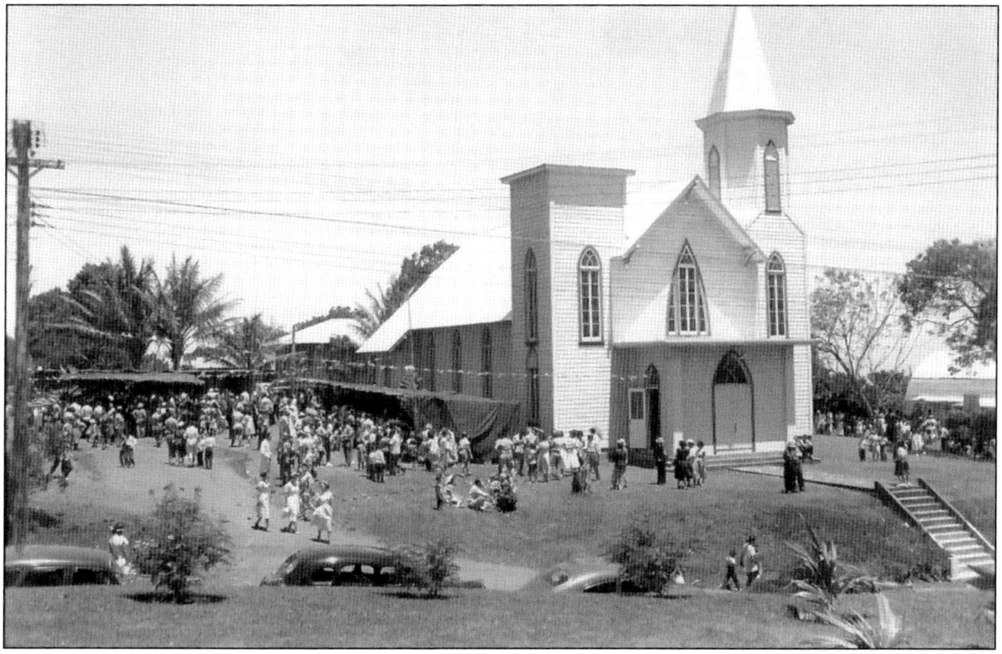

Festa on the Church Grounds. This festival is celebrated 50 days after Easter on Pentecost Sunday honoring the descent of the Holy Spirit to the apostles. Local observance of this tradition originated in Honokaa with the Portuguese immigrants from the Azores and Madeira. In earlier times, there were special newspaper announcements for the Festival of the Holy Ghost train schedule and other transportation to Honokaa. Outside on the church grounds, booths are set up with food and games, and the highlight of the *festa*, the bidding on the *charola*. (CA.) [68]

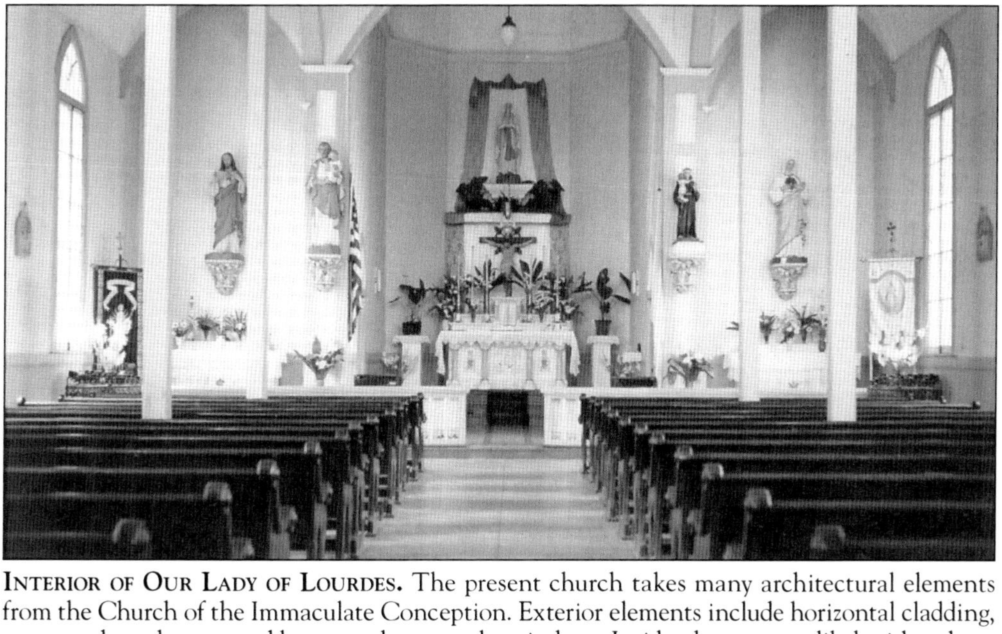

Interior of Our Lady of Lourdes. The present church takes many architectural elements from the Church of the Immaculate Conception. Exterior elements include horizontal cladding, a square-shaped tower, and lancet arches over the windows. Inside, the pews are likely either those of the original church or exact replicas, and the long double-hung windows have been copied with tall apertures. (CA.)

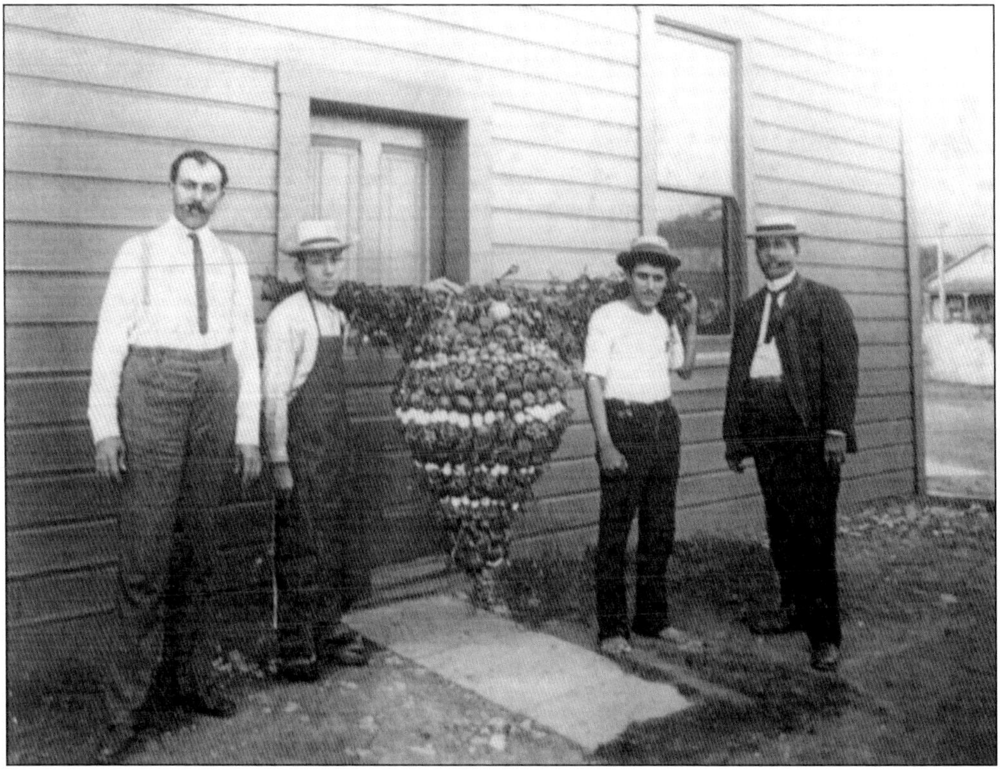

The Charola and the Dove of the Holy Ghost. The colorful bell-shaped charola, an offering of gratitude, is made on a wire frame with fruits and eggs attached with knotted string. The bell's clapper is a bottle of wine. The charola is carried around the church grounds and placed in a prominent place where very active bidding takes place. Below left is the dove of the Holy Ghost. (This one is a paper sculpture.) Below right, Raleigh Martin leans into the booth bidding on the charola. It would be rebid on again and again, with all proceeds going to support the church and charity. (Above, private donor; below left, LM; below right, Martin Collection, NHERC.)

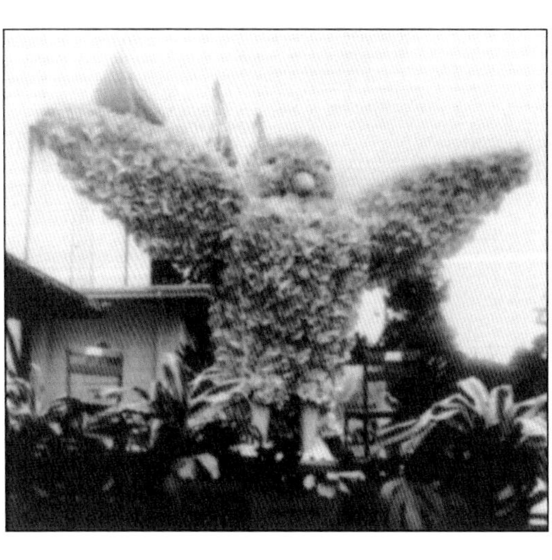

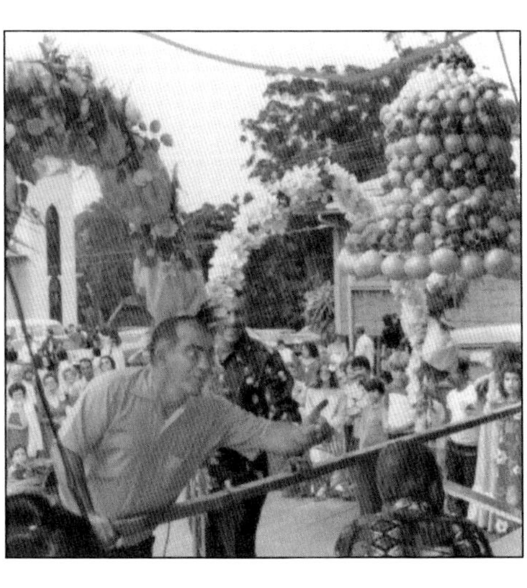

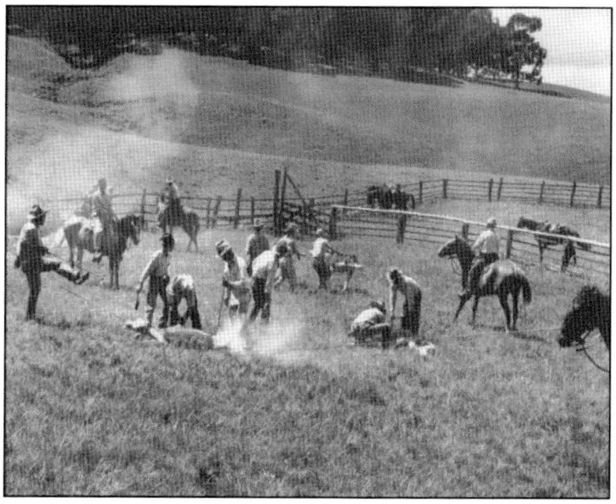

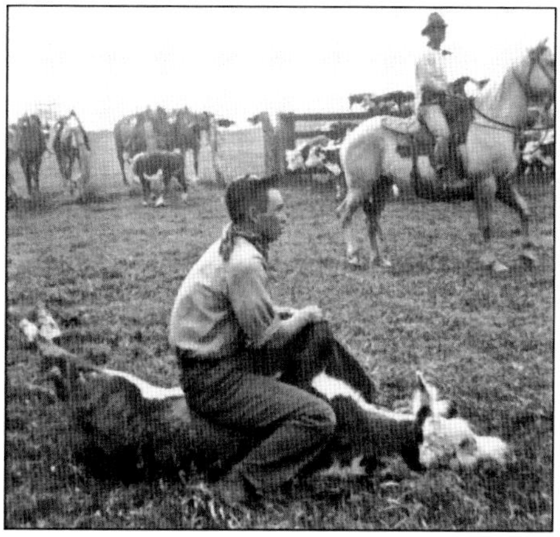

Roundup in Hamakua. Paniolo is a Hawaiian adaptation of the Spanish word *español*o, describing the Mexican and Californian *vaquero* (cowboy) who taught the Hawaiians how to work cattle. In these photographs, paniolo are seen roping, tying up, and readying calves for branding. Today, skilled horsemen and women, as well as aspiring paniolo, compete in the Honokaa Rodeo Arena on land given by Rose Andrade Correia. The stadium is named for this lifetime member of the Hawaii Saddle Club. (Both, NHERC.)

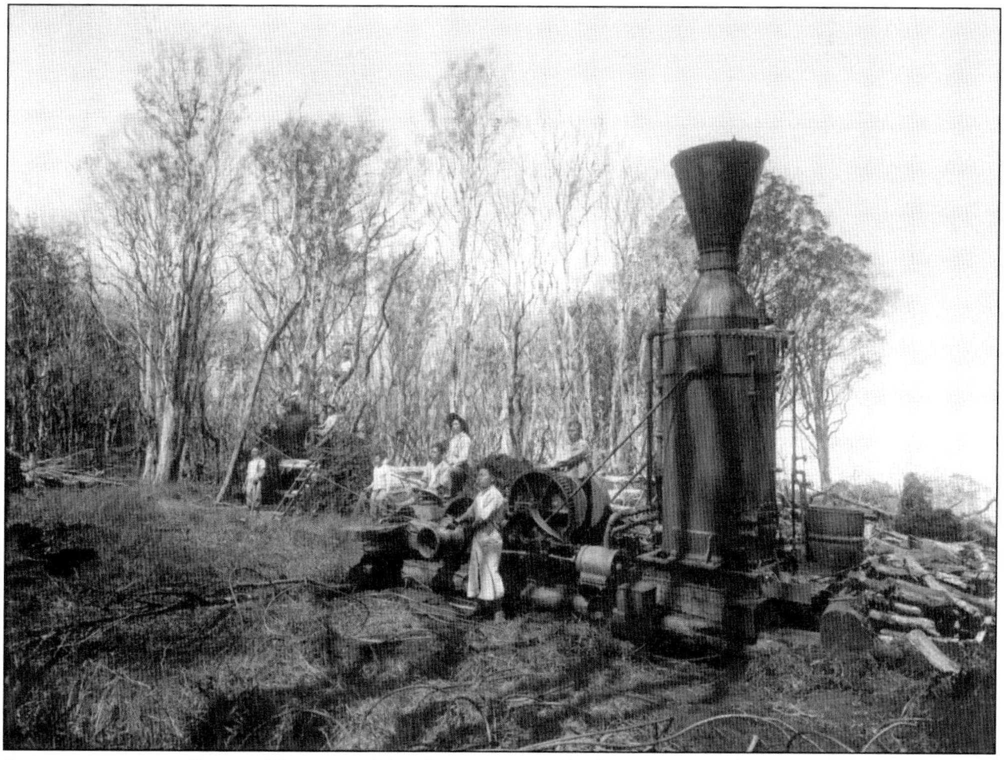

Lumbering and Steam Donkey. Also known as a donkey engine, this was a steam-powered winch. It is shown here being used for logging operations. Rope or cable would be wound around the winch and the cable attached to a log in the woods. The donkey operator would then open a valve, and the log would be dragged ("skidded") horizontally toward a central collection point by the winch. Steam donkeys could also be used to load logs for long-distance shipping and configured to pull themselves to new locations. (NHERC.)

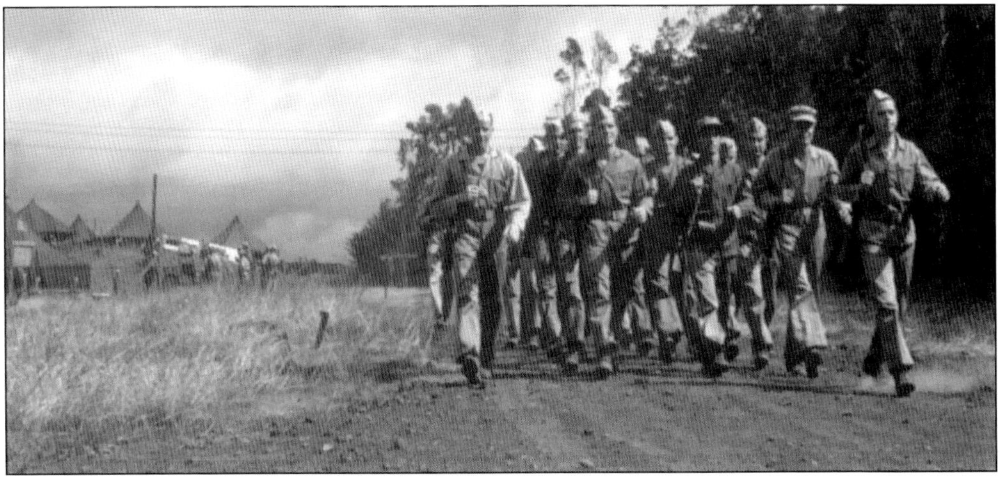

Camp Tarawa Tent City. This site was located on both sides of Mamalohoa Highway, adjacent to the Camp Tarawa Memorial outside Waimea town. Thousands of tents stood on land occupied by the present Lualai subdivision and along the road to the Smart family home, Puopelu. The 137,000 acres of Camp Tarawa extended from Pohakuloa to Hapuna Beach and north to Mahukona. The land was leased by owner Richard Smart for $1 a year. In this photograph, tents are visible in the left background. (Dr. Billy Bergin.)

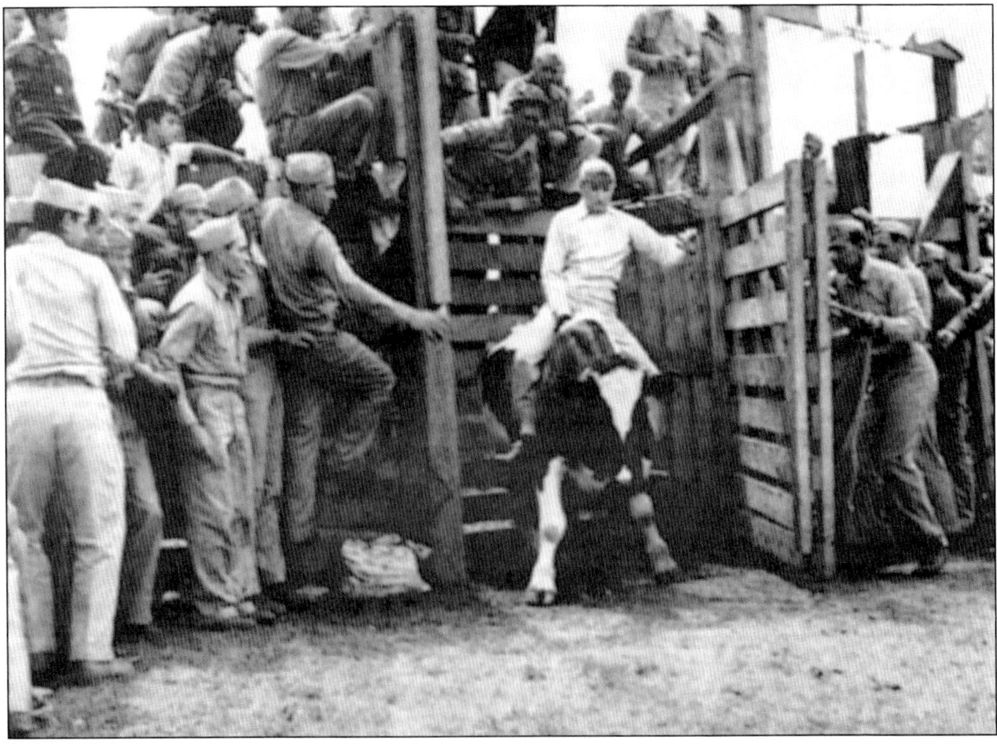

Rodeo. One of the means of making soldiers comfortable in an otherwise strange new environment is the opportunity to engage in activities that they would regularly participate in at home. Fortunately, the Marines and locals at Honokaa and Waimea had a strong commonality in the rodeo. The military command and community organized this event, where a soldier attempts to stay on a bucking animal. (WG.)

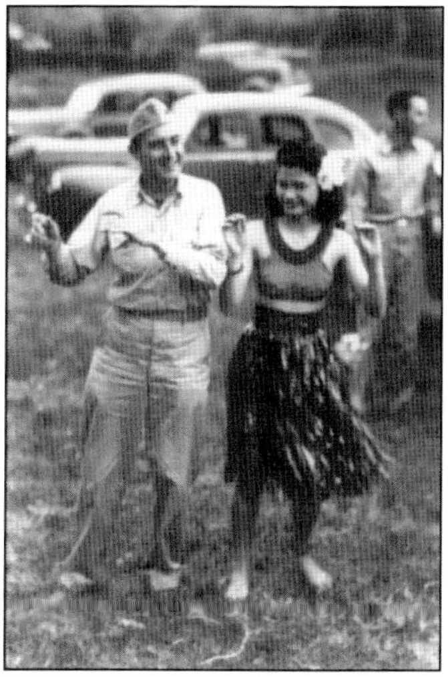 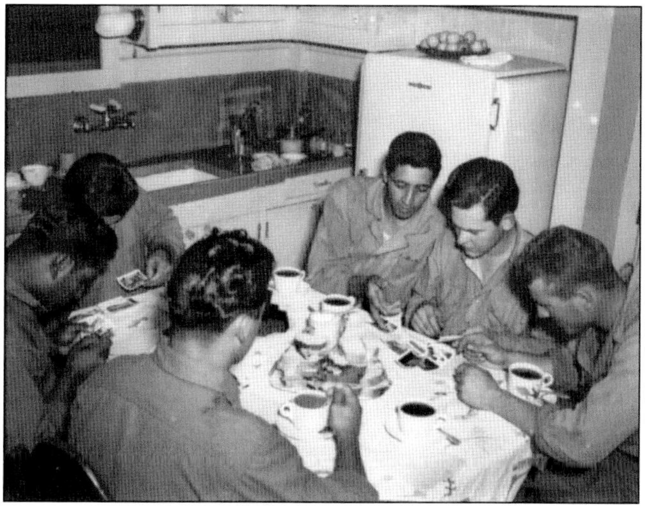

Making the Marines Welcome. Honokaa residents wanted to make the Marines feel appreciated. Everyone understood that the soldiers would place themselves in jeopardy for the common good, or possibly already had. Soldiers were welcomed into local homes for meals and conversation. As many soldiers had previously seen films such as *Road to Singapore* in which Dorothy Lamour, Bob Hope, and Bing Crosby sang *hapa haole* songs and did the hula, they were invited to do the same. (NHERC.)

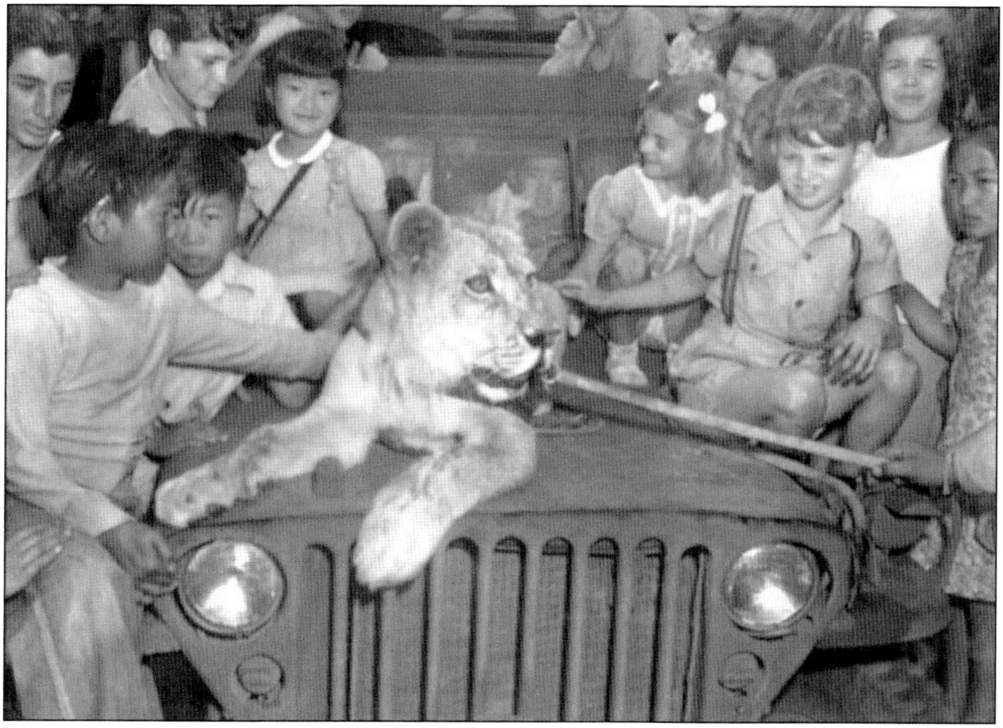

Roscoe the Lion. Children from Waimea on Hawaii Island visit Roscoe the lion during World War II. Purchased as a cub from Los Angeles's Griffith Park Zoo for $25 and later brought to Hawaii, Roscoe was the mascot for the 28th Marines 5th Marine Division at Camp Tarawa. He loved parades, lying draped on the hood of a jeep, and howling to the music. (WG.)

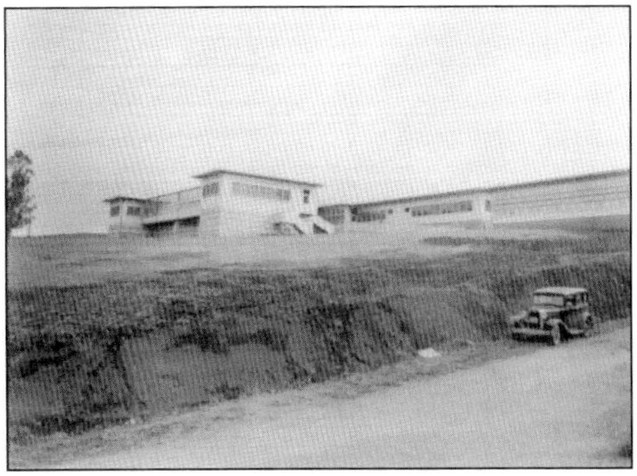

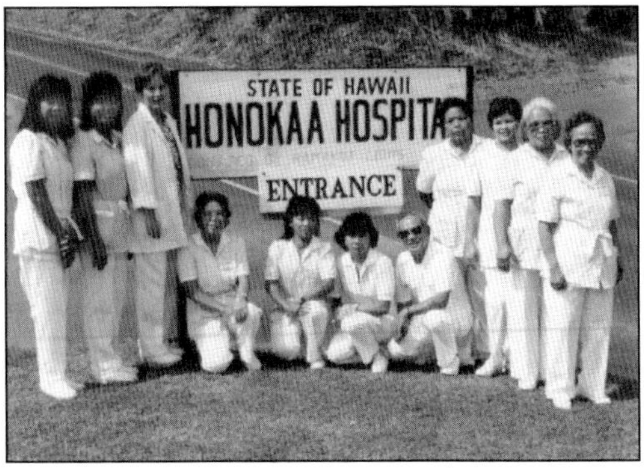

Honokaa Hospital. Before World War II, plantations provided medical care to their employees and families; others went to small private hospitals. The decline of the plantations and the need for medical care in non-plantation areas led to the creation of county hospitals (such as at Honokaa in 1951). Unfortunately, the costs of these facilities soon outstripped the counties' fiscal resources; by 1965, the county hospitals became the responsibility of the State of Hawaii. In 1995, a new 50-bed facility was opened above the original hospital, designed to provide long-term care services; it is now known as Hale Hoola Hamakua (Haven of Wellness in Hamakua). The old Hamakua Sugar Company Infirmary, which became Hamakua Health Center, provides primary care and behavioral health services in a building on lease from Hale Hoola Hamakua. The greater part of the original hospital campus is leased to the University of Hawaii–Hilo for the North Hawaii Education and Research Center, which provides college, vocational, and special interest courses in North Hawaii. At right, in 1992, Honokaa Hospital employees pose at the entrance to the facility. (Left, NHERC; right, Yamato Collection, NHERC.) [70]

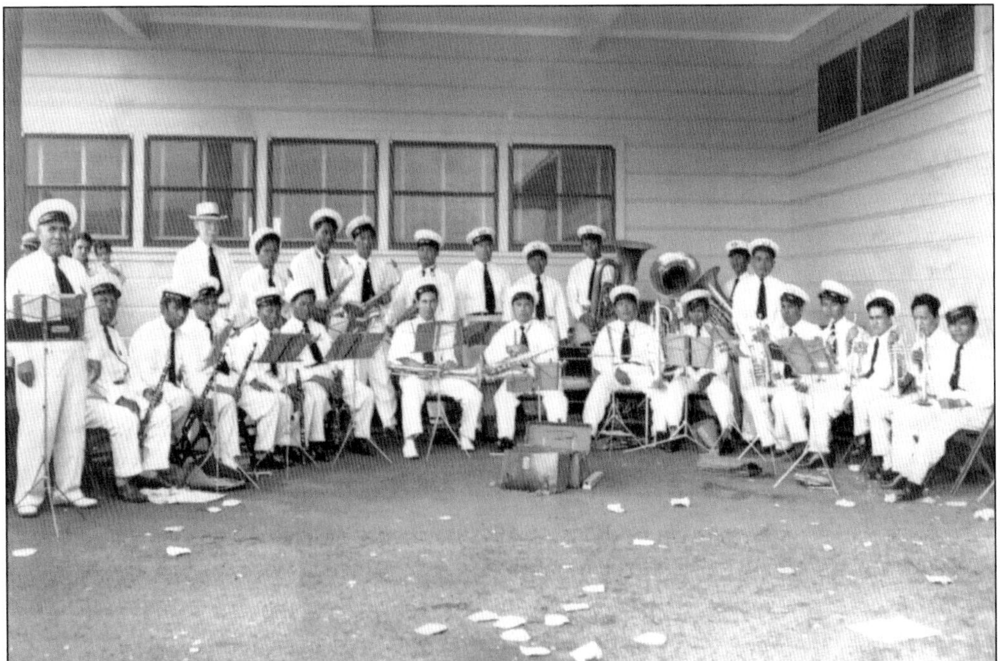

Honokaa Band. Honokaa has the second-oldest community band on the island (established in 1884). Well-known bandleader and owner of Awong Store Alfred Awong is on the left. After World War II, the Honokaa Band was reorganized and became known as the Hamakua County Band. The band is practicing here at the hospital. (Larry Ignacio Collection, NHRC.)

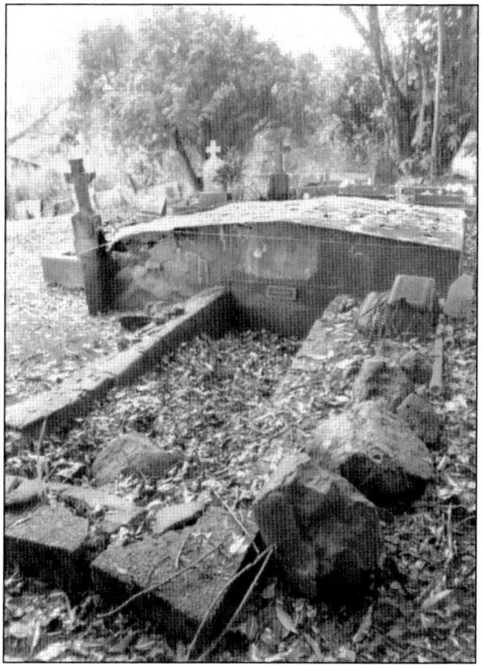

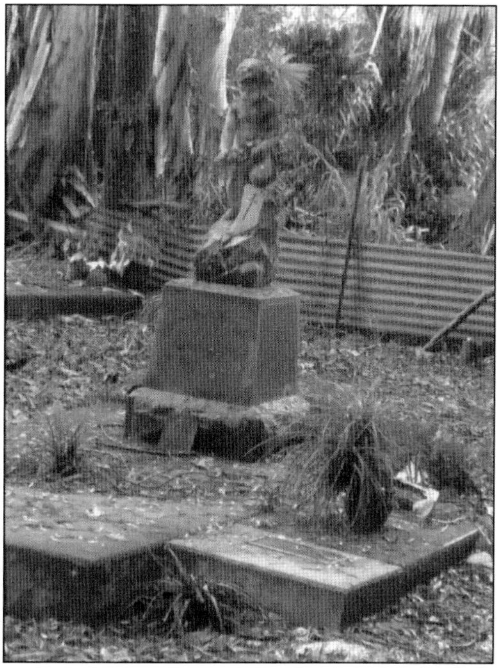

St. Georges Catholic And Botelho Family Cemeteries. Land for the original St. Georges Church Cemetery was purchased off Lehua Road from George Hardy in 1879 and 1886. While the church is gone, the cemetery, containing the 1900 Hardy tomb (left) and graves of other Catholic Honokaa founders, is adjacent to the Botelho family graveyard. Judge Botelho's grave is pictured on the right. (LR.) [71]

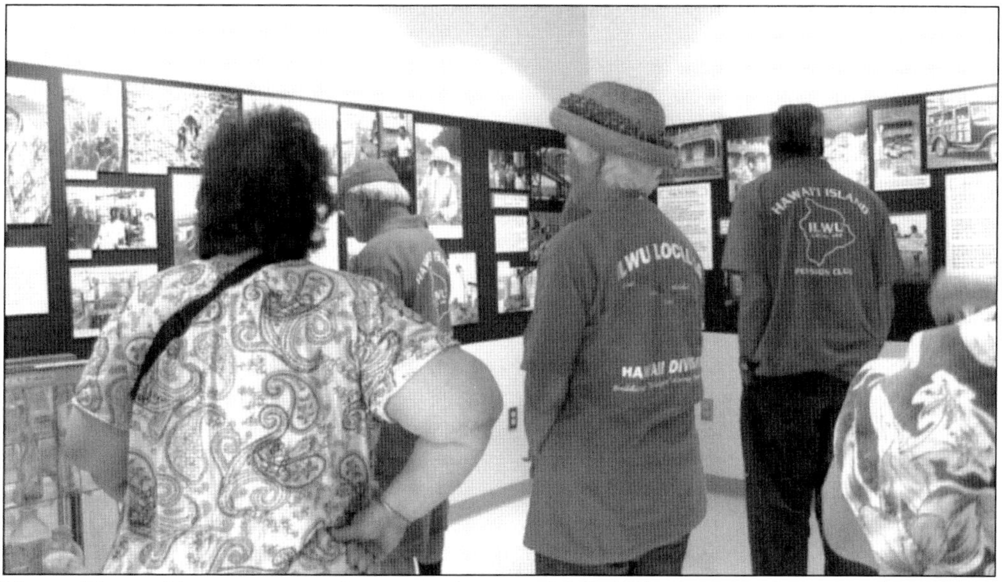

North Hawaii Education and Research Center (NHERC) Heritage Center. The Heritage Center is a depository of Hamakua history, including photographs, documents, artifacts, musical recordings, oral histories, theme displays, and other media that capture Honokaa Town's past. In this photograph, members of the ILWU examine displays at NHERC. The facility is on the ground level across from Honokaa Park. Please come for a visit. (NHERC.) [72]

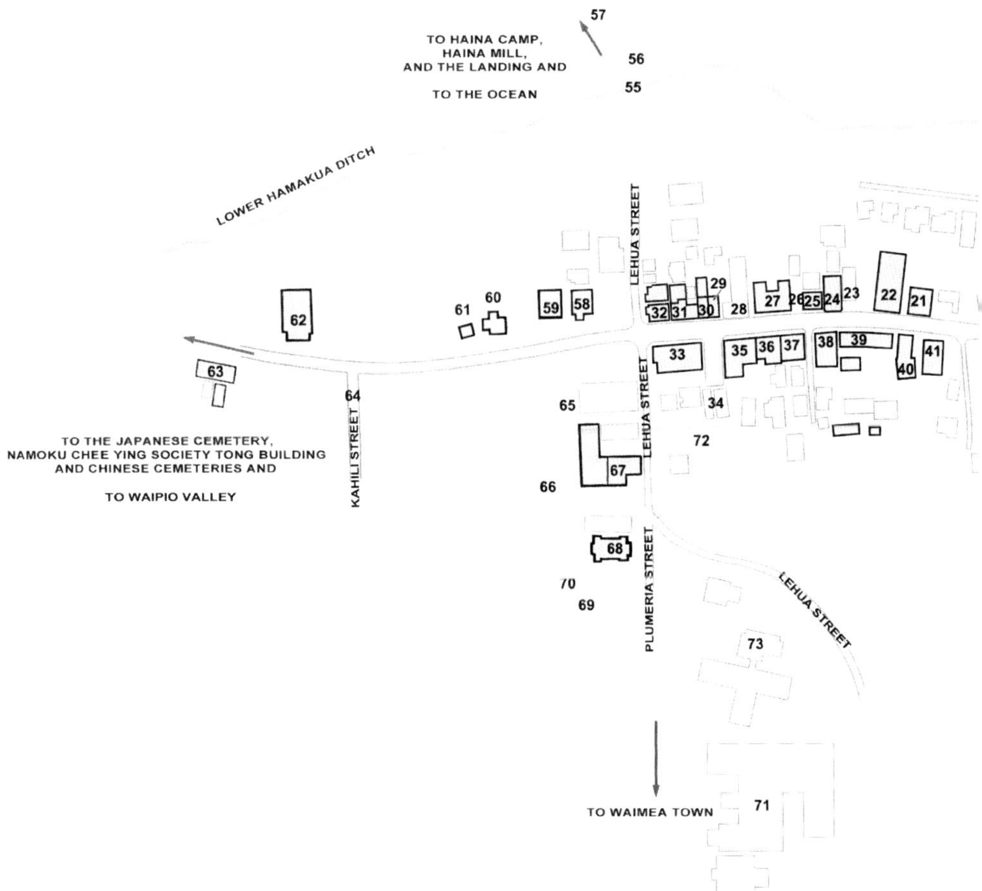

LEGEND

1.Overend Camp
2.School grounds (1889)
3.Anglican Cemetery (1886)
4.Site of old Anglican Church
5.Katsu Goto Memorial
6.State Department of Health, mauka/
Rat Laboratory, makai
7.Hawaii State Library Honokaa Branch/
District Court
8.Fujino Building and residence
9.Nakashima Building
10. Dr. Okada Hospital and residence
11. Dr. Akioka, D.D.S. Office and residence
12. Site of Hawaiian Telephone Company exchange
13. Shingon Mission
14. Ujiki Store, Feed Store, two residences,
and garage
15. Yamato Department Store
16. Harris Sanitary Laundry
17. Hotel Honokaa Club
18. Botelho Annex/original Bank of Hawaii
19. Botelho Building and Garage
20. Site of Dairy Queen/site of Silva Dentist's office
21. Bank of Hawai'i
22. Honokaa People's Theatre
23. Site of Onomura Bar
24. Kuramitsu/Paiva Garage
25. T. Yamatsuka Building
26. Original B. Ikeuchi Store
27. North Hawai'i Community Federal Credit
Union/Old Holmes, Lawson's,
Awong Stores
28. Site of Doc Hill Theatre
29. Hirata Building
30. Kotake Buildng
31. Andrade Building
32. B. Ikeuchi and Sons Hardware
33. Ferreira Building
34. Oshima/Nakamura Hotel
35. Rice Building
36. Souza Building
37. Jesus Building
38. Hasegawa Building
39. Sakata Buildings
40. Takata Building
41. Old Tanimoto Theatre/Harunaga,
Honokaa Theatres
42. Site of Honokaa Shokwai/site of Lindsey Store

HISTORIC HONOKAA TOWN. This map can be accessed at www.historichonokaaproject.com.

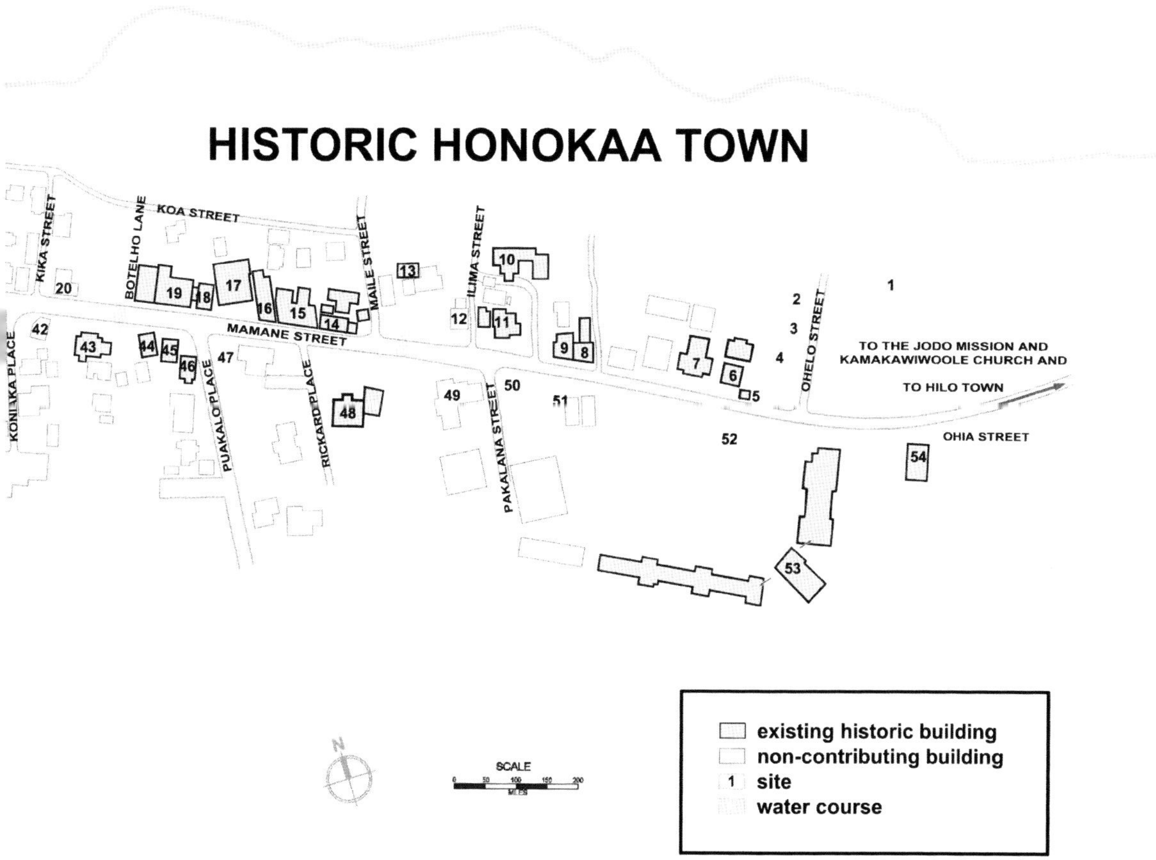

43. Methodist Church/
    former Congregationalist Church/
    site of Lindsey residence
44. Paiva residence
45. Kubo residence
46. Sakata residence
47. Site of Bank of Hawaii cashier's home
48. The Salvation Army/
    former Rickard Hotel and residence
49. Honokaa High/Middle School/former site of Teachers' Cottages/Honokaa Elementary School/former site of Japanese School
50. Pool/site of Japanese School
51. Site of Courthouse, makai/Jail, mauka
52. Site of Lyceum
53. Honokaa High/Middle/
    Elementary Schools
54. Paiva Woodworking Shop/
    former The Country Store
55. The Lower Hamakua Ditch
56. Macadamia Nut Factory/Plantation Store
57. Haina Camp/Haina Mill/Honokaa Landing
58. Fujimoto Flying A Super Service
59. Nagao Coastline
60. Kitagawa residence
61. Igarashi residence
62. International Longshoremens and
    Warehousemens Union (ILWU)
    Jack Wayne Hall
63. K. Kaneshiro Store
64. Site of Camp 8
65. Site of Methodist Church
66. Site of Shingon Buddhist Mission
67. Honokaa Hongwanji Mission
68. Our Lady of Lourdes Catholic Church
69. Catholic Cemetery
70. Site of the Church of the Immaculate
    Conception
71. Honokaa Hospital
72. St. Georges Catholic and
    Botelho Family Cemeteries/
    site of St. Georges Church
73. NHERC Heritage Center

Bracketed numbers within the text correspond to the numbers on this map. (LR.)